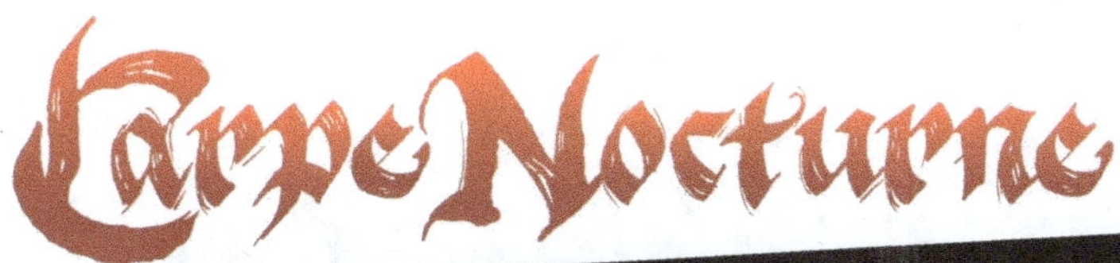

Carpe Nocturne

OTHER THAN THE NORM

VOLUME XII
WINTER 2017

PUBLISHER
Visual Adjectives

EDITOR-IN-CHIEF
Paula Andrews Powles

MANAGING EDITOR
Michael Jack

ASSISTANT MANAGING EDITOR
Zahara's Tangled Web

ART
Feature Editor: Zahara's Tangled Web
Isolde de Mortimer
Noel Rivera
Yasaman Vrd'dhi

ENTERTAINMENT
Feature Editor: Michael Jack
Alexis Marshall
Fairlyinnocent
Hyde Falkenstine

FASHION
Feature Editor: Kathleen Sharkey
Amy Townsend
Emily Bielby

FILM & LITERATURE
Feature Editor: XXX Zombieboy XXX
Axel Karenta
James Donnelly
Jesse Orr
Lisa Fremont

LIFE & STYLE
Feature Editor: Jezibell Anat
Joseph Zuchowski

MUSIC
Feature Editor: Asylum Attendant
Chirality
Dawn Wood
Sergio Manghina
Sonnett57
Trixxi Divine

TECHNOLOGY
Feature Editor: Zannie Campbell
Cosmic

GRAPHIC DESIGN & LAYOUT
Annabella Rios
John David Howard
Zannie Campbell

Subscribe

Never miss an issue.
Have Carpe Nocturne Magazine delivered directly
to your front door or office four times a year.
subscribe@carpenocturne.net

Carpe Nocturne Magazine is available in
Digital and Print editions!
Available in print at Amazon.com, BarnesandNoble.com
and other retailers.

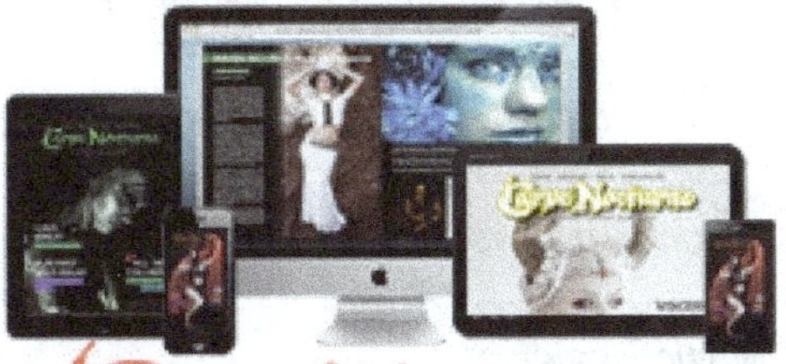

*Carpe Nocturne Magazine Volume XII · Winter 2017
is a publication of Visual Adjectives, LLC
and published four times a year.
All reviews and coverage expressed in this publication
are the opinions of the writer and/or those being interviewed
and may not be shared by Visual Adjectives.*

*Copyright © 2017 by Visual Adjectives, LLC.
All rights reserved.
14280 Military Trail, #7501, Delray Beach, FL 33482, USA.
No work may be copied or reproduced without
the express permission of the editor or publisher.*

Correspondences should be addressed to:

*CARPE NOCTURNE MAGAZINE
14280 Military Trail, #7501
Delray Beach, FL 33482 USA*

E-mail: editor@carpenocturnemagazine.com
www.carpenocturnemagazine.com
p: 561-809-3834 f: 904-701-6272

COLUMNS

ART

ENTERTAINMENT

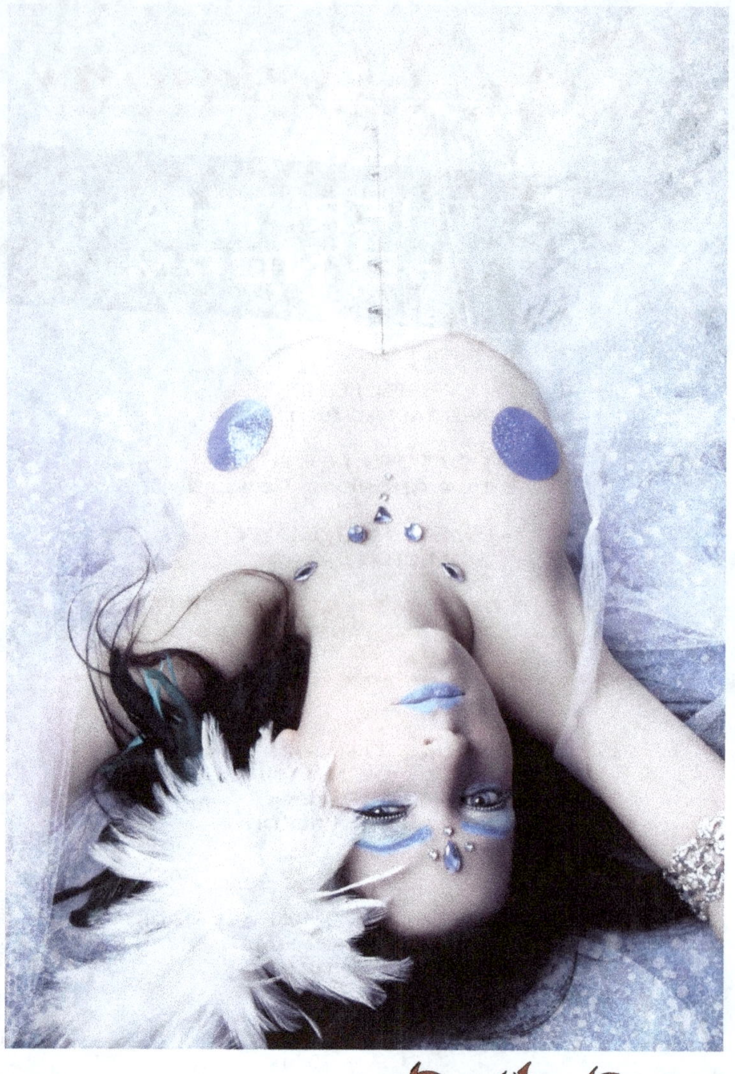

On the Cover

PAGE: 37
MODEL: Tiffany
MAKEUP ARTIST: Gigi Rose
PHOTOGRAPHER: Candylust.org

FASHION

FILM & LITERATURE

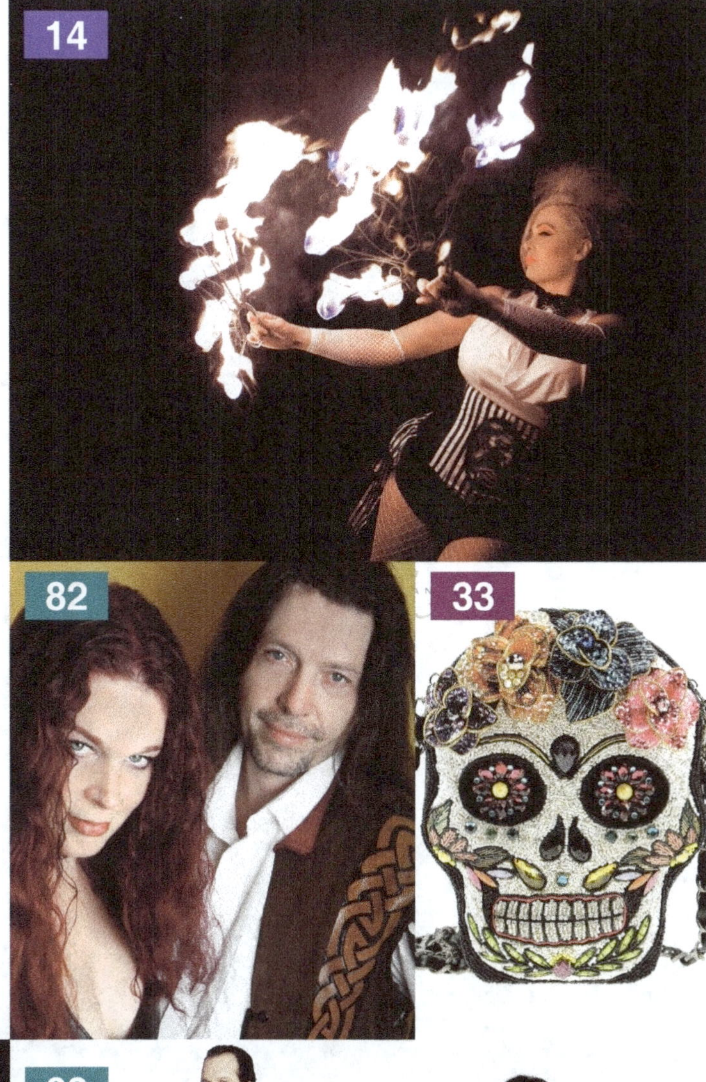

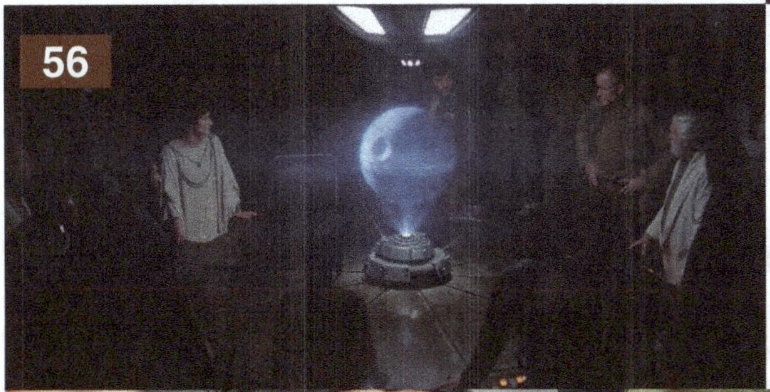

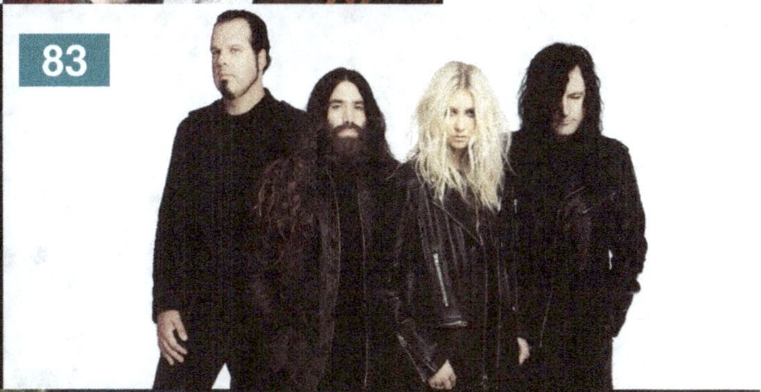

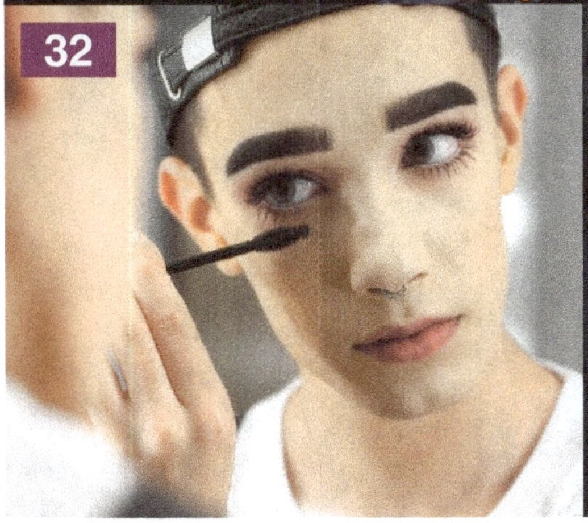

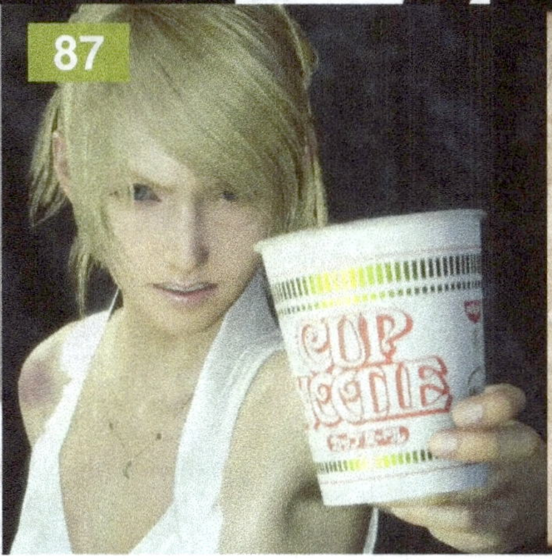

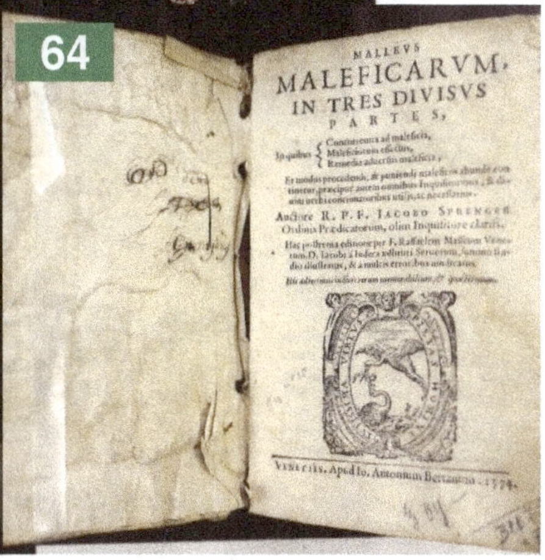

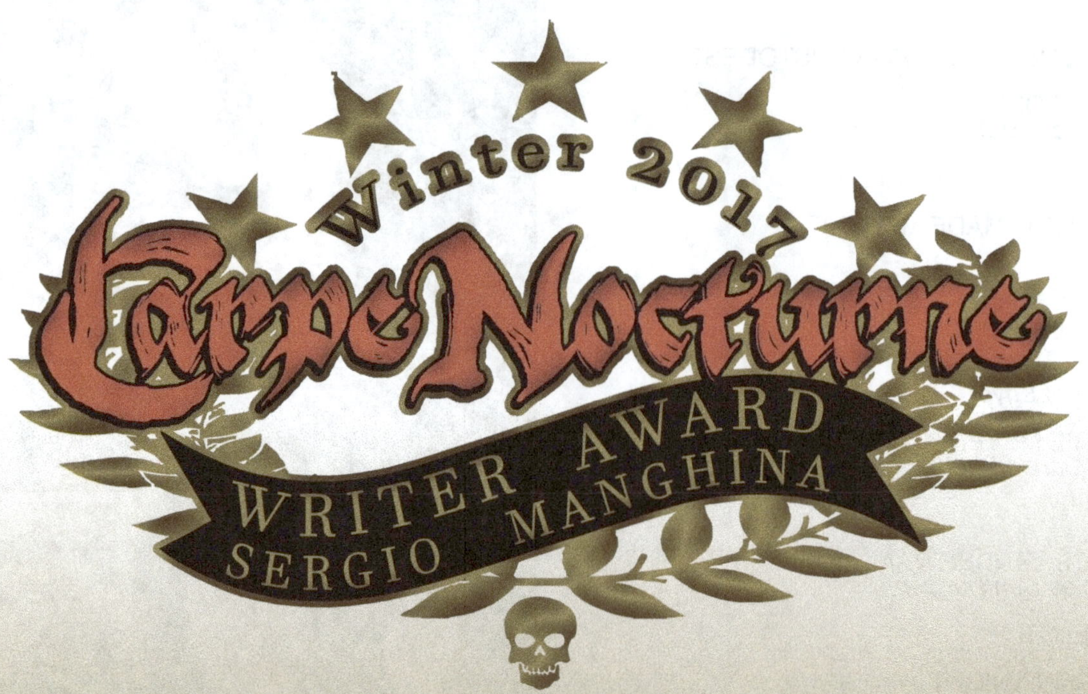

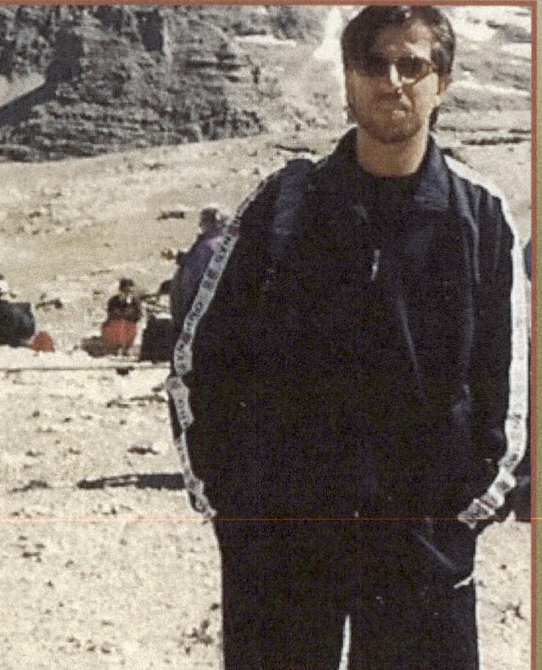

Sergio Manghina is a long time writer for Carpe Nocturne Magazine. From the beginning, he has been one of our most important and most active CD reviewers. Sergio also has to his credit authoring Carpe Nocturne's very first column, "Chained Shadows," which he still writes to this day. Besides the aforementioned column, Sergio also pens our "Amazing Tracks" and "Torn Curtain" columns. His influence can be seen all over the magazine, for he gives the publication a decisive Noir edge. In fact, I would consider Sergio our resident expert on all things Noir. His talents and interests seem boundless, for he often pitches ideas for articles that I have never even considered…like an epic two part piece on Gothic Country or an article on Hipgnosis cover art. I pride myself on knowing my writers, but Sergio's ideas are always a surprise. His articles definitely help to keep Carpe Nocturne "Other than the norm."

Besides the ideas and the columns, Sergio Manghina has a talent for writing that I have rarely seen. His command of the adjective and descriptive phrase is unparalleled in Carpe Nocturne, or almost anywhere else. The way he describes, especially sound, is a form of art. If you follow his work, you know this already. If you do not, do yourself a favor and start reading his columns. To give you an idea, here are a few examples of Sergio's descriptions:

"The dark side of America lives in every song by The Black Heart Procession like a bad thought, a tear, a fist in the face."

"The beat is always slow, atmospheric, disturbing like a lamp thrown on the floor, but still lit."

"These pieces are like phantasmic snapshots in a ghost town that has lost its name among dusted streets and rusting cars, while a radio inexplicably continues to turn on by itself, realizing a dazed and swaying portrait of Americana (Gothic) Noir."

At many writers' best, including myself, they can not turn a phrase like Sergio can. It's a gift. What makes his talents even more impressive, is English isn't even his first language.

For the Winter 2017 Writer Award, I cannot think of anyone more deserving to receive this than Sergio Manghina. He is one of the most dedicated, active, and talented writers we have. Sergio's skills have helped to evolve Carpe Nocturne in ways I have never thought of, and he continues to evolve it. His columns are a cornerstone of the publication, and his articles awe even the casual reader. I couldn't be more proud to call Sergio one of our own, and I'm just wondering when a book is coming.

Besides writing for Carpe Nocturne, Sergio maintains a website on all things Noir, and has been active in various other publications. You can also follow him on Facebook. The links are provided below.

Michael Jack, Managing Editor

http://www.i-m.mx/Lilienthal98/sergiomanghina/
https://www.facebook.com/sergio.manghina ∎

SPOTLIGHT FEATURE

There are a lot of truly talented people out there, especially in our culture. Some use this talent simply for passing the time and personal growth, while others develop their talent to create services, works and objects for others to enjoy. Some post their creations on their website and never try to sell their works, while others use their talents to supplement or create their income. Carpe Nocturne Magazine admires, respects, and supports YOUR TALENT!

Whether you are creating to sell or only for personal enjoyment, LET THE WORLD SEE WHAT YOU'VE GOT!
There is NEVER A CHARGE to be Spotlighted or Featured!

The feature within Carpe Nocturne Magazine spotlights artists, designers, photographers, crafters and others with a creative side.

Does your work relate to the subject matter of this publication. Whether you do what you do for self-enjoyment or to sell your craft, we support you.

Contact: art@CarpeNocturne.net
Subject Line: Spotlight Feature

ARTISTS • COSPLAYERS • CRAFTERS • DESIGNERS • MODELS • MUSICIAN • PHOTOGRAPHER

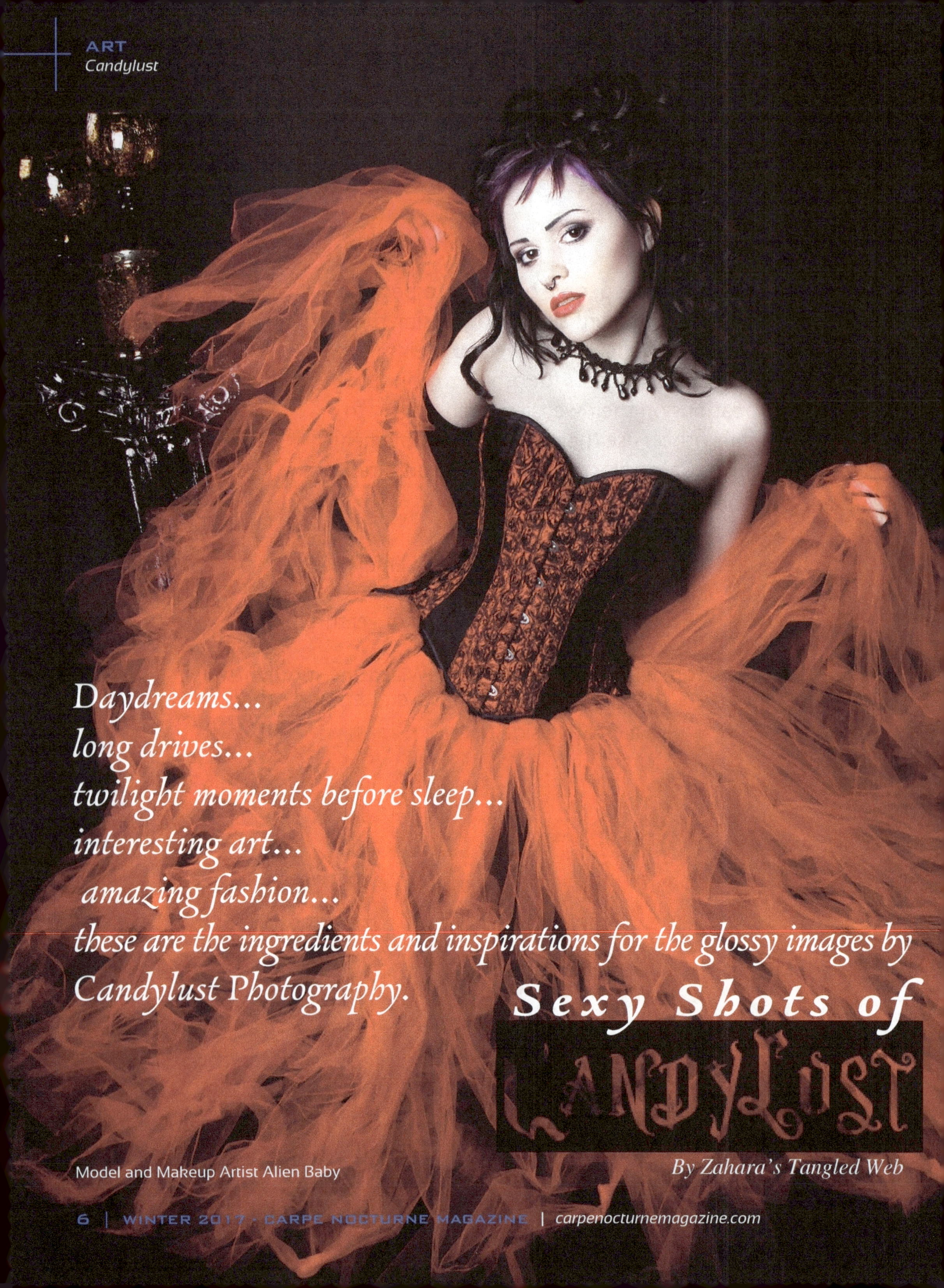

Daydreams…
long drives…
twilight moments before sleep…
interesting art…
 amazing fashion…
these are the ingredients and inspirations for the glossy images by
Candylust Photography.

Sexy Shots of

CandyLust

By Zahara's Tangled Web

Model and Makeup Artist Alien Baby

Based in New York, Candylust has been providing vibrant photographs for a variety of clients, from bands and models to consumer goods companies. "Any time I get to reflect makes me envision myself, my feelings, and how I view the world," says Candace, the woman behind the photography.

Candylust is known for adding splashes of intense pinks, blues, reds, and greens to otherwise dark aesthetics. But Candace's ultimate goal is a simple one: capture each model's beauty. She works closely with her subjects to get their ideas about wardrobe and other elements of the shoot. "I want all of my shoots to have a little bit of everyone involved, so that everyone working on them really gets something out of it on a deeper, more artistic level." Styling the shoot is very important to her, and it's obvious that Candylust has a unique look when reviewing the online portfolio.

One of Candace's favorite shoots is this black and red one with model Alien Baby. Her delicate facial features and alabaster skin set against the dark background is striking. The crimson tulle seems to be spilling from her waist, adding an ethereal element of movement to the photograph. "While the shoot was simplistic, she is so expressive, and she really captures the raw beauty of a goth girl."

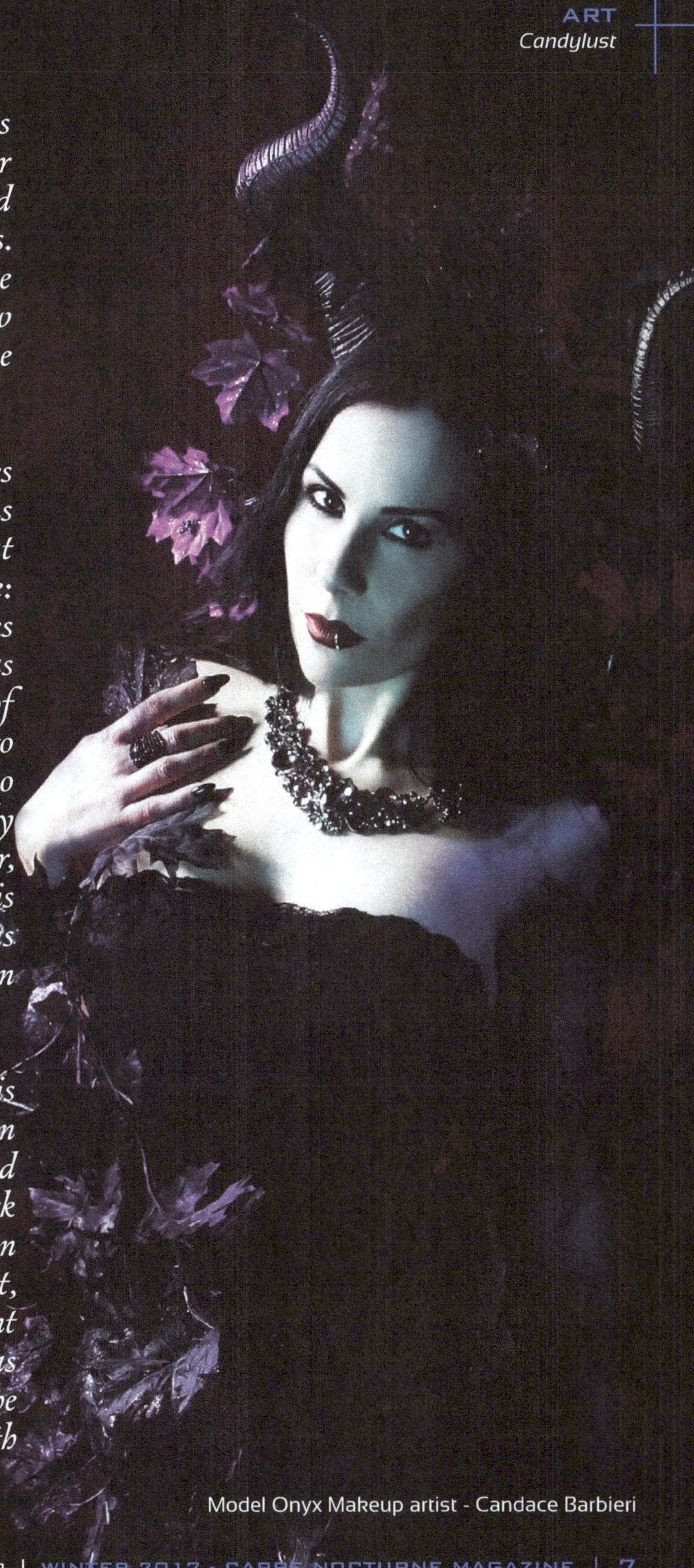

Model Onyx Makeup artist - Candace Barbieri

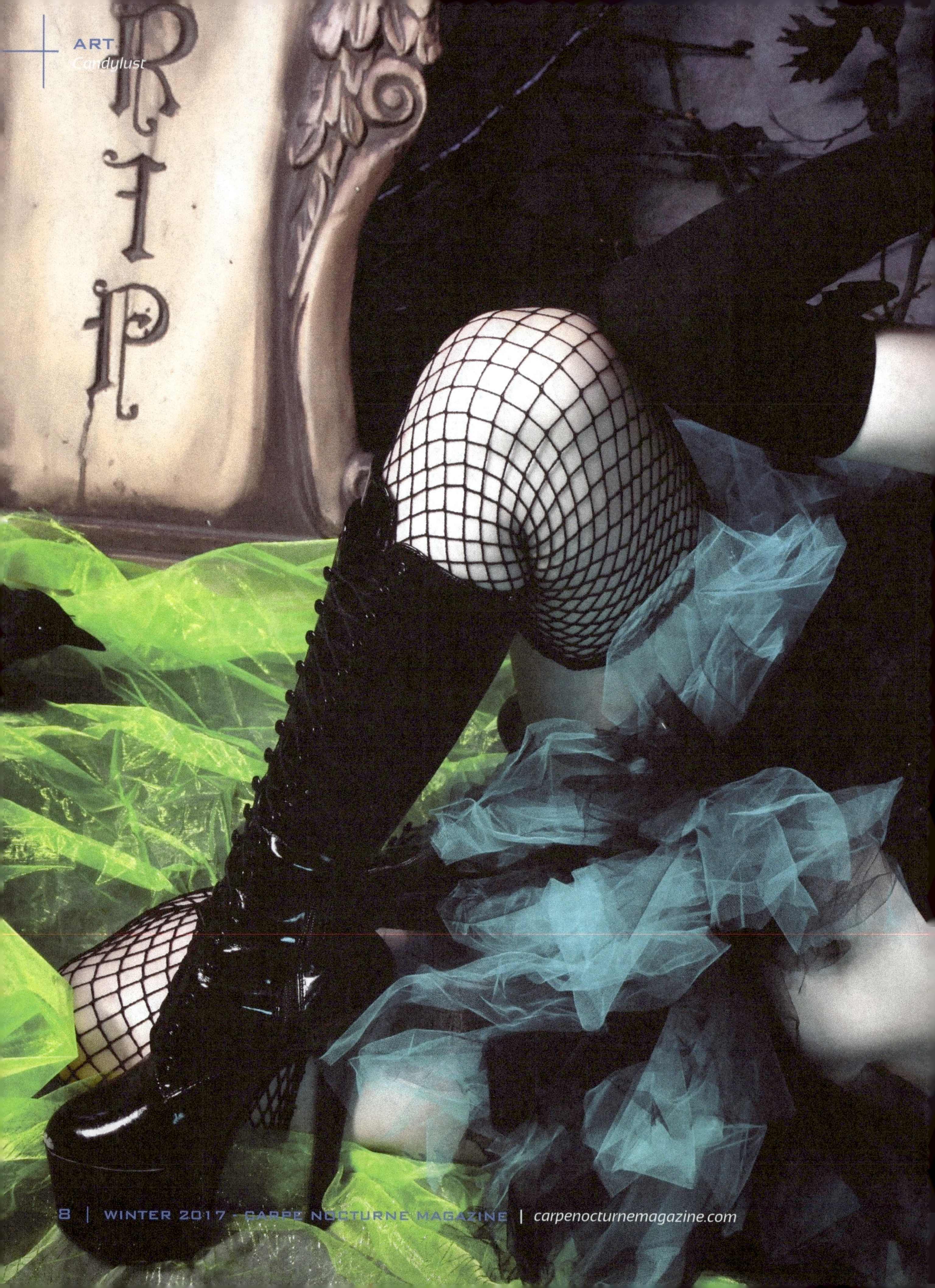

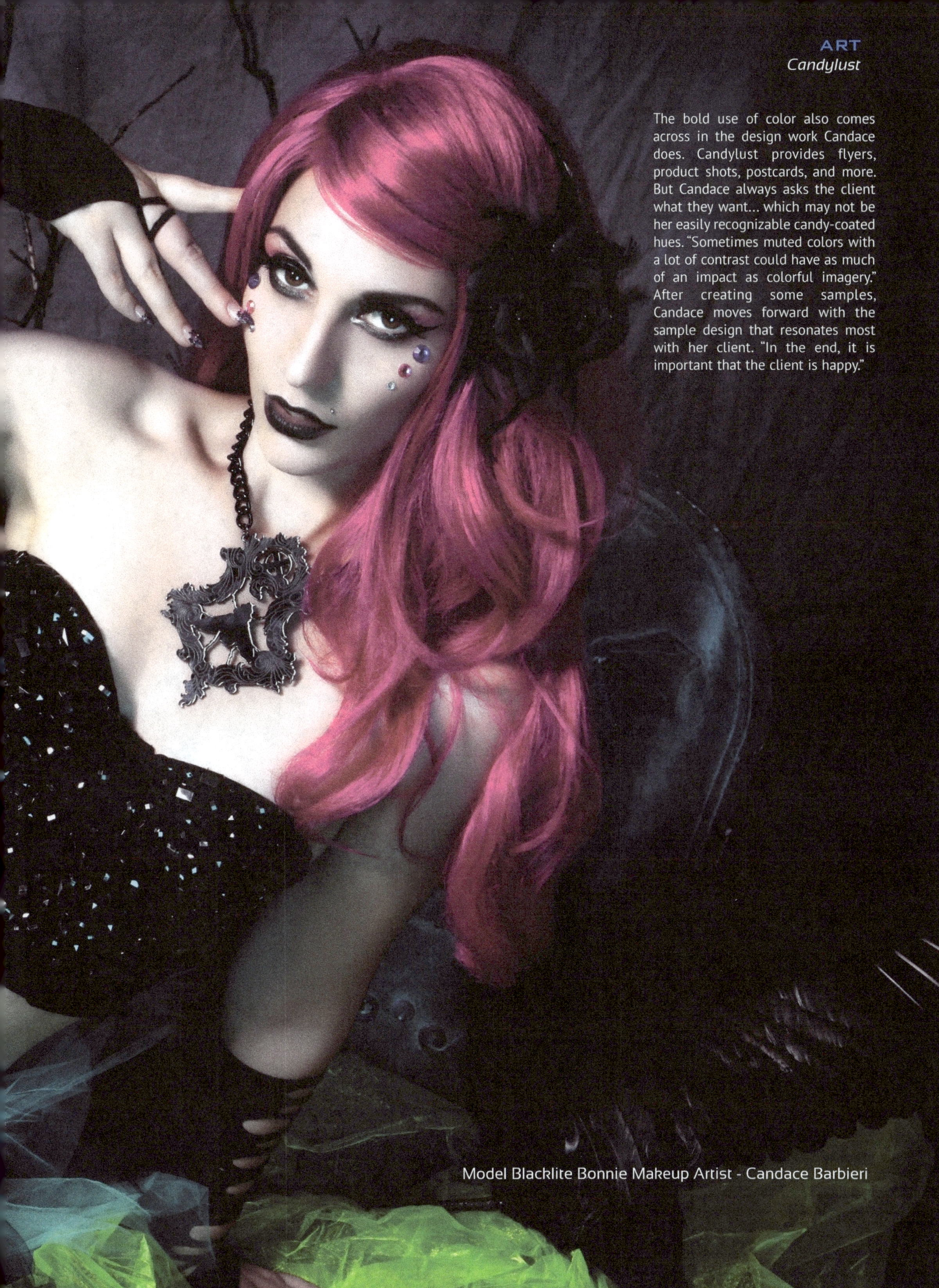
ART
Candylust

The bold use of color also comes across in the design work Candace does. Candylust provides flyers, product shots, postcards, and more. But Candace always asks the client what they want... which may not be her easily recognizable candy-coated hues. "Sometimes muted colors with a lot of contrast could have as much of an impact as colorful imagery." After creating some samples, Candace moves forward with the sample design that resonates most with her client. "In the end, it is important that the client is happy."

Model Blacklite Bonnie Makeup Artist - Candace Barbieri

Fortunately for us, even we can get some gorgeous, gothy pictures of ourselves! Candace loves working with anyone who's interested in hiring her for one-of-a-kind sittings, whether you're into portraits or pin up shots. "I love shooting with people who have never modeled or stepped in front of a camera professionally. It is very rewarding to make someone who didn't think they could be a model into one." After reviewing the images on www.candylust.org, I'm most drawn to the vintage pin up portfolio. I love the curvy feminine poses and interesting backgrounds, including retro kitchens and amusement parks. "I really love the aesthetic of pin up," says Candace. "I try to find ways to make them edgier to stand apart from the usual pin up portraits." She even practices posing herself, so she knows how to coach the models when they get in front of the camera.

What does the future hold for Candylust? Candace has photographed many artists and captured live performances by bands such as Combichrist, Mortiis, Celldweller, and VNV Nation. She hopes to one day collaborate with Mosh, whose looks she finds to be really unique and dynamic. "We can truly make some wonderful creations!" She also aspires to capture Marlo Marquise during a performance. "I've worked with her many times, but never had the chance to photograph her performing." Candace finds her entrancing to watch and an inspiration overall as an artist.

Candace also has a goal to create and incorporate some of her own fashion design into her photography over the next year. "I also want to do a few concept pieces that have never really materialized for me in the past... some involving apocalyptic elements and twisted takes on fairytales."

When she's not behind the camera, Candace spends time with her boyfriend (Tim) and dog (Bear). She enjoys long solitary walks and letting her imagination run wild, coming up with ideas for her shoots. She also loves rollercoasters and crazy nights with her friends. "I used to make music in a band before I discovered photography. I also used to act in short films and even tried making a few music videos." One thing is certain: Candace is a creative force, and we're eager to see what's next for Candylust.

For more information about bookings, or to see examples of design work and photographs, visit www.candylust.org. ∎

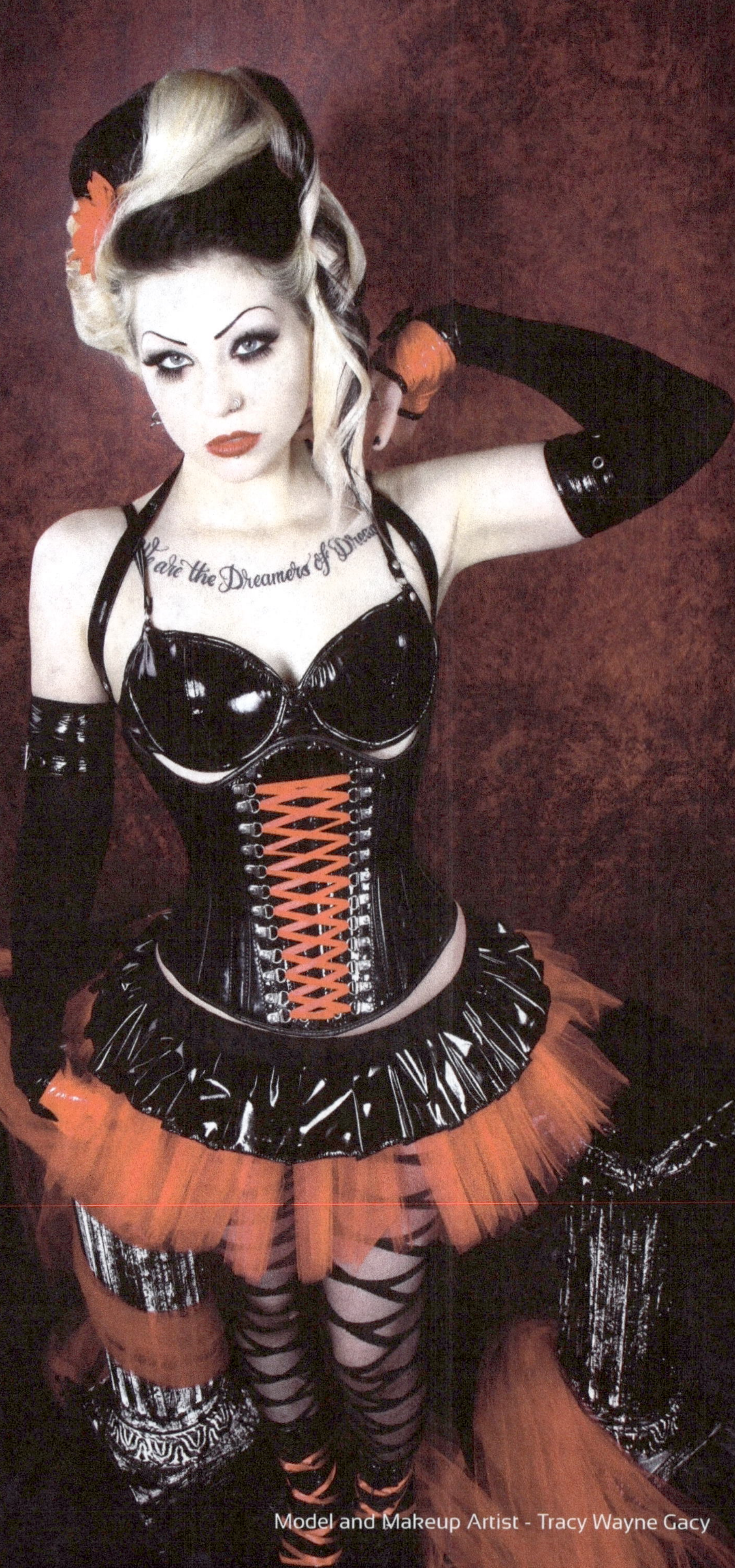

Model and Makeup Artist - Tracy Wayne Gacy

by Michael Jack and Xxx Zombieboy xxX

Weight Loss

So the holidays are over, and you want to lose some extra weight. Or, perhaps, weight is something you struggled with your entire life. You want something that will start shedding those pounds with minimal effort. I hate to tell you, but a product like that doesn't exist...at least not yet.

Losing weight is not an easy task, and it takes continued effort and dedication. There is no substitute for diet and exercise. The old philosophies of drinking plenty of water, cutting the carbs, and eliminating the junk food still hold true. However, there are products on the market that can aid in weight loss. They will not work alone, and only give a minor to moderate boost to achieving your weight loss goals. But, they do help, and can give your weight loss regimen a kick start. These products come in three types: those that curb appetite, those that inhibit the absorption of fats, and those that speed up metabolism. I will explore all three types to help you choose which is best for you.

> "So the holidays are over, and you want to lose some extra weight. Or, perhaps, weight is something you struggled with your entire life."

If it is the quantity of food you consume a day that is your biggest problem, or maybe even the snacking in between meals, then appetite suppressants may be the way to go for you. There are prescription medications available for this, and they mostly all contain the active ingredient Phentermine. Phentermine is an amphetamine, and can be addicting. Avoid if you struggle with addiction problems, if you are pregnant, or if you are trying to become pregnant. If you do not fall within those three categories, then you are probably okay to take this weight loss pill. Available in several different brand names, phentermine has proven to be the most effective appetite suppressant on the market. Again, this pill won't work alone. You still need to watch what types of food you put into your mouth. Phentermine won't help if your diet consists heavily of potato chips and candy. It will help if you regulate your diet to a reasonable daily calorie intake. It will also help to cut out the snacking, because you won't feel hungry. Phentermine will help bring your weight down, and is commonly prescribed by dieticians everywhere. Just watch for possible side effects like mood changes, sleeplessness, or feeling jittery.

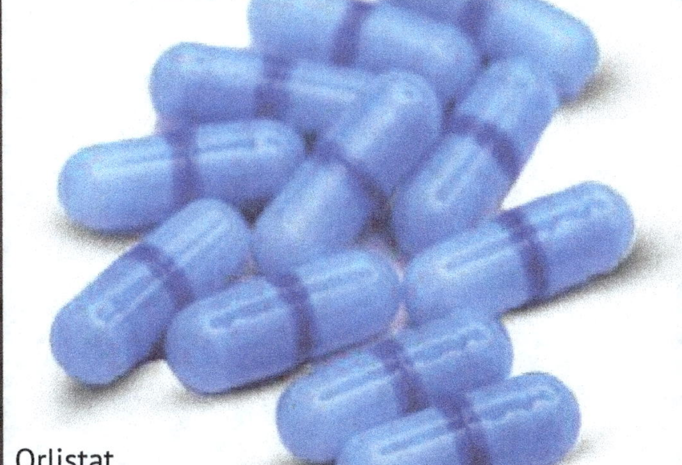

Orlistat

Next up is Orlistat. This medication was originally marketed under the trade name Xenical, and was available only by prescription. Now this product has moved over the counter, you no longer need a prescription, and is sold under the name Alli. Orlistat is kind of unique in the weight loss world. It actually blocks fats from being absorbed by the body. Therefore, you eat candy, and you don't necessarily take in all of the calories consumed in the process. Sounds perfect, right? Wrong. Alli won't block all the fats from entering the body, but it does block some. Alli also brings with it a whole host of unwanted and uncomfortable side effects. Besides excessive flatulence, besides loose oily stools, Orlistat also causes anal leakage. Yep, make sure you have plenty of clean underwear at your disposal. By reducing fat intake, you can reduce the unwanted side effects as well, but...what is the point of Orlistat if you are already reducing fat intake? Alli does work, it will help you lose weight, just be prepared for the side effects that come with it.

If you are feeling disheartened, don't fret. There is still one type of weight loss class to discuss...metabolism boosters. In my opinion,

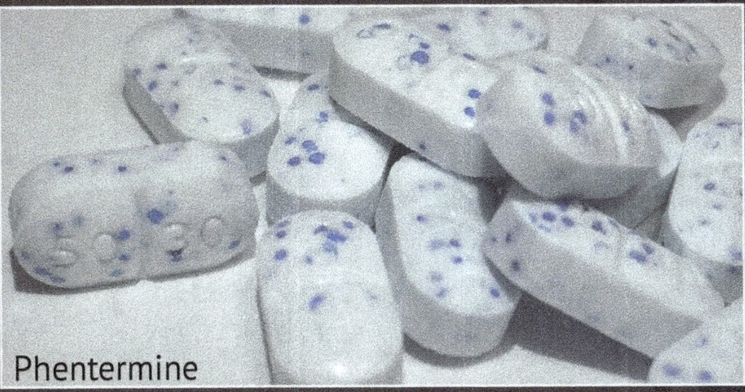

Phentermine

these are the most sensible, however they may not be as efficient as the previously mentioned products. If you are dieting, adding some form of physical activity, then metabolism boosters will help speed along the process to achieving your weight loss goals.

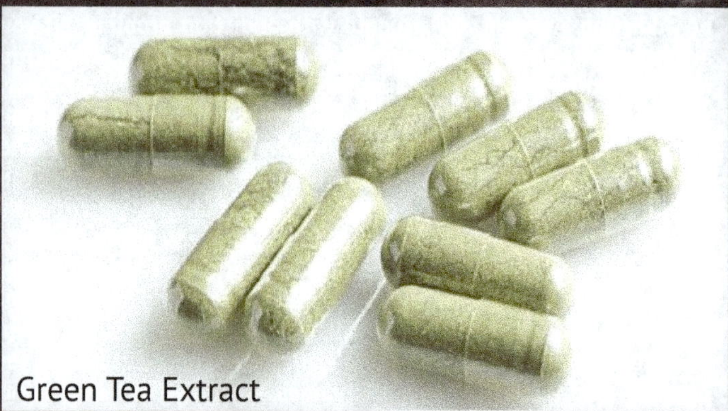

Green Tea Extract

Most of the metabolism boosting products on the market contain caffeine. Yep, my favorite drug. Although I will tell you from experience drinking two pots of coffee a day will not make you skinny, but it will help your body burn fat. On average, caffeine increases your body's metabolism anywhere from 3-11% and increases fat burning by up to 29% A more efficient form of this product comes from the green coffee bean, or unroasted coffee, and you can regularly find extracts at your local pharmacy or health food store. Neither, however, seem to live up to its more powerful cousin, Green Tea.

Green Tea Extract is a common ingredient in many weight loss products on the market, and for good reason. It increases the activity of Norepinephrine, which is one of the main hormones that helps the body burn fat. It also targets the belly more than any other area. Side effects are generally minimal with green tea, and it also has great anti-oxidant properties for overall health. However, like every other product mentioned in this article, green tea will not work for weight loss alone. You need to do the other things as well.

Losing weight is a chore. It takes hard work and determination. There is no miracle cure for obesity, but are there are products that can help. Everyone is different, has different goals, and has different lifestyle habits. Luckily, there are a variety of choices to help with weight loss. I like green tea extract, but that is what would work best for me. Well...and cutting out the beer. That would probably be the biggest help. Phentermine would be my second choice, because it does work. As a pharmacist, I dispense it all the time, and I see the results month to month. Alli is the closest thing you can get to easy weight loss. Just...not sure you want to be walking around with that anal leakage problem. Maybe you do, who knows. The bottom line is there are choices, but all should be accompanied with a sensible diet at least, and an exercise regimen if you can. That is the best way to achieve long-term weight loss.

Mike walks in on Zombieboy eating a Seussian tower of Tagalong Girlscout Cookies

Hrrm? Whu? AH! S@#T! Hi! Um... nothing to see here...
So yeah! Er... weightloss. Right! On it. Um....
Jog. N'....stuff....

...

No? OK... So how to lose weight holistically? Well, there are some options. Though, to repeat what Michael already said, there is no replacement for the only true (and 100% natural) way to lose weight and that is through responsible eating and getting exercise. Period. Sorry everyone but that's nearly the end of the story. However, there are some things that can help.

First, and often overlooked, is the right mental attitude. The word "diet" is nearly a curse word. There are so many negative connotations to it. I mean, think about the word and you just groan inside. It immediately brings to mind thoughts of restriction, hardship, and tiny portions of bland food nothingness with no reward other than the hope that you will look better in that leopard print loin cloth. Or am I the only one that worries about that? Anyway, I would begin first by NOT using that word! Remove the word "diet" altogether. It is just too negative, and upon entering into it, you have already begun on the wrong foot. Now, "responsible" isn't the most fun word either, but let's start there because eating responsible is far better than diet. It is all about mental attitude and having the right drive and confidence. Instead of taking food and turning it into the enemy by labeling it as evil and counterproductive to your slim waistline, try instead to step back and just eat responsible. Cut back a bit on what you already know is bad for you and add a little of the good things. You don't have to starve yourself, and you do not need to quit eating all the things you love. A little can be a great start. And start with the right attitude.

Another thing to examine is pattern and the resulting behavior. Many of us fall into patterns due to our work schedules and life schedules. You learn certain times to eat and drink and certain available sources for those times. It will help you a lot to break the pattern in any way you can to curb learned behavior and thus cause habitual eating or snacking. There is even such a thing as Cognitive Behavior Therapy (CBT) which can help you break such learned patterns. It is not psychotherapy, so don't feel like it is a mental illness you are dealing with. It is a behavior you are looking to break or at least modify. It can also help you reassess

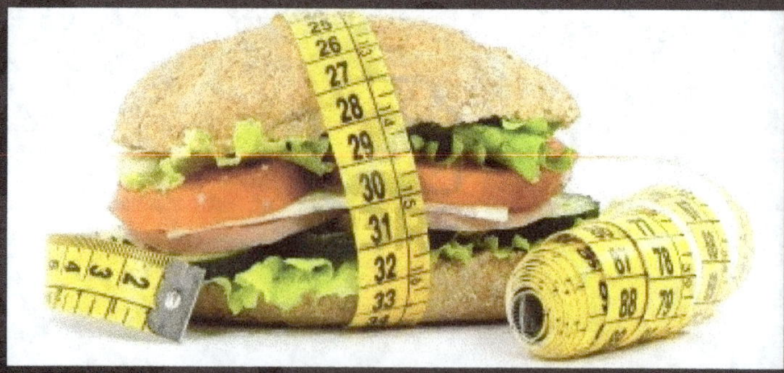

your viewpoints on body image. This is something that can also be a problem in reaching your goals. Having the wrong obsessions over body image doesn't help you. They only set you up for failure. Whether through CBT or not, try to get out of or avoid having any particular obsession with body image. It is ok to want to look good by your own standards. It is not ok to think of nothing else.

Another thing to consider for weight loss and overall health is meditation. I know I mention this a lot in these columns and occasionally even in the zombie column, but there is a reason for that. Meditation is good for so many different aspects of your life.

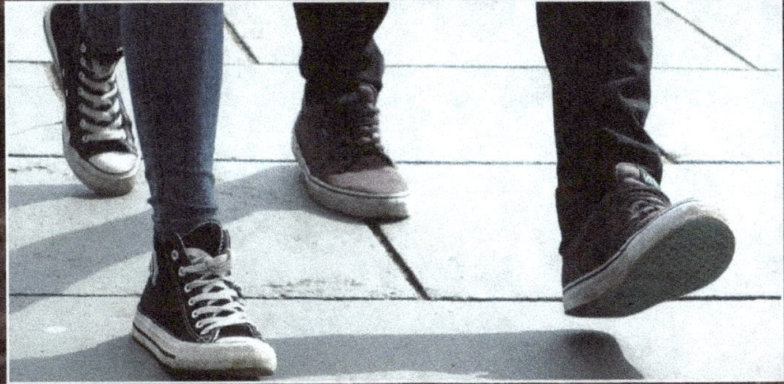

It lowers stress (which let's face it, always leads to eating), it can help establish and maintain a good positive mental attitude, and meditation helps align and center the body and mind. Meditation alone will not make you lose weight, but it will promote and support the things that do such as EATING RESPONSIBLE and exercise.

My next suggestion is to save some money on gas and hoof it more often. Now, I am not at all suggesting that an across town commute to work would be possible on foot. However, there are plenty of times when one has the time and can go through the effort of walking more. Walking is possibly my favorite key to healthy living. First of all, you see more. You experience more. You save gas, wear and tear on your car and you get more fresh air. Walking whenever possible is a huge step. Park further away in that parking lot from now on. Walk the two blocks to see the football game. Leave earlier and walk to work if it isn't really that far. Walking can make all the difference in the world!

Now, there are a few things you can take in that will also help. For example, high fiber foods such as apples and beans. High fiber foods can take longer to digest and will therefore help you stay fuller longer. Also, insoluble fibers help to keep you cleaned out. Side note: if you soak beans first before cooking, it will make you less gassy. Just saying.

Foods that help to increase the metabolism such as ginger root are greatly encouraged. Try it in a tea. And I don't mean ginger flavored tea. I mean actual ginger root IN tea. Add it to the green tea that Michael mentioned when he stole my thunder on the whole green tea thing earlier in this column. Green tea is great! But again... Michael already wrote about it in his section. Michael likes his green tea. And thunder stealing.

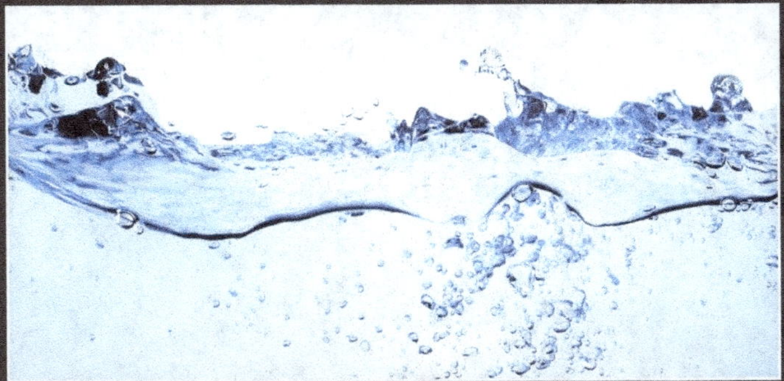

Another thing I mention often... and you know what... here it comes again. WATER! Drink it, swill it, chug it, LOVE IT! Hydration is necessary for good body chemistry, for removal of toxins and for digestion. That and you cannot live without it. So WATER! Stop arguing and drink it.

Now, we would all love to live inside those happy commercials where smiling happy people are unloading massive bags of groceries from the market and smiling while they cook and slice and prepare these wonderful lavish meals and smiling while they all gather around those perfectly manicured spreads of food with the whole smiling family. Actually, this is beginning to sound more like some kind of nightmare to me... but the point is that MOST of us do not live in that world. A good deal of us are probably lucky to grab a sub on the way home. So, although we would like to live that perfect healthy and well-balanced and prepared meal world... let's face it, most of us don't. And of those that of us that could... many of us won't. So there are some supplements that we can take to help replace what we otherwise won't take in.

Omega -3: Decreases inflammation and increases digestion

Amino acids: These fight the desire for carb craving.

Vitamin B: Boosts metabolism, increases vitality and it also helps burn calories more effectively.

Chromium Picolinate: Reduces sugar cravings

I saved the best for last kids...

SEX!

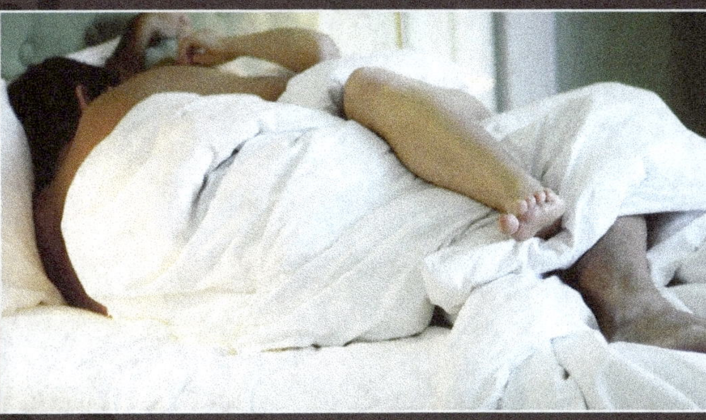

We all want it. We all love it. And it is one of the reasons why so many of us are concerned about weight loss in the first place. It isn't the coronary... It is the coitus!

Seriously though, the average person burns over 200 calories every thirty minutes during sex. Readers of Carpe Nocturne Magazine probably double that because we are damn sexy! And really, isn't your sex partner more fun to climb on and sweat all over than one of those work out machines? So here is what Dr. Zombie recommends for you to lose those love handles. Handle the one you love. Get laid. A lot. A whole... whole lot. Annoy the crap out of your neighbors and roommates and get it on boys and girls. Because once more and with feeling... nothing replaces good exercise! ■

FIRE, FETISH, AND PASSION

An Interview With Nancy Anne
by Michael Jack

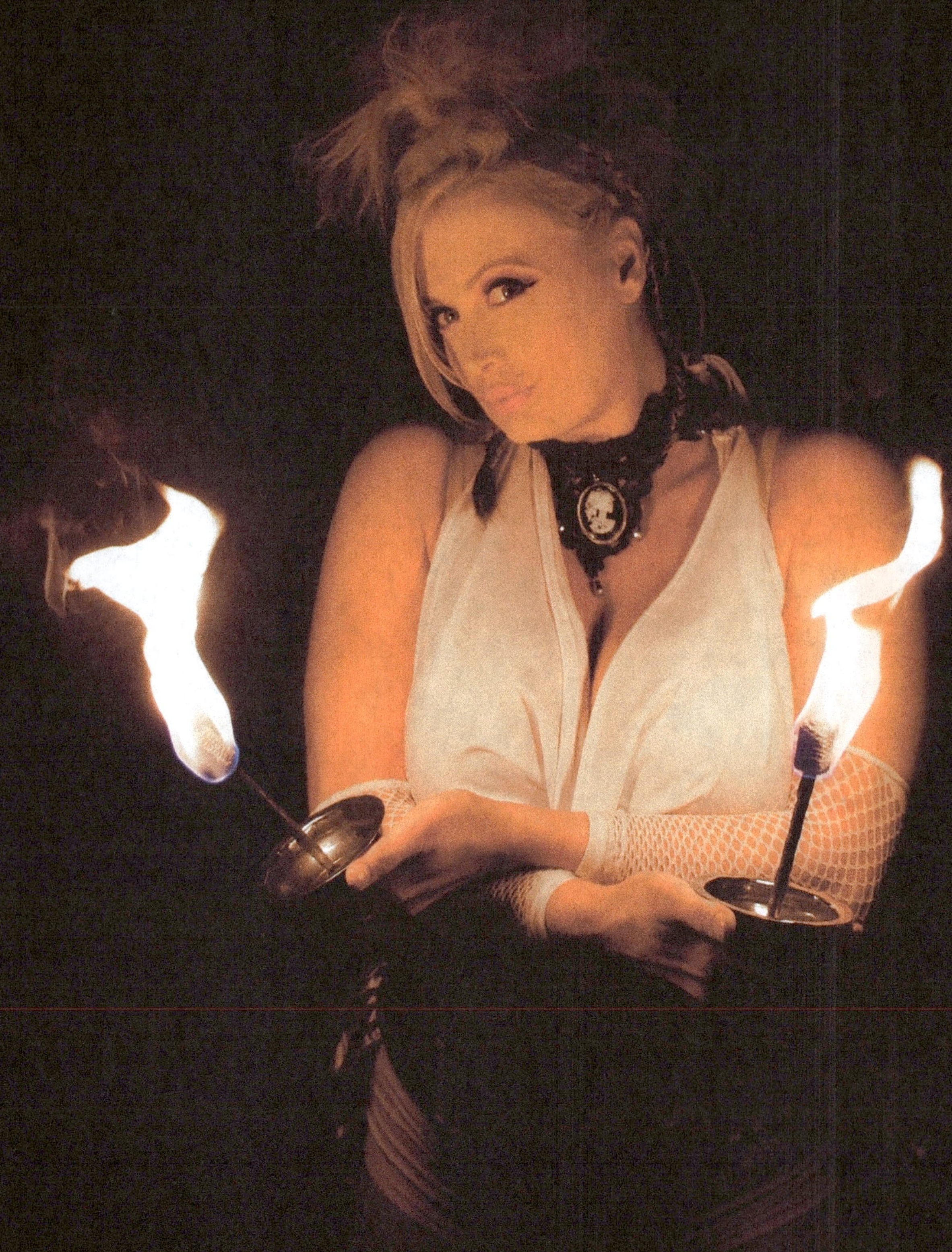

Fire Dancer. Writer. Industrial DJ. Model. Fetish Goddess. Exotic Dancer. These are all talents of the incredibly diverse, multi-skilled Salt Lake City resident Nancy Anne. Readers of Carpe Nocturne might know her better as Sonnett57. Local Utah residents might know her better as DJ Mistress Nancy. No matter you call her, if you attend any local underground event in the Salt Lake City Area, you are bound to encounter Nancy Anne in some capacity. She may be spinning records, greeting you at the door of Area 51's Fetish Ball, or dancing with the Utah Fire Tribe.

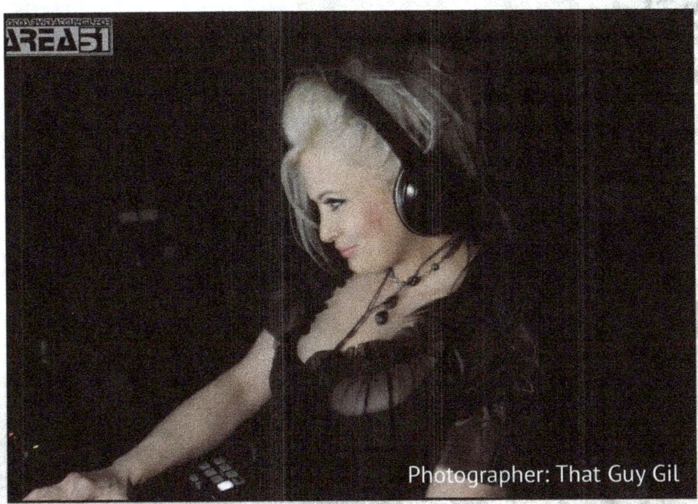

Photographer: That Guy Gil

I first met Nancy over three years ago when I became the Music Editor for Carpe Nocturne. Nancy was one of our longest tenured and most active music writers. She gave the magazine a much needed Industrial edge, and along with our current Fashion Editor, Kathy Sharkey, and myself, comprised the backbone of the music staff for a very long time. Nancy always impressed me with her pure passion for the underground scene, and the under-recognized musicians she was covering. The more I got to know her, the more I realized she was much more than a talented writer. This issue I am excited to bring you my interview with the amazing Nancy Anne.

To begin to understand Nancy, you must first understand the area where she was born, raised, and still resides today… Utah. Nancy is not shy when she describes the sexually repressed and overly religious mindset of the community, why Utah happens to be #1 in the states for porn downloads, and why the fetish balls are becoming more popular. She states, "Once people wake up from their religious beliefs, or stray from the path of the church, they often go into a sort of rebellion, because sex is a natural thing. We all have desires and fantasies, and you can only deny them for so long. What you will see at the Area 51 Fetish Ball presented by Blue Boutique is people escaping from these beliefs without judgment. They are here for you to be yourself and feed your desires – of course they must be done inside of Utah's strict

laws." Those strict laws include no spanking. However, the restrictions have relaxed over recent years, and you may now find vacuum beds, rope demonstrations, wax, piercing play, and adult toys for sales at the events.

If you are lucky enough to attend an Area 51 Fetish Ball, expect Nancy to not only greet you at the door, but to also see her face on many of the promotional flyers for the event itself. She explains the experience. "It is sometimes quite fun to see a newcomers reactions to the video that plays which shows them of what is happening inside the club. During my breaks you can find me on the dance floor as sometimes I can be quite the exhibitionist. Like the popular Informatik songs says, 'I get turned on by Watching you Watching Me'." As for themes, there are many, but Nancy describes her best-loved. "I would have to say the "Medical" theme is my personal favorite. The reason for this is that you can do so many different things with it. There is something very sexy about exploring another body with tools from this theme."

Being a self-proclaimed exhibitionist, it shouldn't surprise anyone that Nancy is an exotic dancer as well. As I mentioned before, the laws in Utah are strict. Dancers must wear pasties and a three inch wide thong in the back. There is no customer to dancer contact, no lap dances, and customers must be at least three feet away from the stage. This leads to certain challenges, but Nancy always has a way to spin things in a way to promote the darker cultures. She explains, "it forces us to become more creative in our performances and music choices. I love this aspect as we are often in control of the music we dance to. I will take any opportunity I can get to spread knowledge about our underground music and love to share it with people who may have never heard it before. There is something really gratifying when you are dancing in a club like this and play an artist like Modulate. I watch

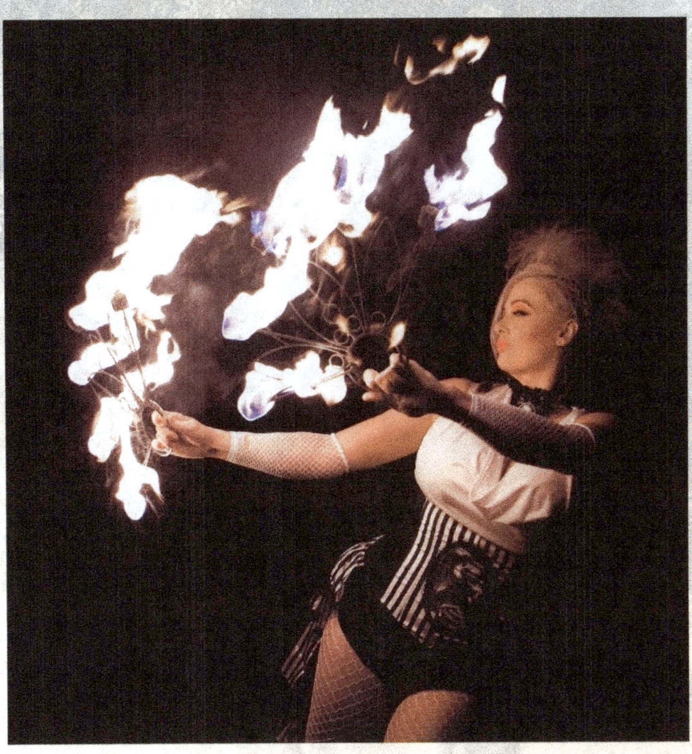

Photographer: Kathryn Frederick
Hair: Paul Chance

people's heads bounce and bodies react to what they are hearing, and when they ask, "who sings this song?" the feeling is like being tipped a 100 dollar bill. The only thing that is more gratifying is performing to a song like this and the customer already knows it."

From the dance floor, to the stage, to the sand beneath her feet, Nancy Anne awes with her skills. Certainly the most dangerous, and perhaps the most beautiful, is her performances as a fire dancer with Utah Fire Tribe. I had to ask what drew her to this art form, and she responded, "Back in 1998 I came across my first group of "Burners" and I was amazed, excited and even a little turned on by the craft as I find it very sexy. Life happened and I had some adventures and lessons to learn that took me away. It was always lurking in the back of my mind. Once you "light up", it stays with you."

Fire dancing is so much more than performance, Nancy explains. It is a mindset, and way to live your life. Through many personal struggles and hardships, Nancy found peace within this community. She elaborates, "I not only became part of a radically inclusive fire spinning group, a new way of thinking was installed. The experience has made me have a brighter outlook on things. I now am living life by The 10 Principles of Burning Man, and have not been a happier person. I am stimulated to grow, accomplish goals and learn in ways that I could not even imagine. There is so much creativity, love and encouragement to be yourself in the "Burner" community."

If you think the art form is dangerous, Nancy will agree with you wholeheartedly. "It will burn you eventually," Nancy explains, but she credits her tribe member Phil Olsen as summing it best. He told her, "Fire is alive, you have to respect it, because though you can know its patterns it can surprise you with what it wants to do." One of the biggest pieces of advice Nancy can give is learn how to treat a burn if you are taking up fire dancing.

Photographer: Tony Matinez

HEY LOOSERS
It's That Holiday of Love Again!

Get The BITCH What She DESERVES

Lingerie
Fetish Wear
Body Piercing
Shoes
Men's Shirts
Love Oils
Unique Gifts
Sexy Dresses
Body Jewelry
Adult Tools
& More...

Blue Boutique
Open every stinkin day
1080 E. 2100 S.
485-2072
http://www.blueboutique.com

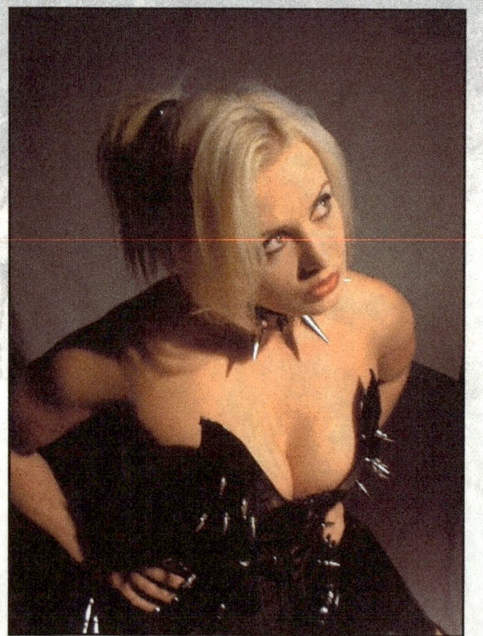

Perhaps the talents Nancy Anne has been longest known for are her skills at writing and as an Industrial DJ. Besides Carpe Nocturne, Nancy is senior writer for SLUG Magazine, a local based publication from Salt Lake City. She has interviewed countless musicians, and her motives are always to help the struggling artists.

As for the best and worst part about being a writer, our own Sonnett57 explains, "The best parts about writing is spreading knowledge, becoming more informed about what is going on with the musicians in the community, as well as the history behind their careers. There is nothing greater then to hear about classical industrial music from the artists that created it.

The worst part is, you are going to be critiqued. There is always going to be someone pissed off about what you had to say – even if the entire piece was written in a positive light. Let's face it, we have many elitist in our community and there is always going to be that one that knows more about their favorite artist than I do. People are passionate about the music, and it is impossible to please everyone. I write for free and the reward is knowledge and experience. If they can do better, I challenge them to start writing and sharing what they know."

Photographer: Tyler Newman

Very well said, Nancy. She further elaborates about the music, and challenges that face her as a DJ. "Records are like relics to me, treasured and put on a shelf. I am very hard on my CDs, and prefer them, but today's technology is forcing me to go to mp3 and use my TRAKTOR software. You cannot mess around with the music I play too much without the threats of getting lynched. The people here in Salt Lake city want to hear every note as it was created by the artist—at times I feel more like a human jukebox than a DJ."

If you go to see Nancy spinning (or maybe no longer spinning) the records live, expect to hear some old-skool Industrial music. Her go to song is "Targeted" by Intermix. That should give you an idea of what you are in for.

Yes, Nancy also models, but it has to be for a cause. She doesn't do any commercial modeling anymore. Instead, she states, "I consider myself to be more of a fetish clothing spokesperson now. The only modeling I do is for fundraising. There is an orphanage in Guinea Bissau, Africa that I was in a calendar for, so that was fulfilling. I have recently done some shoots for Utah Fire Tribe and will do almost anything that helps promote the music."

For me, that last response basically sums up who Nancy is. She does what she does for enjoyment, but more importantly to help people, and to help the underground communities she so dearly loves. This has always been Nancy's underlying motivations for as long as I have known her. She writes, DJ's, dances, models, and always to help someone else out. Even when her daily life struggles are at an extreme, Nancy thinks of everyone else. I think our world needs more people like her, and our cultures need more people willing to promote like she does. When asked how she manages the positive mindset even during her worst times, she replied, "It is simple. I am an entertainer, I love to perform, and I care about my community. I stay positive for others to have a good experience. To see others enjoying themselves and enjoying the music shuts out what I personally may be feeling at the time."

If asked, it is not surprising what Nancy states is the biggest challenge she faces...finding the time to do it all. Any reader of this interview could have guessed that, but we certainly thank you for trying. ∎

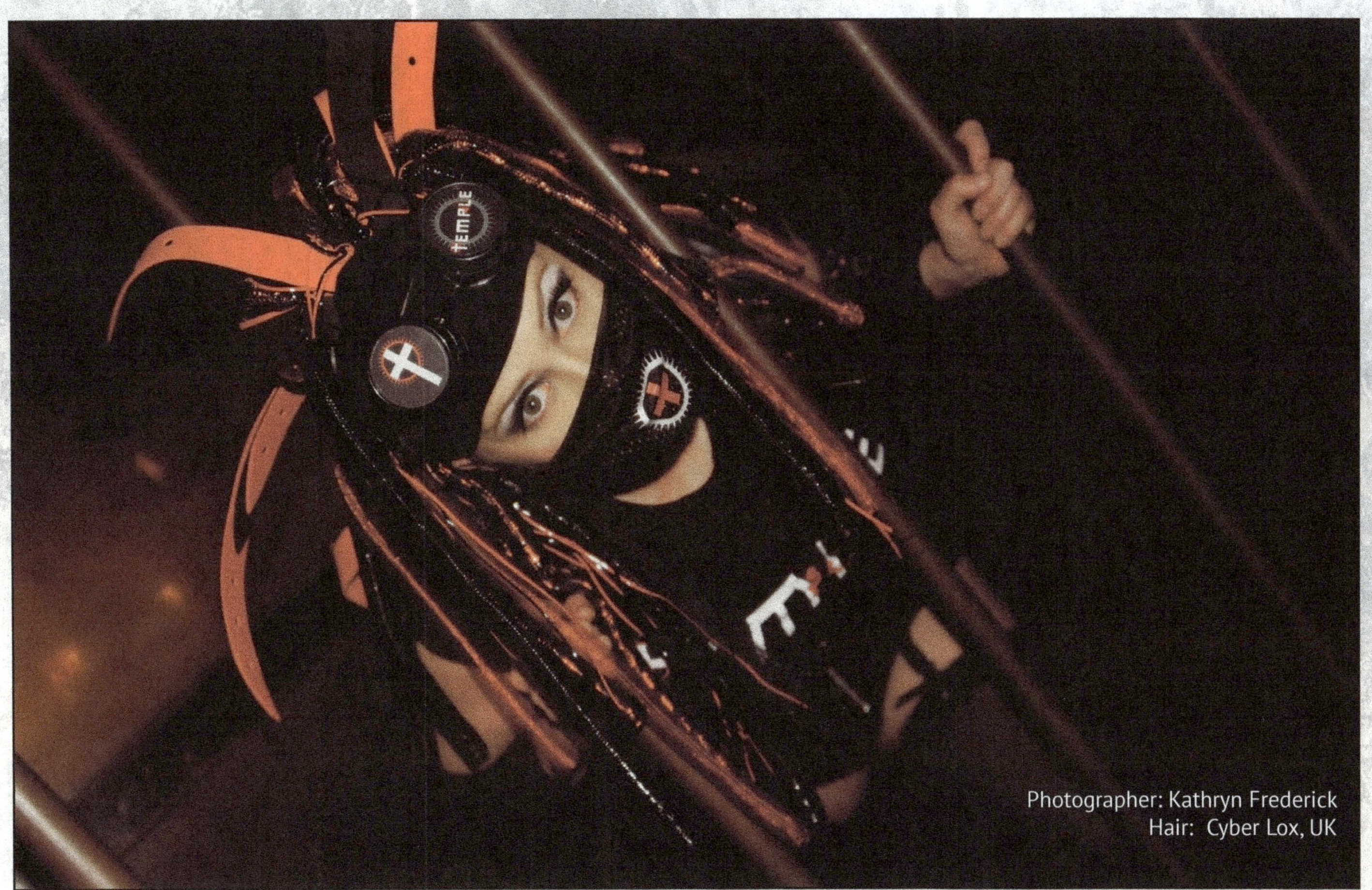

Photographer: Kathryn Frederick
Hair: Cyber Lox, UK

PAPER DOLLS AND GLITTER ARMIES
AYRIA AT THE TOKEN LOUNGE

By Asylum Attendant

I am always down for any opportunity to dance around to the sound of female fronted electronic groups in stompy platform boots and pink glittery goodness. Luckily, Jennifer Parkin of industrial pop musical project Ayria has that in common with me. So, when Detroit became a last minute addition to her Fall 2016 Paper Dolls tour, I knew I could not miss the extravaganza. Glitter army represent!

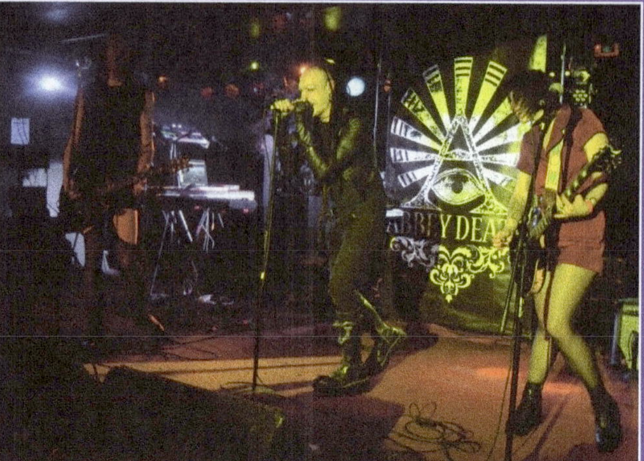

The show was at The Token Lounge in Westland, Michigan, a venue I had never been to before. The space was not very large, but the lighting was splendid. The sound was not perfect. The crowd was quite diverse. There were some hipsters, quite a few Eldergoths (who were adorable), an epic top hat guy and the lovely Cybergoth girl who was front row center. There were not a lot of people there, most likely because the show was the last one added to the tour. The benefit to this was being able to get super close to the stage and having a clear view of the bands.

First up was Goth rock band Abbey Death, featuring the lovely Valerie Gentile, a model/musician and Carpe Nocturne favorite. She really is a firecracker on and off the stage and I could not help being drawn into her infectious energy. Valerie's husband and bandmate Abbey Nex has a crazy powerful voice that I was not expecting, but the band put on a great show. The next opener was Inertia, a dark electro-rock group from the UK. Apparently half of their band was stuck in customs, so only two members made it to the show. This did not detract from the quality of their performance in any way. Lead singer Reza Udhin was really getting into it, almost like the show was a spiritual experience for him. I was getting major Depeche Mode vibes from the dark synthpop instrumentals and Reza's voice and that made me very happy. My friend and I were admiring the attractiveness of the guitar player. He had mad skills, too.

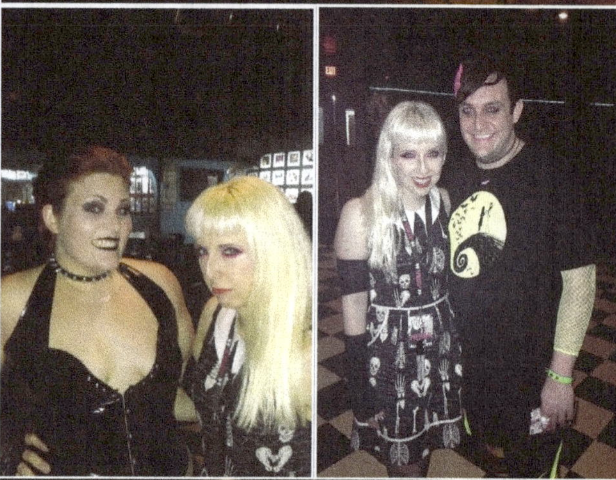

People finally went on the dancefloor and close to the stage right before Ayria came out. It is so surreal to see someone you have idolized for years literally feet from you. The show opener was a song from the new album, *Paper Dolls*. Everyone was jumping around and dancing. There were some sound issues that Jennifer had to address with the audio tech, but they were quickly resolved. She was so sweet about it. I might have had a diva moment in the same situation!

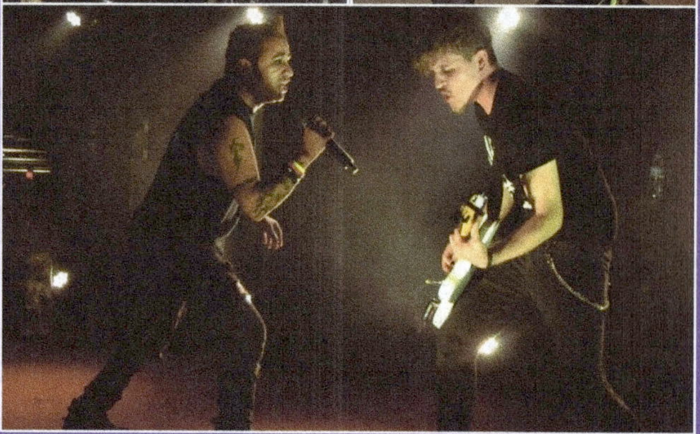

Photography by Digital Racket

Ayria played all of my favorites, like "Bad List", "The Gun Song" and "Plastic Makes Perfect". I had a moment with Jennifer when she pointed to me and smiled as I sang along, knowing every lyric. Ayria's high energy electronic pop lends itself to many dance breaks and I do not think I stopped moving the entire show. Jennifer talked to the crowd a lot, joking that she would take us all back to Canada with her after such a tumultuous election. Sarah Stewart on the keys was super cute and fun to watch. The show actually made me take notice to songs I had not before, such as the danceable "Crash and Burn". The live version is just plain badass!

We thought Ayria was done and the crowd began to shout for "Winter Love Song". Ayria came back out for two encores of "Blue Alice" and "Six Seconds", which really was the perfect ending. Jennifer came out to meet all of the fans after the show and we had a wonderful heart to heart. She liked all of my sparkly jewelry and I told her how her music got me through my rocky teen years. She was very sweet and genuine in her spooky bone dress and she encouraged me not to give up on my dream of becoming a music artist. All in all, the bands put on a phenomenal show and I have now met two of my three major music idols (Kerli and Jennifer Parkin…I am still coming for you, Emilie Autumn). Detroit loves you Ayria!

http://digitalracket.tumblr.com ∎

PART TWO

GOTHIC COUNTRY

by SERGIO MANGHINA

#1...THE DENVER SOUND AND OTHER ODDITIES.

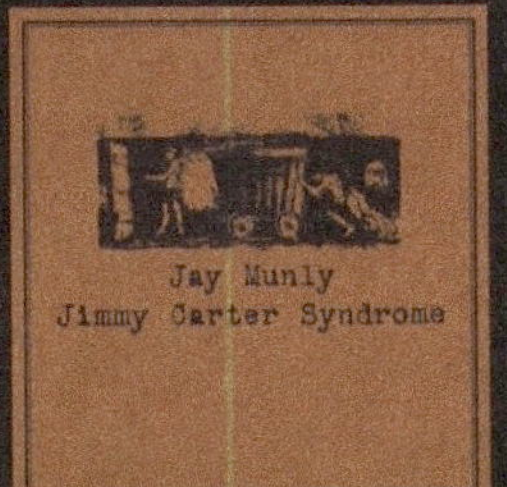

"Introducing the Denver Gentlemen" was recorded in 1995 and subsequently published in 2001. Definitely, it is the first act of the so called "Denver Sound," and probably of Gothic-Country itself. Actually, The Denver Gentlemen were born several years before - in 1988 - as a small bizarre orchestra lead by Jeffrey-Paul Norlander (piano-vocals) and guitarist David Eugene Edwards. Their music was a sinister Gothic-Cabaret also able to flirt with a marked noir mood, at least in some episodes. Jay Munly is another key figure in the Denver scene. Singer songwriter, banjoist, guitarist, he plays alone or as animator of two different bands: Munly & Lee Lewis Harlots, and Munly & Lupercalians. He's also member of several other acts, such as Scott Kelly & The Road Home, Denver Broncos UK, and Slim Cessna Auto Club.

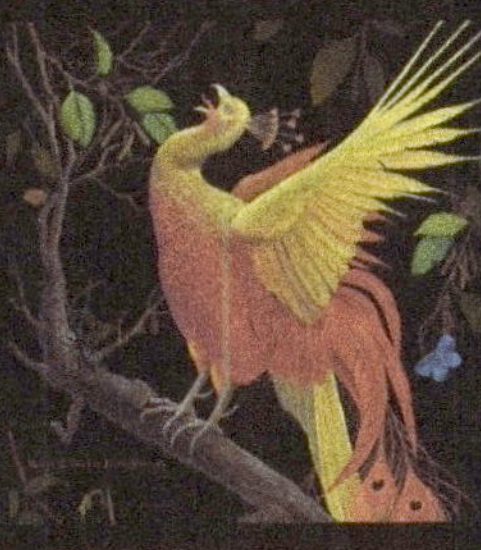

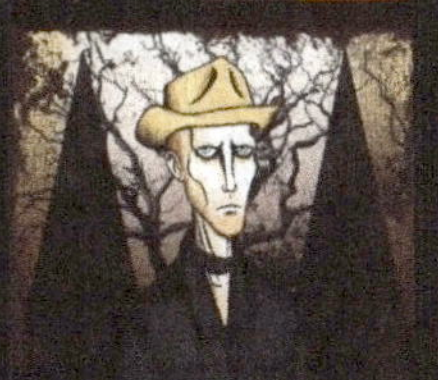

In addition, this circle of musicians based in Colorado, are entwined with each other into a complex frame of groups including also Kalamath Brothers, DeVotchKa, Tarantella and who knows what else... However, the very crucial band of the entire lot are the guys of 16 Horsepower. They are another creature of David Eugene Edwards, ready to distill an infusion of country, gothic, folk and gospel in debt with Nick Cave, Warren Zevon, Jeffrey Lee Pierce. Edwards intones insane preachings, macabre and desperate, immersed in a nowhere land between the Delta and the border of an imaginary Far West.

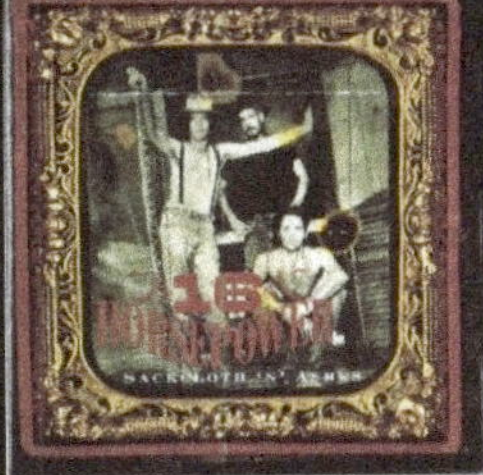

"Sackcloth & Ashes," "Low Estate," and "Secret South" are the smoking gun of the high quality of an (underrated) band out of any scheme. Once he closed the 16 Horsepower adventure, Wovehand - the new band of Edwards - starts an exploration of new musical territories. Maybe it is true that things already exist, but only when someone gives them a name do those things gain an accomplished shape.

#2...WUTHERING HEIGHTS/THE WOMEN OF DARK AMERICANA

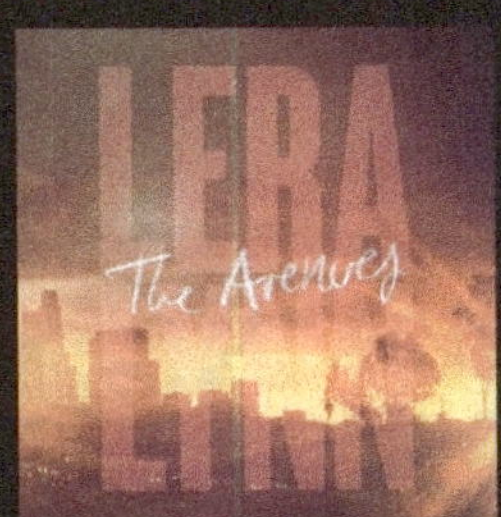

1-LERA LYNN-THE AVENUES/ Label:Caroline Records 2014
It's so hard to resist the charm of Lera Lynn. Instead, it is so easy to be objective about her. Behind the form of the appearance, Lera is abundant in substance as a singer and songwriter. Simple and sophisticated at the same time, maybe she's the real new icon noir. She is even the "bar singer" in the cast of "True Detective."

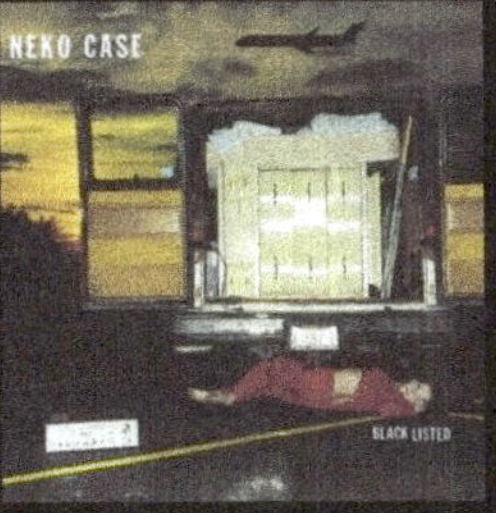

2-NEKO CASE-BLACKLISTED/ Label:Bloodshot Records 2002
Neko Case lists among her influences Angelo Badalamenti and David Lynch, two big beautiful names of the neo-noir. If "Furnace Room Lullaby" certified her dark mood, "Blacklisted" puts pen to paper with no preambles or shyness that she's the Queen of Country-Noir. Dangling twang guitars and dramatic, nocturnal tones. Haunting. Wrapping. Even dangerous. Handle carefully.

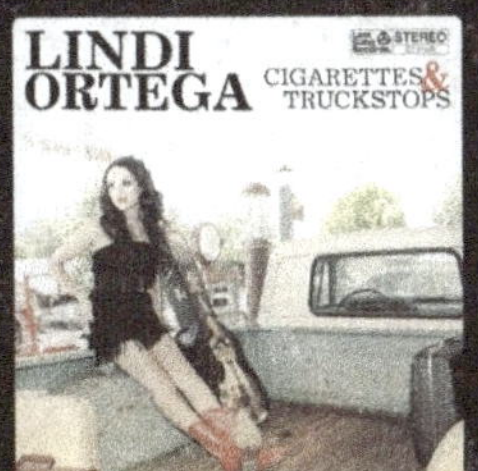

3-LINDI ORTEGA-CIGARETTES AND TRUCKSTOPS/Label:Last Gang Records 2012
The bad girl of country-noir from Toronto, but resident in Nashville, owns great assets as a singer, songwriter, and musician. A song like "Murder of Crows" - just to say - runs in perfect balance between music and its related video (black & white, of course) in pure goth-country with a pinch of her Mexican blood.

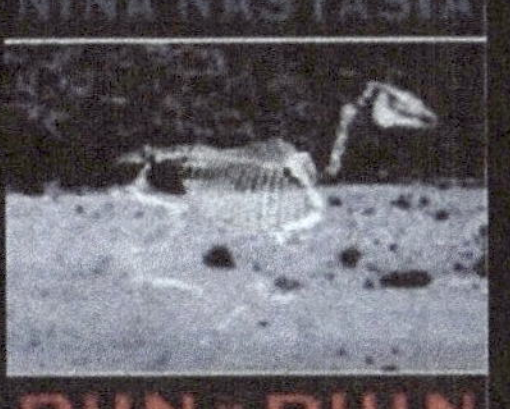

4-NINA NASTASIA-RUN TO RUIN/ Label:Touch and Go 2003
Nina is chamber gothic-folk, harsh and sharp as a blade. Born in California of Italian-Irish ascendants, and now based in NY, Nina Nastasia is an outstanding artist, but she's also reserved and introspective. Her songs tell of losses and conflicts, have deep words and above all an original points of view.

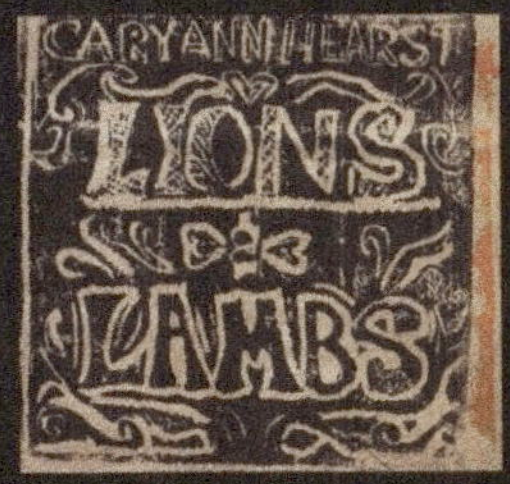

5-CARY ANN HEARST-LIONS AND LAMBS/Label:Shrimp Records 2011
Cary has a great temperament and a remarkable natural stage presence. For this, it is highly recommended to watch the amazing videoclip of "Hell's Bell." Alone or with her husband Michael Trent (as Shovels and Rope), her Southern Gothic mood is effervescent and intriguing.

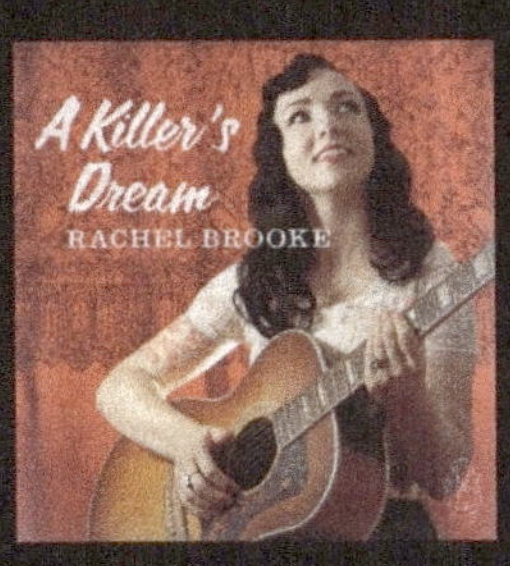

6-RACHEL BROOKE-A KILLER DREAM/Label:Mal Records 2012
Yellowed pictures found and brought to new life, subtracting the black letters of an old calligraphy. Rachel is an eclectic time-traveler trapped inside a vintage radio on the dresser, filled with old jazz and bewildered country. Squeezing the inner blues inside, her American Gothic soul drips out.

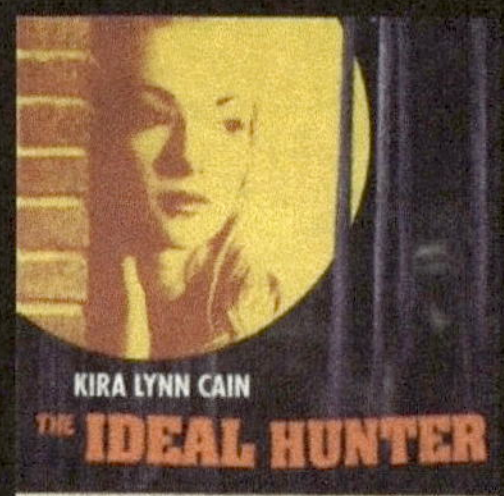

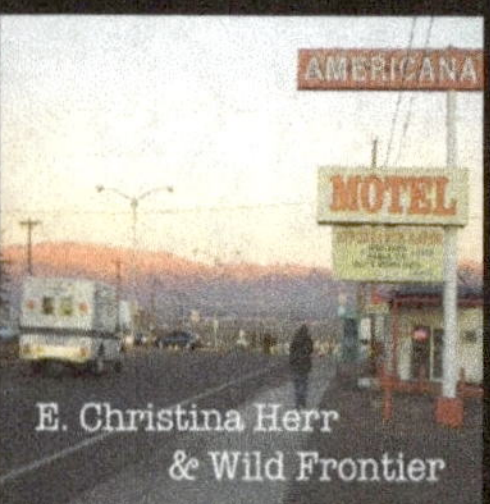

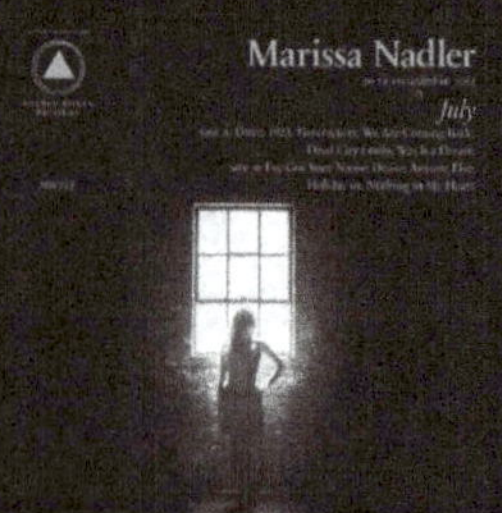

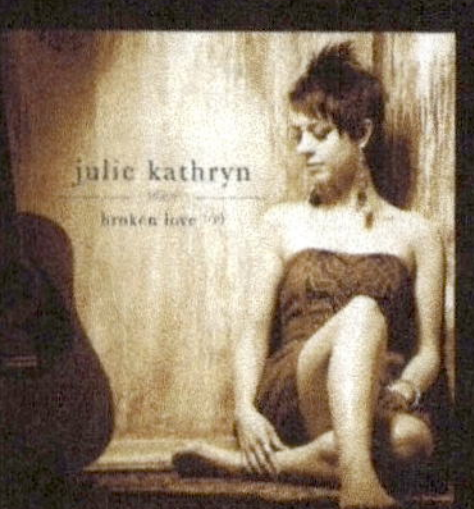

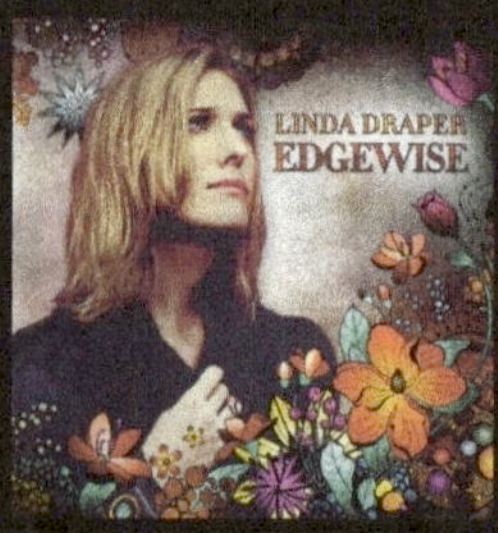

7-KIRA LYNN CAIN-THE IDEAL HUNTER/ Label:Evangeline Records 2008
Kira really looks the part of a femme fatale in a crime film, and her voice is a transparent whisper inside ballads and waltz-like lullabies. It is a rich chamber-folk set, languid and nostalgic thanks to unusual instruments such as a vibraphone, a glockenspiel and even a musical saw.

8-CHRISTINA HERR & THE WILD FRONTIER-AMERICANA MOTEL/2012
Western Gothic, Country-Folk, Rock'n'Roll, Spaghetti Western and then all things ranging from Gram Parsons to Bruce Springsteen passing through Townes Van Zandt. Her songs are similar to messages in a bottle abandoned among the sand of the desert waiting for some solitary rider or an unlucky songwriter to find it. They go from New Mexico and straight to the heart.

9-MARISSA NADLER-JULY/Label:Sacred Bones 2014
Marissa is the more atypical and eclectic female singer in the neighborhood of Dark Americana. Her mezzo-soprano voice distinguishes atmospheric compositions able to touch the chords of different genres and influences including goth and dream-pop, but also with relevant echoes of country and folk. She gives full meaning to a word sometimes a bit inflated, but seeming invented specially for her: ethereal.

10-JULIE KATHRYN-IN THE BUCKET (EP)/BROKEN LOVE (EP) Not On Label 2010-2012
Her ballads have a superior quality like certain precious fragrances or sensual rustling dresses. All these songs contain a color or at least a spark, from "Banks of Eden" and "Break My Heart" to the title track 'Broken Love." Her songs are dramatic stories for passionate hearts inside a country-noir frame, suspended between an original folky inspiration and seducing shades of jazz, embroidered around her delicate voice.

11-LINDA DRAPER-EDGEWISE/Not On Label 2013
Linda loves a certain English folk - Nick Drake, Jacqui McShee, Pentangle - but has also assimilated entire seasons of Joni Mitchell. Linda writes amazing melodies pointed by her masterly guitar. She has a sepia-toned dark-folk, shy and somber that finds its apex into a song like "The Shadow of the Coal Miner" dedicated to The Man In Black Johnny Cash.

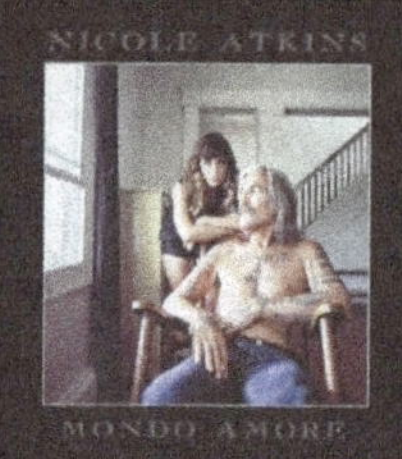

12-NICOLE ATKINS-MONDO AMORE/ Label:Razor & Tie 2011
A special mixture of roots-rock/country-folk often built over remarkable melodic solutions. This is the distinctive mark of Nicole Atkins. However, "Mondo Amore" turns mostly on her dark side, thoughtful and shady, giving a classy and sensual pop-noir with gothic nuances.

#3...AMERICAN & GOTHIC/ THE DARK SCREEN OF TV

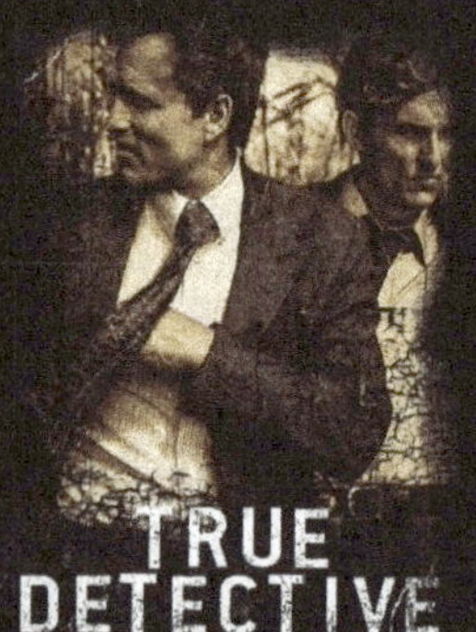

1-TRUE DETECTIVE
STUDIO: HBO 2014
TRUE DETECTIVE-FIRST SEASON
DVD HBO 2014
The show follows two detectives of the Louisiana State police and their fierce hunt of a dangerous serial killer. But also - and above all – it is a gloomy journey inside their dented souls. Dried dialogues, morbid landscapes, great neo-noir atmosphere, even dirtier than usual, everything is bleak. Nothing is in focus since the opening credits, and then - cherry on the top - the theme song by The Handsome Family. It is the definitive Southern Gothic series of our times, at least the first season.

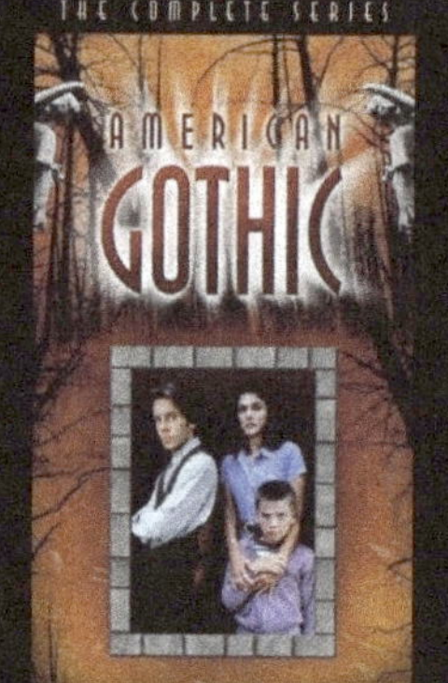

2-AMERICAN GOTHIC
STUDIO: CBS 1995
AMERICAN GOTHIC-COMPLETE SERIES
DVD UNIVERSAL 2005
Maybe someone still remembers the terrible Lucas Cole, sheriff of the imaginary Trinity, a small town located somewhere in North Carolina. He's the negative hero of this series, not to be confused with the currently aired drama of the same name. Sadly, American Gothic, had little success and was soon deleted from the tv-screens. Yet, that story was intriguing enough to be still remembered today with a pinch of regret. It conjugated horror and supernatural, dosing appropriately fear and suspense, in an original way.

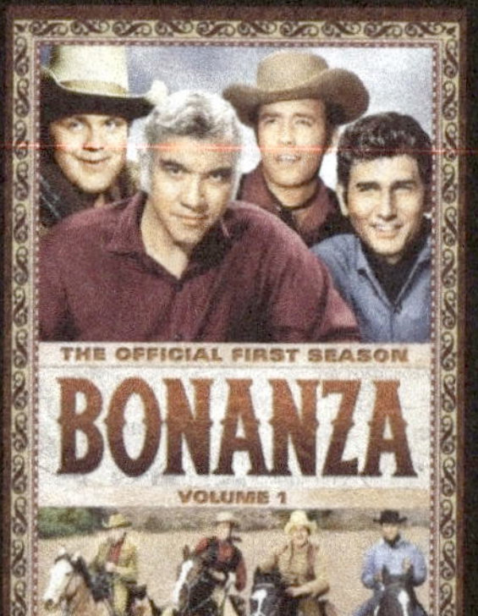

3-BONANZA
STUDIO: NBC 1959-73
BONANZA - FIRST SEASON
DVD PARAMOUNT2009
About the term Bonanza, the Merriam-Webster says: an exceptionally large and rich mineral deposit. The Cartwright Family and their Ponderosa Ranch are at the center of this famous series, but this show runs on different roads aside the usual topics of a classic western, touching on unusual topics. It includes more than one frontier story, dusted with a peculiar gothic patina. In particular, two episodes - "Hoss and the Leprechauns" and "Song in the Dark" - are excellent examples of it.

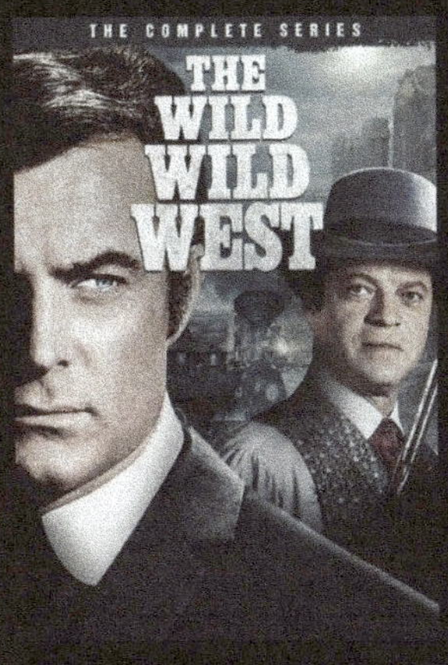

4-WILD WILD WEST
STUDIO: CBS 1965-69
WILD WILD WEST-THE COMPLETE SERIES 1965
DVD: PARAMOUNT 2008
James West and Artemus Gordon as secret agents have, moreover, the duty to protect the President of the USA - Ulysses Grant. They travel in a private train, often incurring in the characters more bizarre and threatening of this world, equipped with infernal machines and crazy inventions. Spy stories and science fiction are the spicy essences for this tv-show.

A precursor of this strange mix of Jules Verne and western movie can be found in a forgotten novel written by Edward S. Ellis in 1868. In 1999, Barry Sonnenfeld realized a movie starring Will Smith and Salma Hayek was based on that legendary series. Many have forgotten "Wild Wild West," and yet steampunk germinated its first flowers right among these four seasons and 104 episodes.

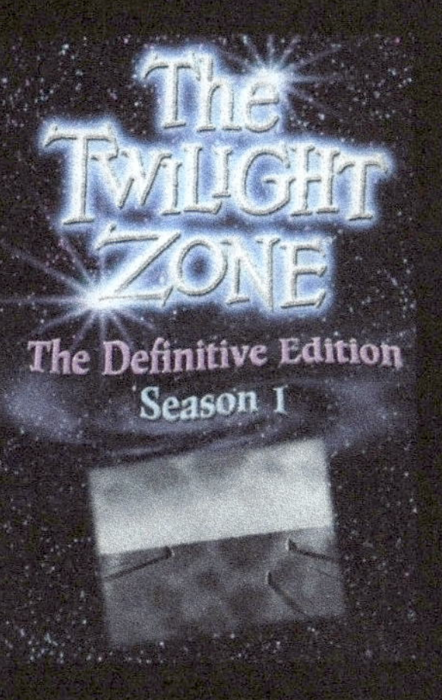

5-THE TWILIGHT ZONE
STUDIO:CBS 1959-1964
THE TWILIGHT ZONE-COMPLETE SERIES 1959
DVD SONY 2013
Paradoxically, one of the more appreciated sci-fi series of all times included, at least for the classic seasons (1959-1964), is one of the best examples of Gothic Western in tv. Created by Rod Serling, it amalgamated weird stories of horror, science-fiction, supernatural, noir, joining intelligent plots and generally an accurate staging. Episodes like "Showdown With Rance McGrew," "Mr. Denton On Doomsday," "Execution," "Walking Distance," " A Hundred Yards Over the Rim" and "Dust," are the episodes to look for.

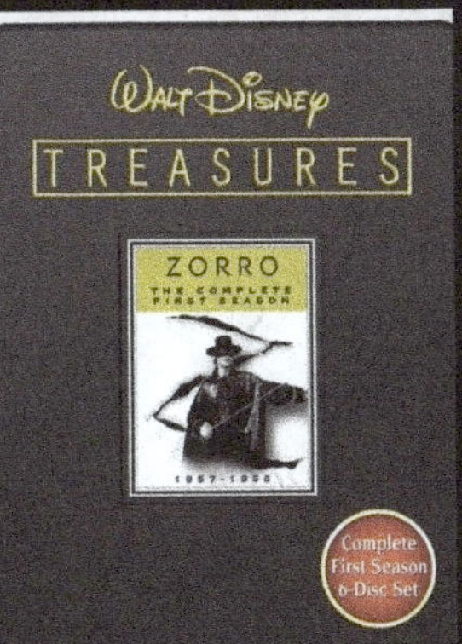

6-ZORRO
1957-59
Studio: WALT DISNEY 1957-59
TREASURES: ZORRO – FIRST SEASON
DVD WALT DISNEY 2009
Zorro, the creation of Johnston McCulley, is the precursor of many masked justices, including Batman, and with evident gothic elements. The original show with Guy Williams has been a planetary success during its run, and still now. Those apparently innocuous stories, hide a double bottom of masonic signals less recognized, scattered here and there, starting from the zeta sign passing through the secret society called Eagle Feather that plots in the shadows. The Spanish Los Angeles is the setting of intrigues and mysteries that go beyond the raids of Zorro, and the good nature of the Sergeant Demetrio Lopez Garcia. ∎

Get your music reviewed
music@carpenocturne.net

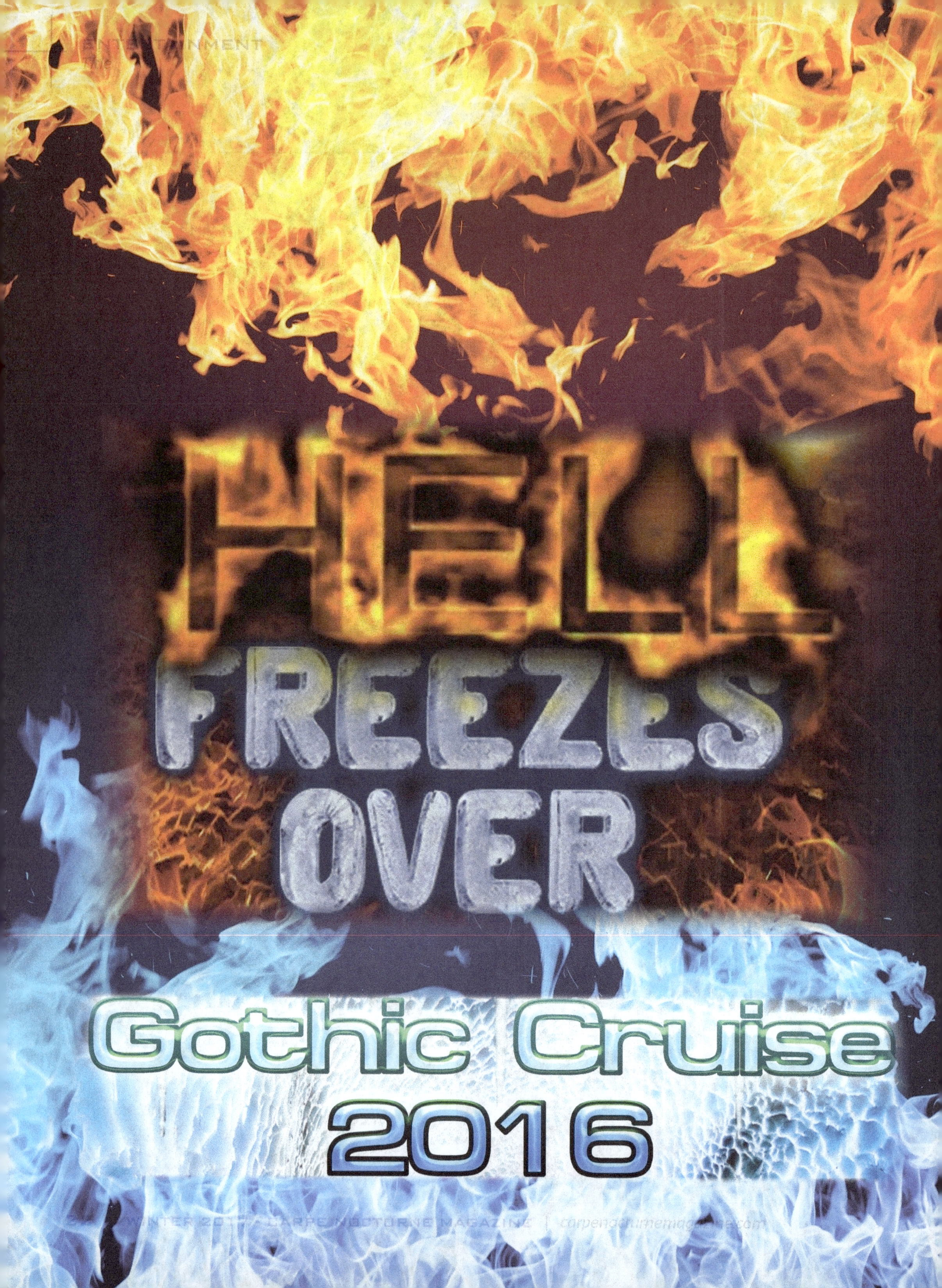

HELL
FREEZES
OVER
Gothic Cruise
2016

By: Owner of the Gothic Cruise Zaida Bourque and Carpe Nocturne writer Fairlyinnocent

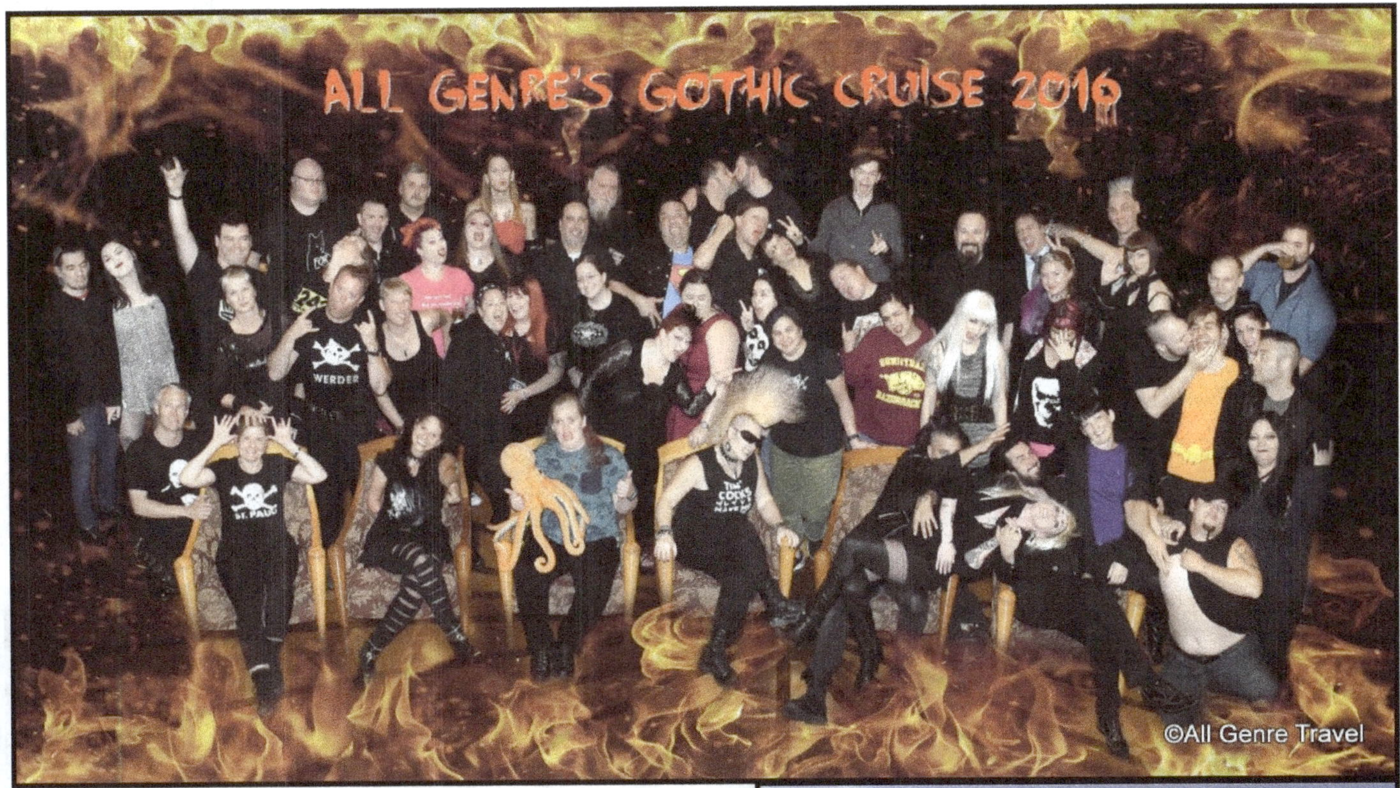

Bands: The Gothsicles, Voltaire, Stoneburner and Hopeful Machines

DJ Aesthetic Official Gothic Cruise DJ

Guest DJ: DJ Steven Archer of Ego Likeness

The cruise this year was on the Carnival Cruise Lines, Carnival Legend August 16th and it was beautiful! Our journey was a round-trip 7 night Alaskan excursion to Tracy Arm Fjord, Skagway, Juneau, Ketchikan, and lastly Victoria British Columbia.

We were delighted to have Voltaire added as a last minute performer only a few days before the cruise was set to sail, who delivered a top notch extended performance for us! We hope to have him back again! The Gothsicles performed an energetic show of brilliant music and a few new songs were debuted. Hopeful Machines and Stoneburner delivered hours of eye candy videos choreographed to live mixed danceable music in surreal setting. This left one with the dilemma of... dance and miss the video performance... or watch the video performance and try to dance in place? Decisions, decisions!

True to form our bands hung out with us every step of the way creating a sense of family amongst our group. From dinners, sitting and having a few drinks, to shore excursions and dancing parties. Steven of Ego Likeness finally got his white pony and celebrated his birthday on board with us all and we have the photos for proof!

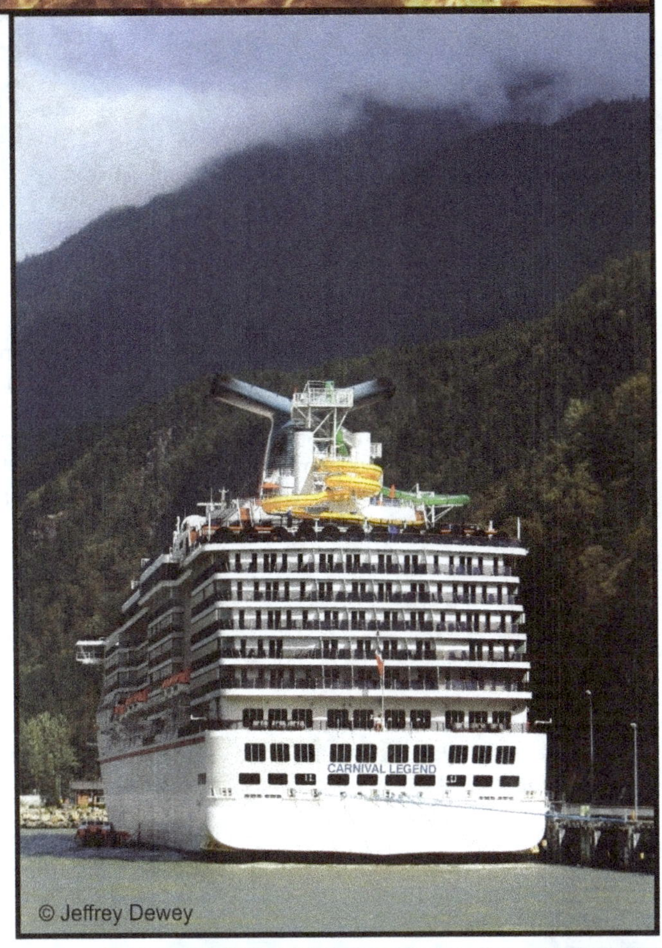

© Jeffrey Dewey

August 15 2016 - Pre Cruise Party, The Edgewater Hotel Seattle, WA- Located directly over the water on its own pier and stilts, the hotel is within walking distance to many must see sights such as Pike Street Market, Chihuly Glass Gardens, Music Museum, the Space Needle, the aquarium, and more so most cruisers arrived a few days earlier to take in those sites and the local Goth scene. Our meet and greet dinner was at Paddy Coyne's Irish pub just a few blocks from the hotel. This is a fun time to purchase merchandise like T-shirts, CDs, lanyards, and any other interesting items that might catch your fancy. You can get fun pictures with band members and have them sign your purchases or chat about all the music you will hear while on board during the cruise. Many of us enjoyed otters at the aquarium, night time city views from the space needle and shopping at the New York Xchange. We also took in an impromptu Voltaire show while in Seattle followed by Resurrection at the Baltic Room.

August 16 2016 - Boarding the ship and welcome aboard orientation. This is a really important event to attend as this will help with what to expect, the ins and outs of how things go on board in regards to our group, how to handle problems, and just a great way to figure out what is happening in general and if any changes are going to occur. Great time to mingle, activate a bar card, get drinks and relax for the rest of the activities ahead. Fire and Ice DJ Party "Old Meets New" is the theme for this nights gathering.

August 17 2016 - A full day at Sea allows for time to go to a spa, sit on the balcony, enjoy the views, or just catch up with long-time friends you have not seen since the previous gothic cruise. This was also an afternoon for "Vamps and Sirens" dance party, followed later that night with a Dune inspired concert by Stoneburner.

August 18 2016 - Tracy Arm Fjord, Viewing of Sawyer Glacier - We sailed down the Tracy Arm Fjord. A Fjord of about 30 miles in length with natural waterfalls along its sides, the fjord ends in Sawyer Glacier. We enjoyed warm blankets and specialty coffees and hot chocolates provided by the cruise line while we viewed this awe inspiring glacier as we cruised passed the icebergs and ice formations in the fjord.

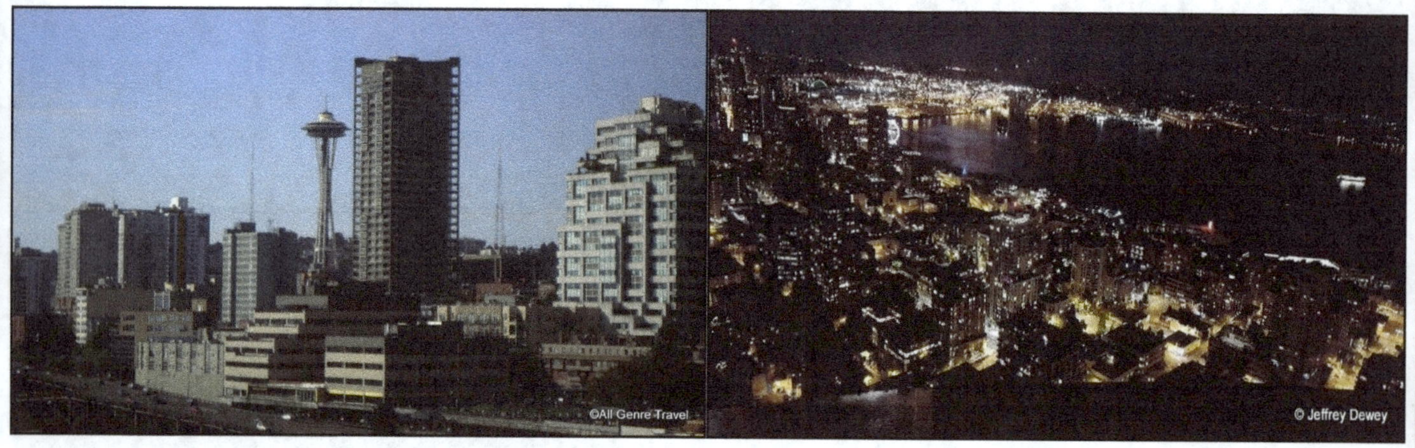

August 19 2016 - Skagway - This location had a lot of options for folks to do and see. The White Pass Train ride was a freezing success, including the viewing of a juvenile bear on the side of the road on our bus ride up to the summit at the Canadian border. Our driver stopped for photo ops, from inside the bus of course! Also in Skagway there what is known as "Prostitution Shacks" that housed prostitutes that came hoping to seek fortunes. They shared their income with pimps and madams and lived in tents, boarding houses, and the shacks called cribs, and some were brought here as "white slaves" from foreign countries. Some suffered disease, attacks, and even suicide. Also of interest in Skagway was a hotel called The Golden North Hotel. It is rumored to be haunted so there were some cruisers who did make sure to take photos and visit that location. Some cruisers opted to tour the Skagway Cemetery on their own called the Gold Rush Cemetery of which was fascinating as well as quite old and breathtaking. There are a lot of old tombstones to read and explore with that creepy haunted aura floating about, yet it is peaceful and serene. This is the oldest cemetery in Skagway and many of the town's famous Gold Rush characters are buried here.

August 20 2016 - Juneau - One of the tours available here was the Whales and Ales tour where you can go for a day of viewing whales and Mendlehall Glacier and ending at a brewery for beer tasting! Based on the photos this was a fantastic tour to take to see whales up close that you may never see at any other time.

August 21 2016 - Ketchikan - This was another area full of adventure! Many of us took the Lighthouse, Totems and Eagles tour. The boat ride out into the sounds was just stellar. There was no shortage of eagle spotting in their natural habitat. This was a tour filled with old history and a lot of great stories from our guides. The evening was another dance party called "My boots are taller!"

August 22 2016 - Victoria BC - Arriving at night, quite a few gothic cruisers disembarked for night life and some took the opportunity to just relax on the ship for our farewell party or pack to go home. There is a door decoration that matches the theme of the cruise every year. This year's was Fire and Ice and the winner was Paris Reilly, her door was AMAZING!

August 23 2016 – After the cruise each year cruisers can either go back to the post hotel and chill for a day or two, or take flights out to go home. The post cruise party was at the Hard Rock Café in Seattle, WA and The Edgewater Hotel. This is always a sad time to say goodbye to all the new friends and old. But on the plus side you know you will probably meet up again the next year.

This particular cruise did not have the usual amount of late night parties or bands due to the nature of locations visited. Most cruisers wanted to get out early when in port to explore and do tours. This was an Alaskan cruise, one of unbridled nature, sightseeing, and on most peoples bucket lists. As always come out and join the family of Goth cruisers and bands who love to party, dance, travel, and just have fun!

Book the 2017 cruise now because the theme is HELLYwood. Leaving from Los Angeles for 7 nights to new ports Cabo San Lucas, in port here for two days, and Puerto Vallarta this is going to be such an adventure. Also bands onboard performing some fantastic kickass music will be Covenant, Haujobb, and Lights of Euphoria. So don't be shy, come make new friends, and have a trip of a lifetime.

Cruise booking: All Genre Travel: gothiccruise.com

Band information for Gothsicles: www.thegothsicles.com/ and www.facebook.com/thegothsicles

Band information for Voltaire: www.voltaire.net and www.facebook.com/VoltaireFanPage

Band information Stoneburner and Hopeful Machines: www.stoneburnerband.com/ and www.facebook.com/stoneburnerofficial

Sponsorship of the Gothic Cruise: Carpe Nocturne Magazine ∎

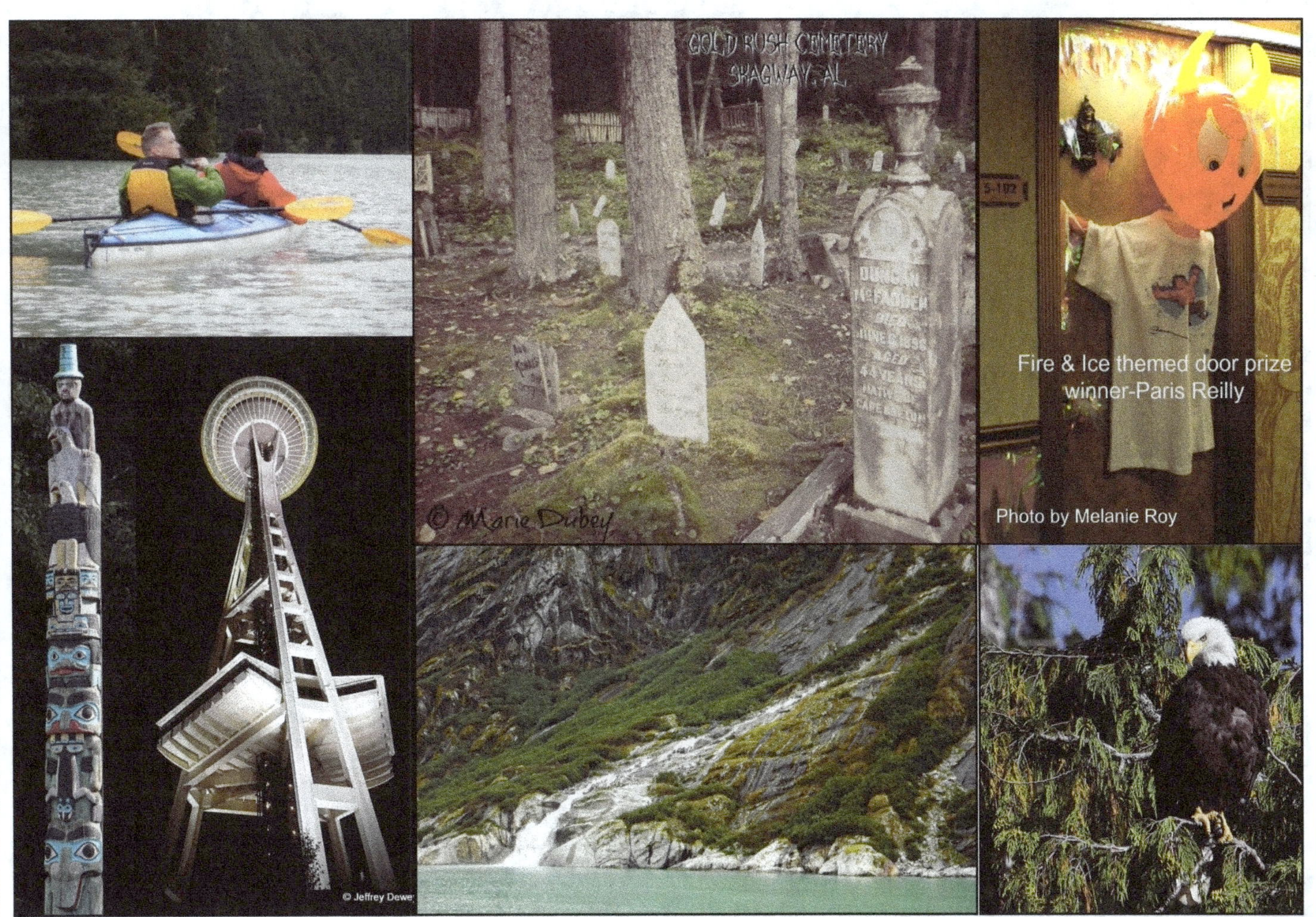

Fire & Ice themed door prize winner-Paris Reilly

Photo by Melanie Roy

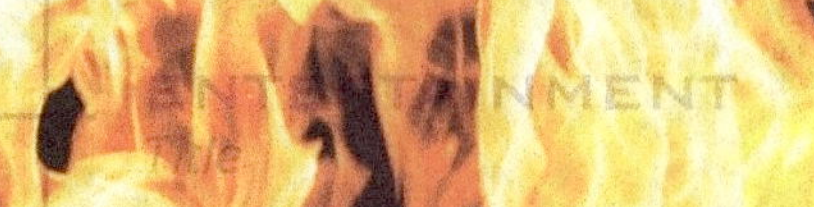

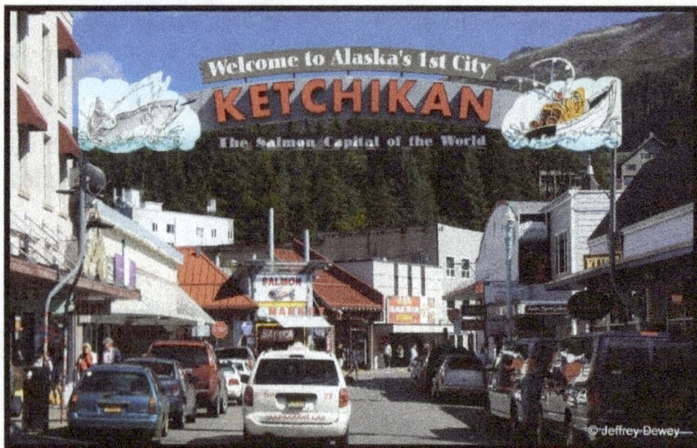

Photo by Melanie

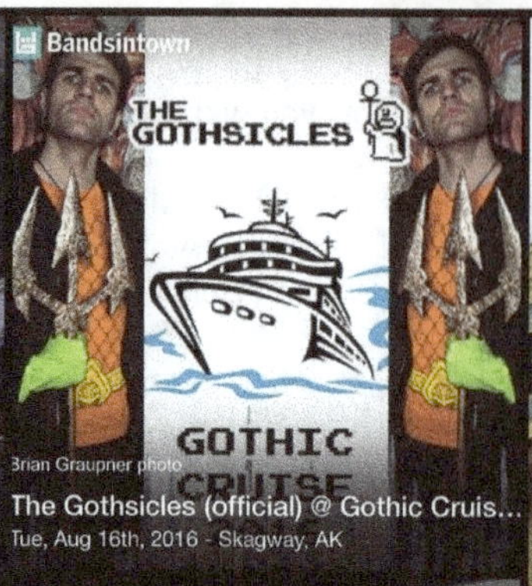

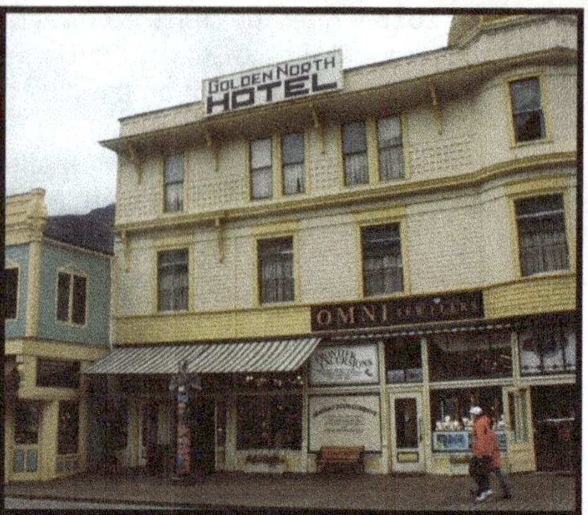

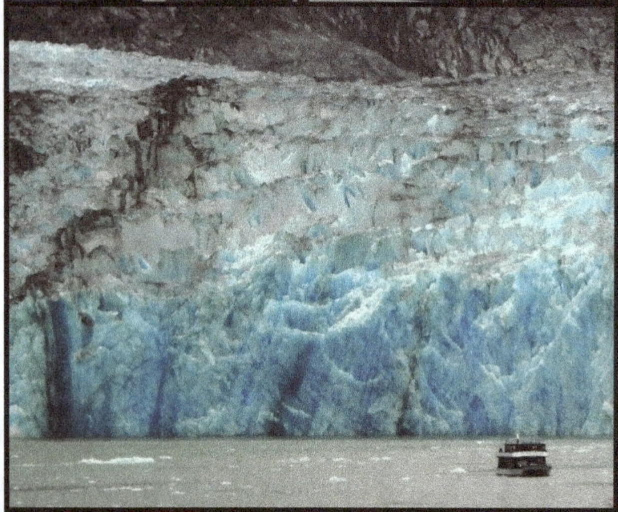

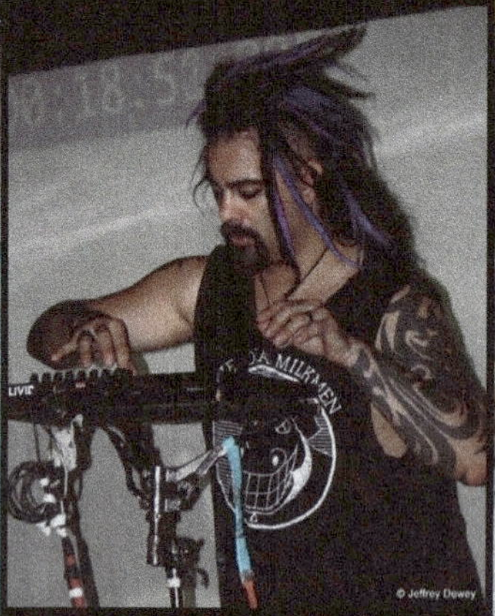

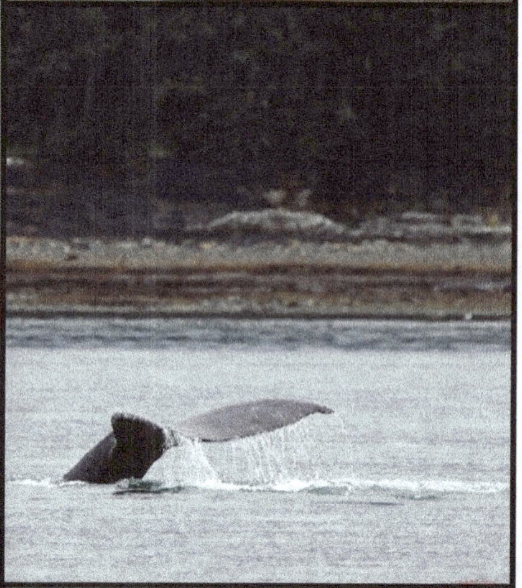

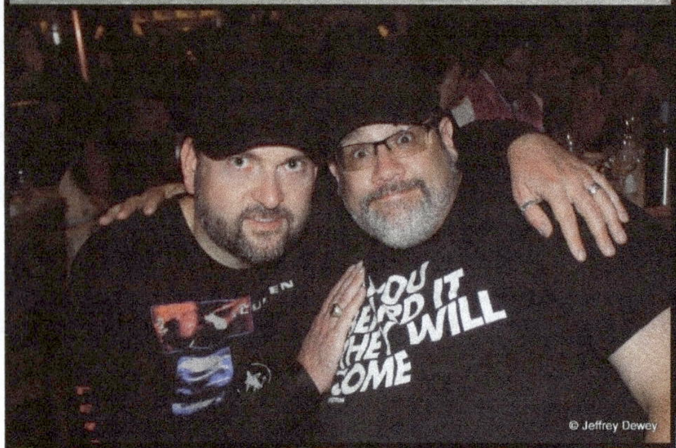

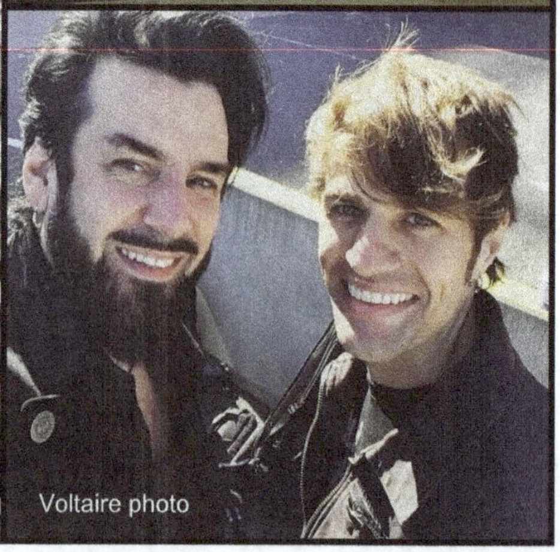

Voltaire photo

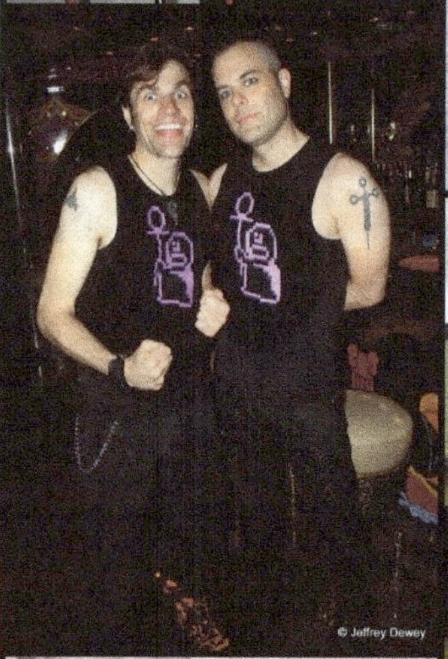

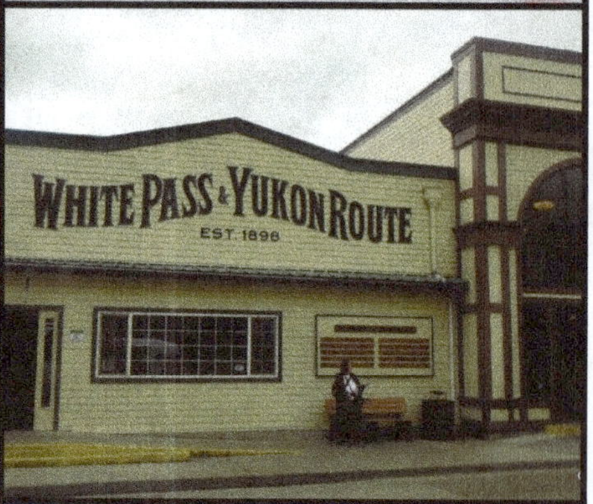

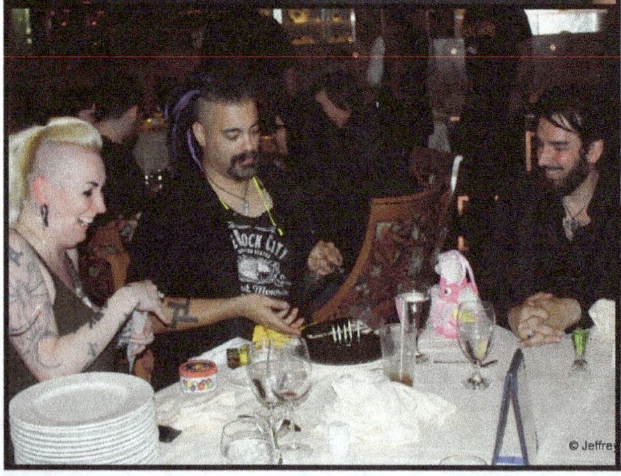

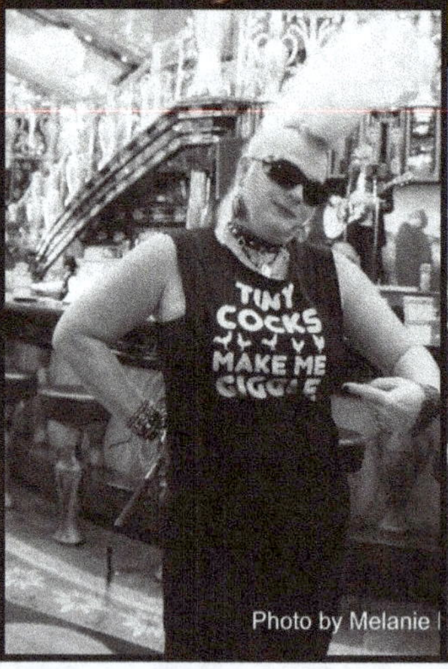

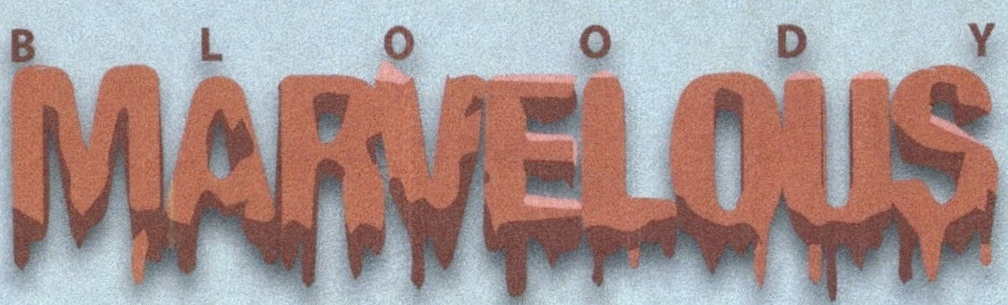

BLOODY MARVELOUS

by Xxx Zombieboy xxX

TARANTULAS

"There was an old lady who swallowed a spider. That wriggled and wiggled and tickled inside her; She swallowed the spider to catch the fly; I don't know why she swallowed a fly - Perhaps she'll die."
- Unknown

continued to be served and even savored. At roughly 12-20 cents per arachnid (or a few hundred riels), they are a cheap "tasty" treat for the more adventurous amongst you.

Now, I have never eaten this crunchy critter myself. The first time I ever even heard of such a thing was from some random documentary in my days of endless Discovery Channel addiction. I will never forget the image of the British guy (aren't most of these guys British?) crunching on the legs. Supposedly, this is the best way to begin. You twist off the legs and munch them like Cheetos.

Then there is the abdomen. While some reviews and videos I have perused describe this experience as something you will never want to repeat, there was a surprising amount of relish and desire to dive once more into the black belly of the tarantula. Often the abdomen may be filled with mealy tasting eggs, but when prepared properly with any number of exotic (and often strange) recipes, this can be

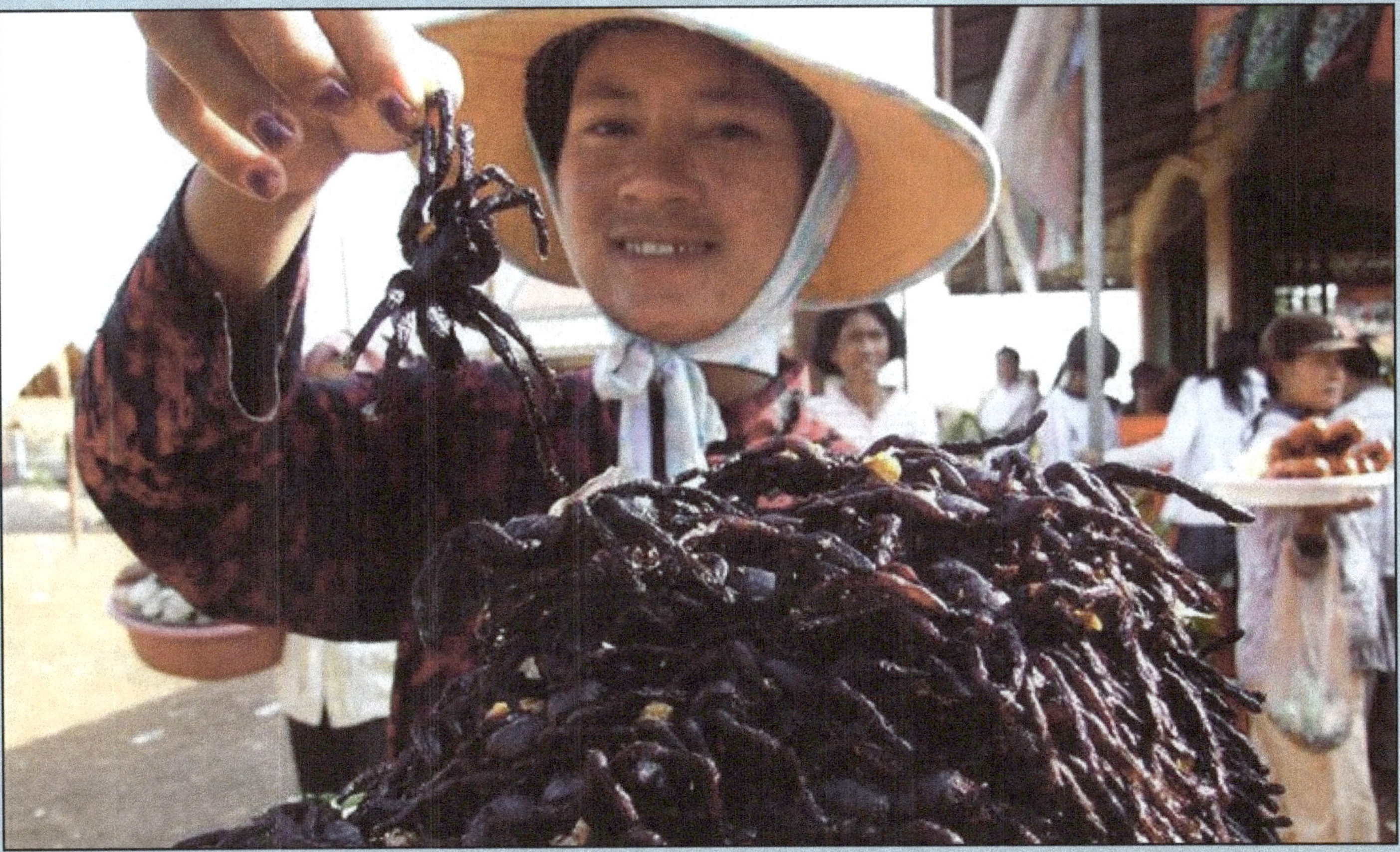

So after binging briefly on a series of films featuring my personal greatest fears (arachnids), I decided to focus this entry of Bloody Marvelous on a Cambodian delicacy that is gaining popularity with tourists, and has been favored by locals for generations. The eating of tarantulas.

Called A-Ping, it is served in street markets as a novelty to visitors, and as a treat to Cambodians. Though eaten sporadically throughout history and in several parts of the world just as sporadically, the popularity of eating A-Ping grew out of the food shortages during the Khmer Rouge regime of the 1970's. What began in necessity

overcome with the burst of flavorful protein. In fact, a number of brave adventurous souls likened the experience to eating soft shell crab.

Though often served in restaurants, I myself would choose to head just north of the capitol city of Phnom Penh to the smaller town of Skuon, which is known for these crispy treats and pick them up from countless roadside vendors. Here, your little foray into exotic treats will also support families used to a daily wage of about $1-3. And really, who doesn't want to increase the supposed number of spiders you will (willingly or unwillingly) ingest in your lifetime? Maybe they go good with Phnom Penh Stout? ■

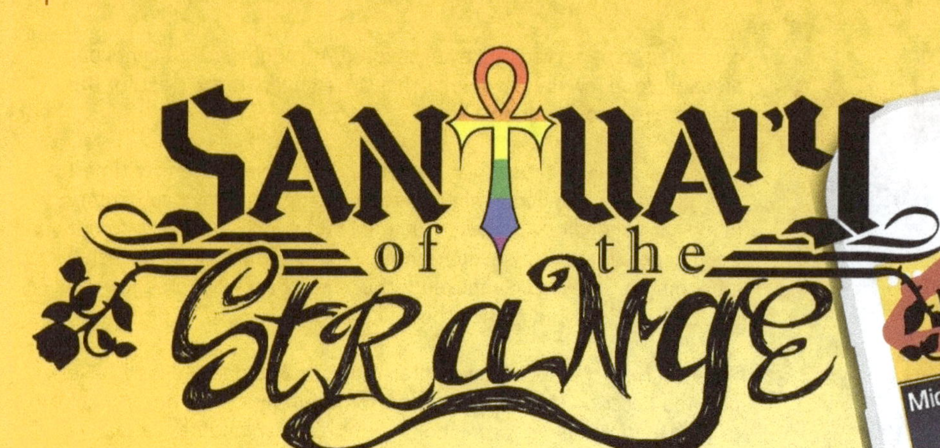

SANCTUARY of the STRANGE

by Asylum Attendant

Is dating an enjoyable experience for anyone? I think we all dread putting ourselves out there, meeting up with complete strangers and facing rejection. I personally do not have the time or the energy for finding love, but I have learned some things about LGBTQ dating over the years that I would like to share. The trashy dating app Grindr will not be discussed. Breathe easy everyone.

The downright horrifying part about LGBTQ dating is that another person's sexual orientation can be almost impossible to figure out without asking them. So, unless you are at a gay club, you are pretty much playing a game of Russian roulette that could completely blow up in your face. How reassuring. Luckily, we live in a world in which people are much more accepting of the LGBTQ community than in the past. If you have ever hit on a straight person and been politely turned down, then you know how embarrassing it can be. Not to mention the assholes that react badly or violently to a romantic advance from the same gender. Can't people just wear name tags with their sexual orientation on them?

There is always online dating, which seems safer than guessing at a person's sexual orientation. I tend to attract a lot of freaks who believe that my feminine appearance makes me a slut. Guys either wanted to sleep with me or wanted nothing to do with me since I was not masculine enough for them. I do not recall meeting a decent person through online dating so I gave it up. The most disturbing part of my experience were all of the gay male profiles I came across stating that they were not interested in femmes. That kind of attitude or exclusionary preference is extremely damaging to the LGBTQ community and encourages gay men to mask their femininity. We already face enough discrimination without dividing ourselves further.

One thing all LGBTQ people can probably relate to is their lovely and kind friends trying to set them up on dates. "Oh, I have a friend that you should meet. You guys have so much in common. I think you would be great together." This is all fine and dandy until you meet the mutual friend and the sparks do not fly as predicted. This type of dating situation feels very forced and unnatural. Neither party wants to let their matchmaker of a friend down. Plus, just because we are both gay does not mean we will automatically be attracted to one another. I do try to have some self-control and standards. I appreciate the friendly help in the love department, though.

I have had terrible and quite a few dating experiences, which has likely turned me off to the entire idea. The only guy I would consider, a former boyfriend, still pretends to be straight around his family. I wonder why we never had an actual relationship. I am open to love, I just do not seek it out anymore. Throwing myself at the cute guy at work and buying him Starbucks every day was a desperate look. I am so much better than that. It is high time that someone throws themselves at me. I'm ashamed to admit that I would absolutely go on a date with anyone who bought me a Cotton Candy Frappuccino. There went my standards. ∎

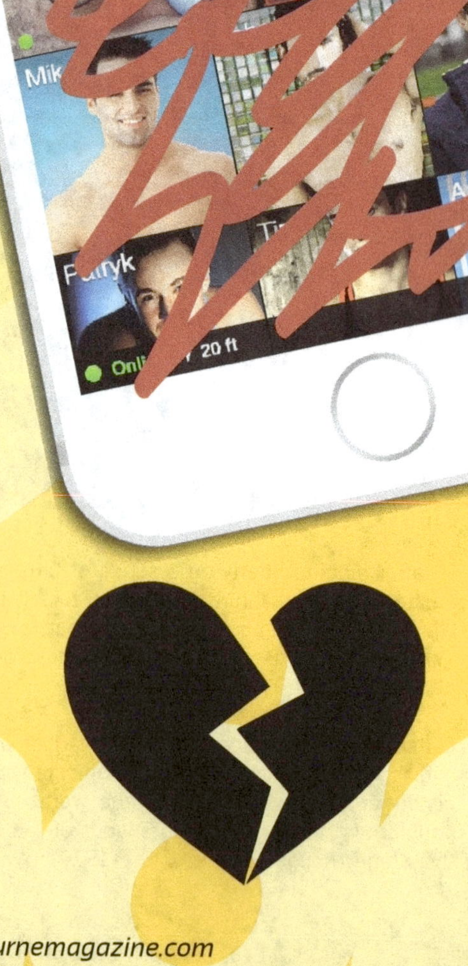

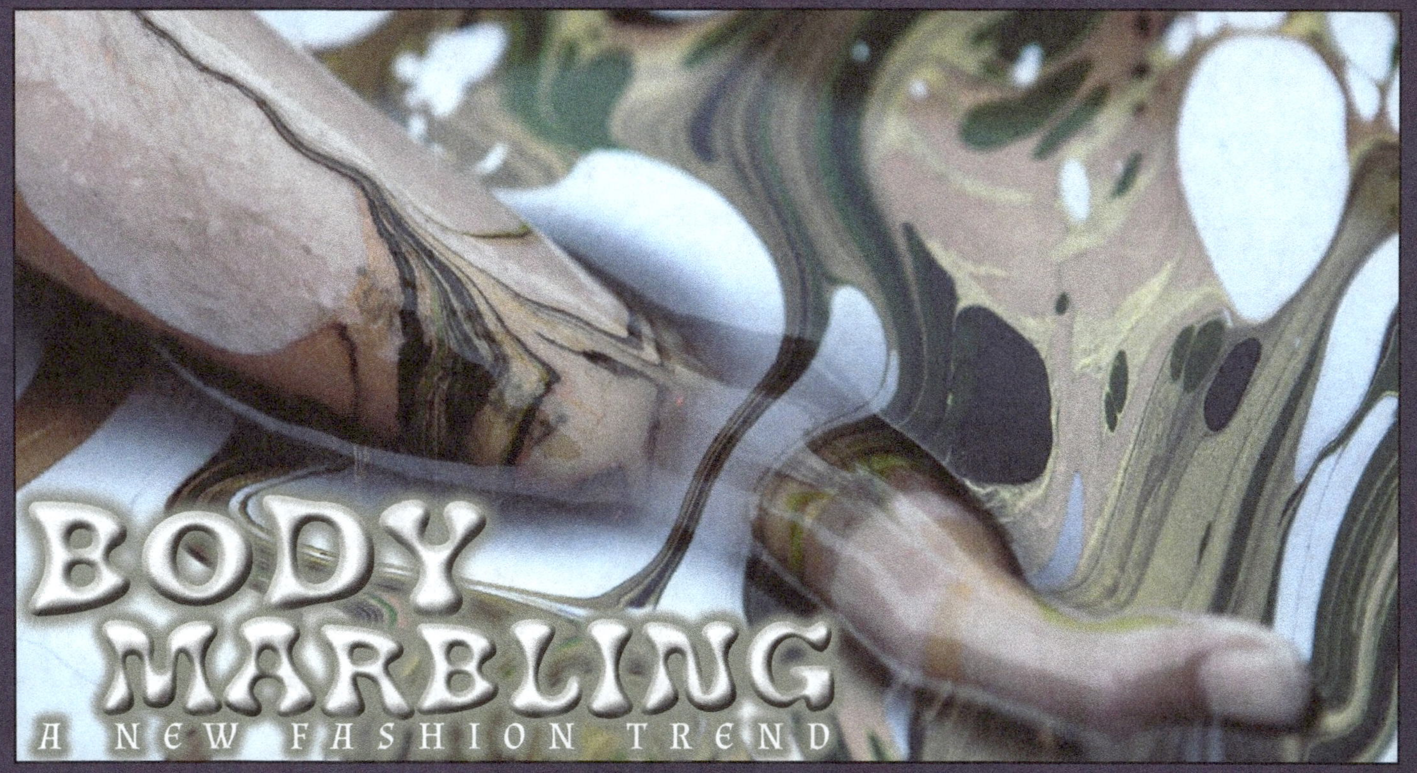

BODY MARBLING
A NEW FASHION TREND

by Kathleen Sharkey

Tattoos have been a fascinating form of fashion accoutrement. Individual pieces of artwork worn proudly by creator or palette. The only problem appears when someone else admires your beautiful artwork and decides to have the same ink indelibly added to their skin. Then your one of a kind piece of skin art is no longer one of a kind. Temporary tattoos are another way of displaying art but so much of it appears to be cartoonish most of the time, and again you have the undying problem of not having an individual piece of art. Welcome Body Marbling.

In the summer of 2016 Body Marbling started appearing at festivals all over the US. This amazing artwork provides an ever changing possibility of design on the wearer's skin with the added bonus of being washable. The idea for body marbling was started by the Black Light Visuals Company (www.blacklightvisuals.com). From the website this is how it works: 1st acrylic paint floats on a fluid's surface, 2nd pigments are manipulated into patterns and designs and finally colors transferred directly upon dipping. To do this on the body one must dip their skin into a container of water combined with salt. This combination allows the paint to adhere better to the skin. After the solution dries, during which the paint has been dripped and swirled into designs in another liquid, the skin is placed into this "hydro-dye" and then slowly removed from the liquid. Finally the area is placed in regular water to be rinsed.

The artist who started the idea is Brad Lawrence, who at the age of 23 was told he could no longer create the art he had come to love due to Chronic Tendonitis. Inspired by his friend Michael Zach to find a different way to create art they came up with the idea to create Body Marbling and Black Light Visuals was born. One only has to go to the website to see the beauty and love for the art that they create. Plus there is the added bonus that one can hire Black Light Visuals for events and parties.

So now we know where the concept of Body Marbling came from but the beauty and art that is Marbling, where did that appear. It is my great fortune to have gotten to meet a young man who creates this beautiful art on paper so I wanted to give you, dear reader a background on the historic and beautiful art that is MARBLING.

CN: Could you introduce yourself to our readers?

Curtis Splan: Hello, my name is Curtis Splan and I'm an amateur water marbler and general hobbyist here in Sacramento, California. I've been marbling for a few years now and have participated in several international events through the vast network of water marblers around the world. I currently work for the State of California within the state retirement system, and help them to manage their business intelligence systems.

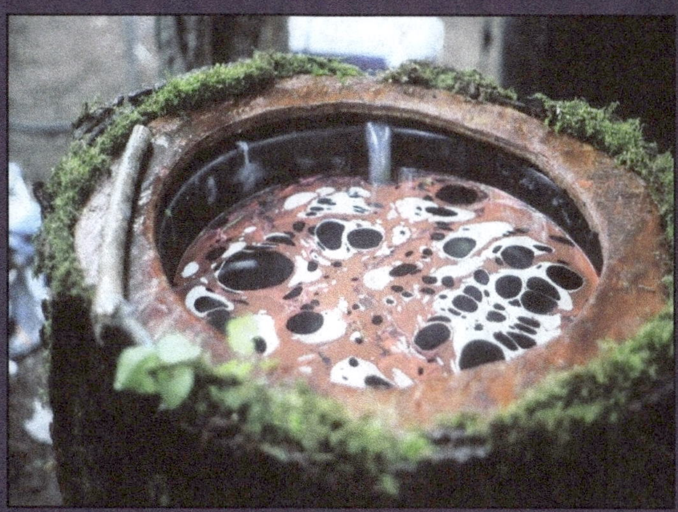

CN: Could you give us a little background on marbling art?

Curtis Splan: The art itself is most recognized in 16th to 20th century hand bound books within the actual end pages. These are the colorful pages (or patterns) found either on the cover, on the fore edges of the pages themselves, or the book end pages (which sandwich the beginning and ending of the book.) When books were still handmade, these were considered an embellishing touch by the bookbinders. Using marbled sheets of paper also helped to hide all the messy parts of binding the book, thus increasing their quality and presentation.

The history of marbling itself is just as interesting as it is mysterious. The earliest extant examples of marbling are found in Turkey, dating back from the 15th century. However, each country which has adopted marbling has brought a new spin to it; added new materials and processes, as well as the artistic mediums which have been marbled. The Europeans brought brilliant and timeless patterns to their marbling; the Turkish brought the calligraphy and all manners of beautiful flowers. The Japanese adopted an early form of marbling called Suminagashi which uses traditional Sumi ink and plain water. These traditional styles of marbling--when added to beautiful handmade Japanese paper--are so amazing; they were even used as the backing of all royal documents for several Japanese dynasties.

Unfortunately, until the 19th century, many of the earliest pages (older than 15th century) of this beautiful art form were virtually lost. Due to industrialization and mass reproduction, the bookbinding business was quickly in decline—and along with it—the demand for water marblers. In a mad dash to save this vanishing art, several

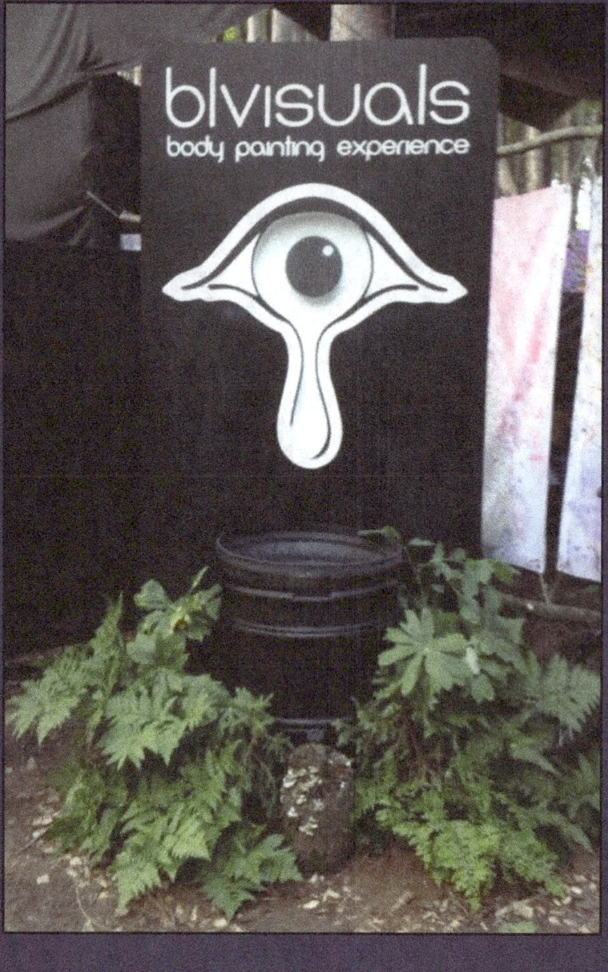

notable marblers published the vast majority of their trade secrets during highly competitive times, with hopes to spurn the art further. These efforts literally saved this fading art. Within the golden age of information technology, many of these old books, techniques and recipes have been recovered and shared to those interested in furthering this amazing art. I consider myself part of this resurgence.

CN: How did you get started doing marbling?

Curtis Splan: To be completely honest, I just saw a YouTube video which came up as a recommended video. Between the grace of the music, the dance of the ink and the flow of the water, I just watched it over and over-- and I was hooked! I ordered my first water marbling kit from Galen Berry (a well-known and respected marbler in Oklahoma, OK) and I took the plunge. I have been marbling ever since!

CN: What do you think of marbling temporary tattoos?

Curtis Splan: I think it is awesome and looks like great fun. One of the amazing things about water marbling is that it has an unlimited list of mediums (with the proper preparation) which could be marbled. In the marbling community, we call it 3D dunking: whether it be a piece of wood, ceramic, masonry, or—yes, even a human arm. If it can be submerged in water—even momentarily--it can be marbled!

So there you have it. If you are looking for an amazing style of art to create take a look at water marbling. Hey, and if you happen to be at one of the amazing events where body marbling is happening try it out, it could be right up your individualistic alley. ■

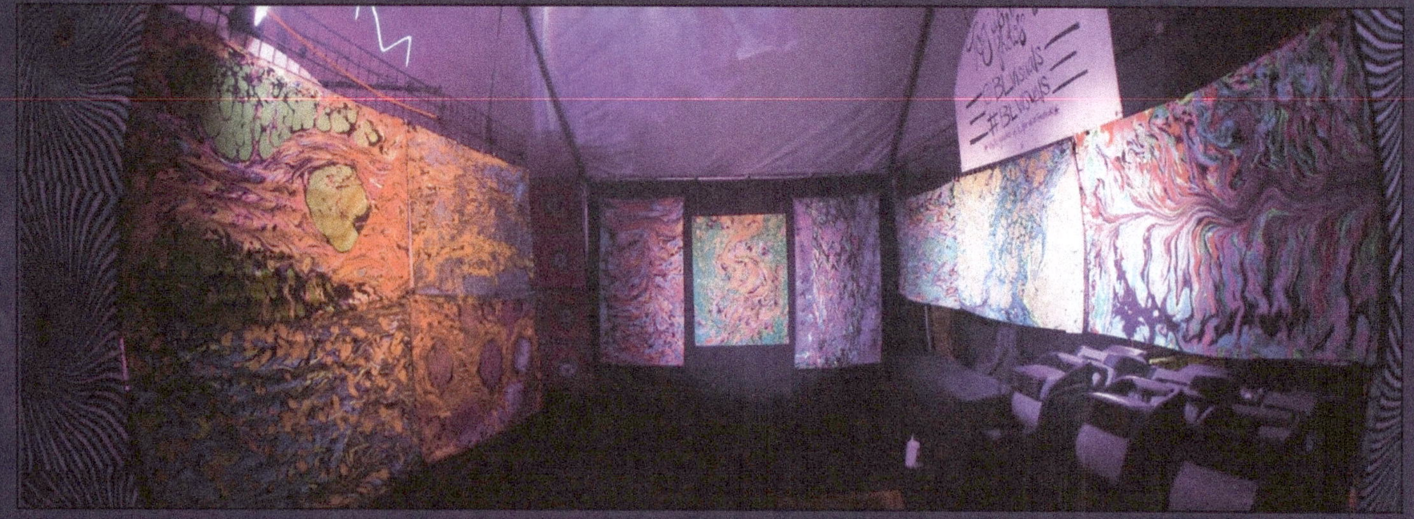

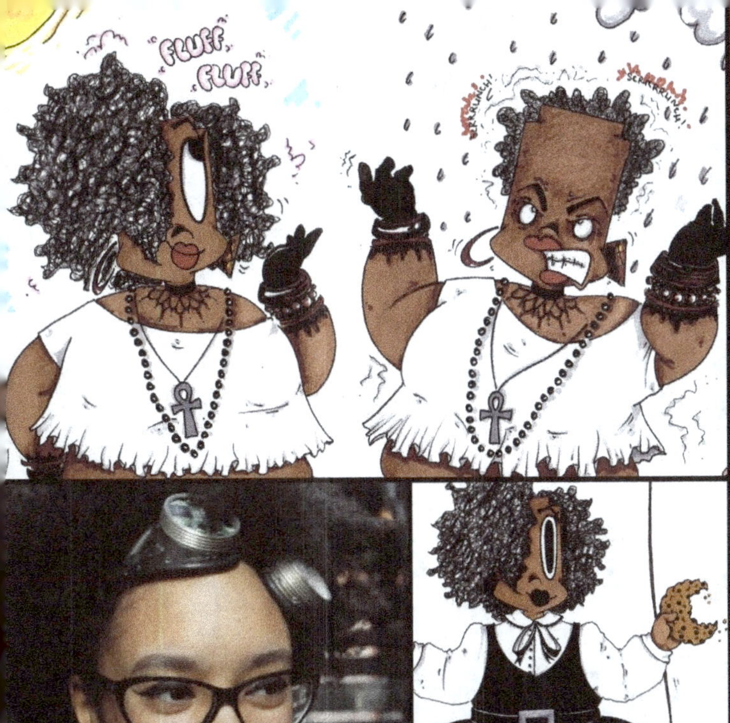

Dining with Dana is an alternative/goth blog and webcomic series started in 2014 by Calyn. It features a Fat Bat, Rabid Reader and Sweet Chef, her freaky friends and six limbed mad scientist dad. Since then, it has become a resource for the underrepresented in the alternative subculture. The character, Dana Dillipede, was created in 2007. As her personality grew, so did her size as she is affectionately called "Fat Bat" by the community. Dining with Dana has plenty of resources for goths of color, such as positivity, fashion, and musician posts. "Although I've always had an affinity for both Goth and Punk, I do not attach myself to any subculture in particular. However, the two - along with many others - are seen as predominantly white. This is mostly due to misrepresentation. Comments about melanin in regards to style and music usually come from the monochromatic image put in the forefront of many scenes. I did not grow up in a place where solely my race was questioned; rather, it was mostly my person as a whole that provoked confusion. There are plenty of POCs playing a crucial role in alternative subculture. The trick is to find them." I have been following Dining With Dana for quite some time, and it has been a huge inspiration to see like-minded people come together in one place where we can truly be represented.

Where to find Dining with Dana:
http://diningwithdana.tumblr.com/
http://diningwithdana.net/

JASON & THE G.O.C.'S

Martanna Lunna is an eighteen year old aspiring makeup artist. She became interested in extravagant makeup a year and a half ago because of a well-known makeup artist in the goth community, Drac Makens. "She was my biggest inspiration, and when I got to speak to her it was such a huge motivation." Martanna got bored with doing her makeup the exact same everyday until she got the confidence to shave off her eyebrows. "Being in the gothic subculture has been bittersweet, but mostly on the sweet side. All my friends and a lot of strangers love my creativity, and I inspire other goths to be more creative. There isn't anything that brings me more joy than to inspire!" She cites herself as her own main inspiration for her extravagant looks. Martanna's goals for the future are to hopefully become a licensed hair and makeup artist.

Where to find Martanna:
Thecolorfulwitch.tumblr.com

Jason a.k.a Night Fever King is a writer and aspiring film maker from Louisiana. When he's not writing for Carpe Nocturne, he's attending college for forensics. He can be reached at nightfeverking@gmail.com ∎

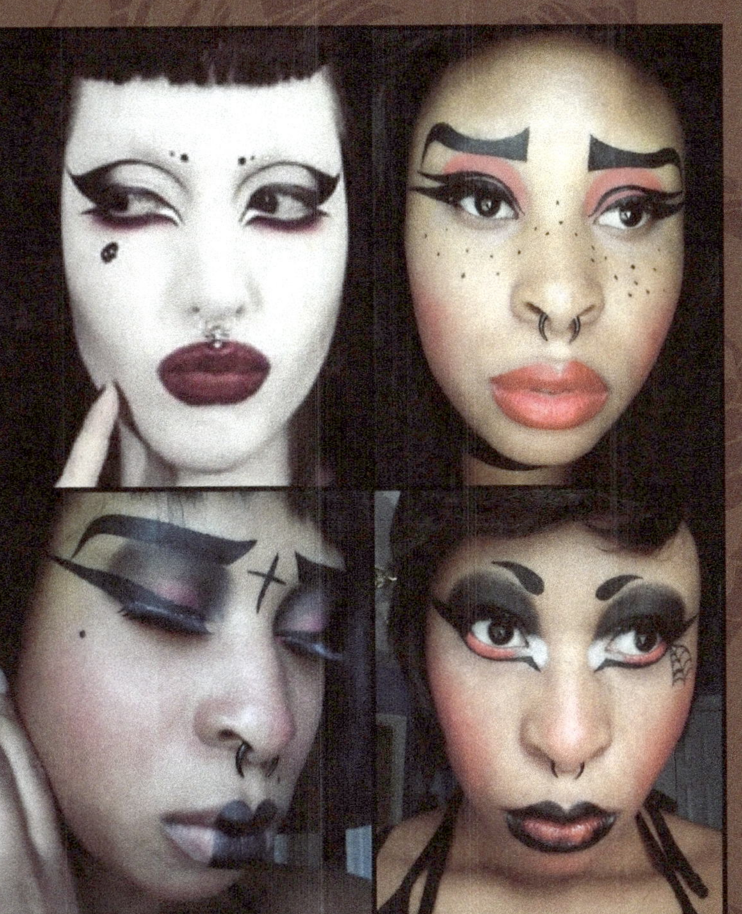

I would never have imagined that I would see a guy in makeup in a CoverGirl commercial. I know the world is becoming more progressive, but this is uncharted territory. Makeup is certainly not marketed to men, so this was a truly shocking and revolutionary event to witness. This first male CoverGirl is James Charles and he is slaying the beauty world all while navigating through his senior year of high school. I did not even know how to use eyeliner at his age.

17 year old James only started doing makeup about a year ago. He has almost one million followers on Instagram, where he posts subtle and more extravagant themed makeup looks. His looks include skulls, mermaids and even a human Ouija board. James embraces his masculine features and likes to enhance them, such as his accentuated eyebrows. It is important to note that a lot of men who wear makeup are not trying to look like women, but just want to get creative with their appearance. James falls into this category.

So how did CoverGirl become privy to James' talent and stunning confidence? James had his senior pictures done and was not happy with the results. Oh, can I relate to that. So, he asked the photography studio for them to be redone and brought his ring light along this time. The gorgeous photos went viral and CoverGirl took notice, scooping James up to be the face of their So Lashy mascara. He's joined the likes of Katy Perry and Ellen DeGeneres as a national spokesmodel for CoverGirl cosmetics. A man in makeup is no longer weird.

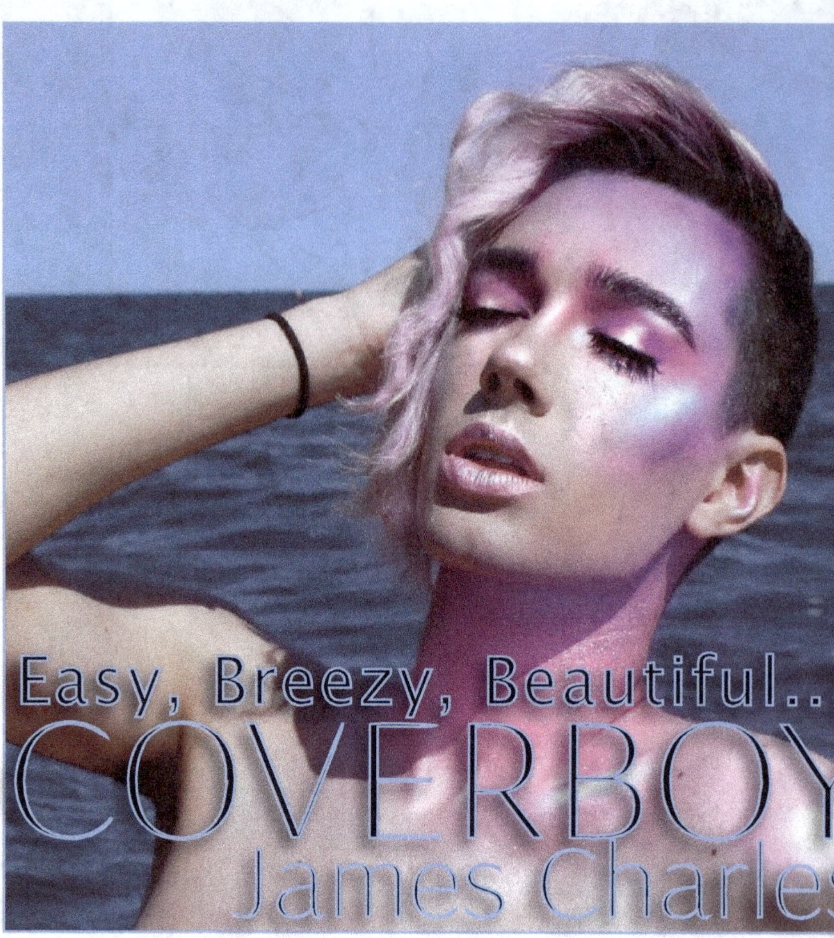

by Asylum Attendant

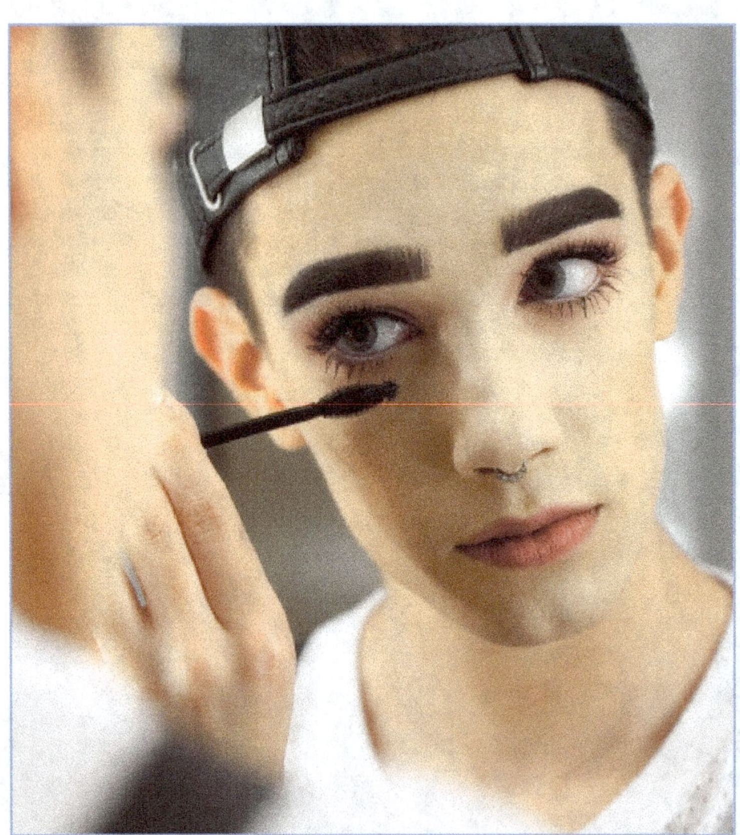

James has been openly gay since the age of twelve and is not shy with sharing his exuberant personality in makeup tutorials he posts on YouTube. He is completely self-taught and started out doing hair and makeup on his friends. James is still a regular teenager in so many ways. He has to juggle schoolwork around photoshoots and deal with boys who are just interested in him to gain attention on social media. However, his hometown of Bethlehem, New York has been super supportive of James' overnight success.

One of James' signature looks is faux freckles. A lot of people try to hide their freckles, but James thinks they are youthful and fun. He also embraces a bold highlight, which is right on trend in the beauty world. Even though he loves to experiment with extravagant looks, James rarely wears makeup outside of his house. He is comfortable with his gender and does not use makeup to impress anyone else or look more attractive. This makes James a great role model to people who feel that they must wear makeup to be accepted by society. Naked faces are just as beautiful as painted ones.

I'm very excited to see what James Charles' career will become. He's persuading society to think about makeup in new ways and celebrating equality on and off the television screen. CoverBoys everywhere can look to James for strength and inspiration. You better work! ■

M A R Y   F R A N C E S
Designer Handbags for a Cause

by Kathleen Sharkey

So many times the fashion industry is raked across the coals for the abuse of cheap labor in the production of their wares. So it is a beautiful thing to see people of the fashion industry making amazing things of beauty and training people how to create the same beauty while supporting the cottage industry. Mary Frances

80's out of her own home. Over time she moved into other accessories and heavier duty bags. Scarves, bottles and belts and jewelry joined the heavily beaded handbags. More recently, and as the demand for her bags have gone up, the Mary Francis Company released 5 design lines per year; Resort, spring, fall, summer and

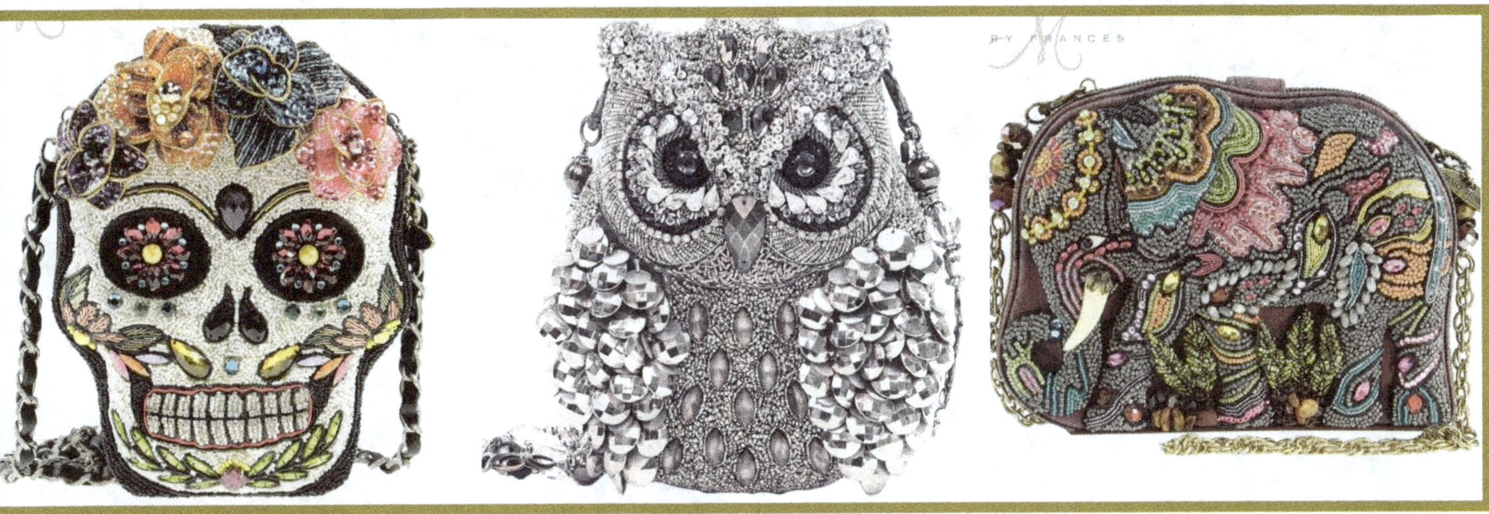

has always been about supporting those artisans all over the world who produce items in the cottage industry. The handbags that are created in this way are hand beaded works of usable art whose creations bring money to the artisans of third world countries.

For twenty years Mary Francs has brought her bohemian bags to life, each one as brilliant and unique as the last. From phones to faces, from ice cream to crowns these bags are stunning pieces of wearable art. Inspired by the art of San Francisco, where she grew up, Mary Francis has had her artistic endeavors displayed at Paris Fashion week and many famous women own Mary Francis bags. Eva Longoria, Paris Hilton and a variety of fashionable women carry these amazing purses. But then again I first came across these beautiful bags at Dillard's, so they are available to those of us who are not so famous.

Mary Francis began he foray into handbag creation in the early

Winter/Holiday. She has also started creating other purse like accessories; pill containers, mirrors, wallets and a variety of other amazing pieces.

Pictures of these purses do not do the real pieces justice. For anyone looking for a one of a kind art object you should go to Mary Francis's website at http://www.maryfrances.com/ . Her website has all of Mary's newest objet d'art and even some of her sale items. The items are on the pricey side but worth every penny for these beautiful pieces. So if you are looking for that one of a kind piece that matches your one of a kind personality you can definitely find it in a Mary Francis design. ■

Fairy Tale Dresses For Every Bride

By Samm Sanity

The designers at Alfred Angelo have created a new collection of wedding dresses inspired by the Disney princesses, yet again. The new collection is scheduled to launch January 2017, with two additional limited edition dresses launching in June in celebration of Disney's Fairy Tale Weddings and Honeymoons' 25th anniversary. They will all be available for purchase on the official Alfred Angelo website. This new collection also debuts dresses inspired by Pocahontas and Mulan, who have never before been embodied in previous years. Meaning all princesses are included for the first time.

Each dress is designed to reflect each princess' charisma, strength, and beauty. And they sure are beautiful with organza skirts and beaded bodices.

Ariel's dress is a stunning mermaid dress with an embroidered lace bodice and flowing tulle skirt. Details such as pearls and caviar eggs add that touch of under the sea elegance befitting a princess of the sea. Or the air.

Cinderella's is a simple ball gown styled dress

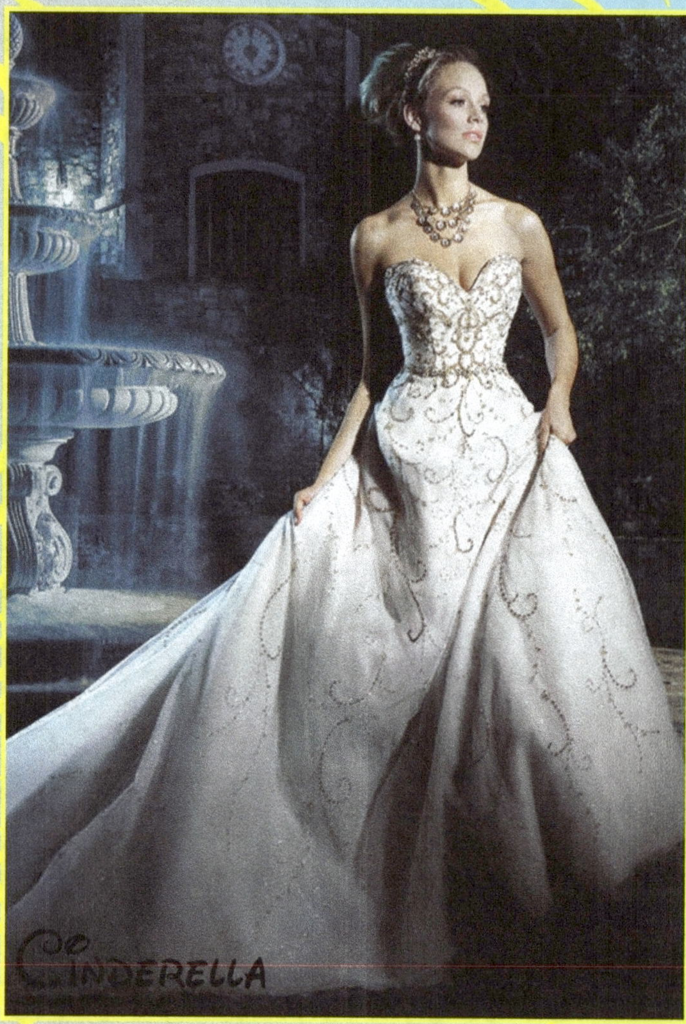

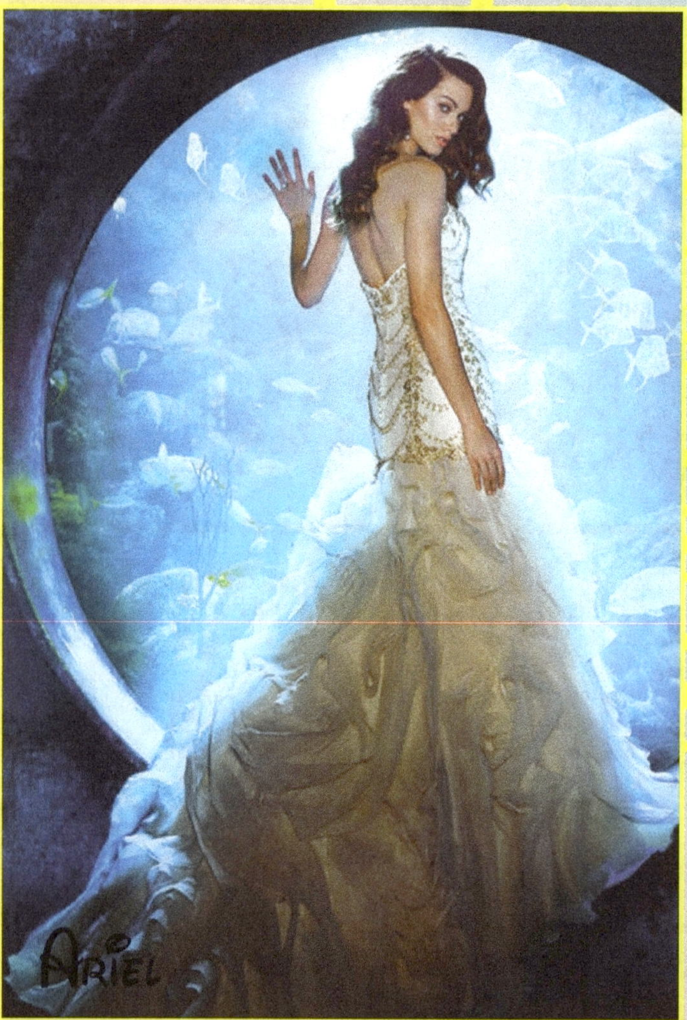

with a pearl and rhinestone beaded, sweetheart neckline. The bodice is beautiful embroidered lace, and that lace continues down the skirt. This dress is sure to make you feel like Cinderella dancing across the grande hall, while your step sisters get their eyes pecked by pigeons.

Pocahontas' design reflects her own Disney dress perfectly. The dress features a tulle one-shoulder strap over a sweetheart bodice. The entire dress is decorated in corded lace with a crystal and rhinestone beaded medallion on the waistband. This dress is perfect for Pocahontas' debut. Ten year olds shouldn't be getting married, but you know, shit happens.

Now, Belle is one who has not only a dress in the official collection, but is one of the limited edition ones releasing in June. Her collection dress is gorgeous with a draped skirt and embroidered lace. Her limited edition one is very similar to one released in 2011; I personally like this design. The only differencing feature are the

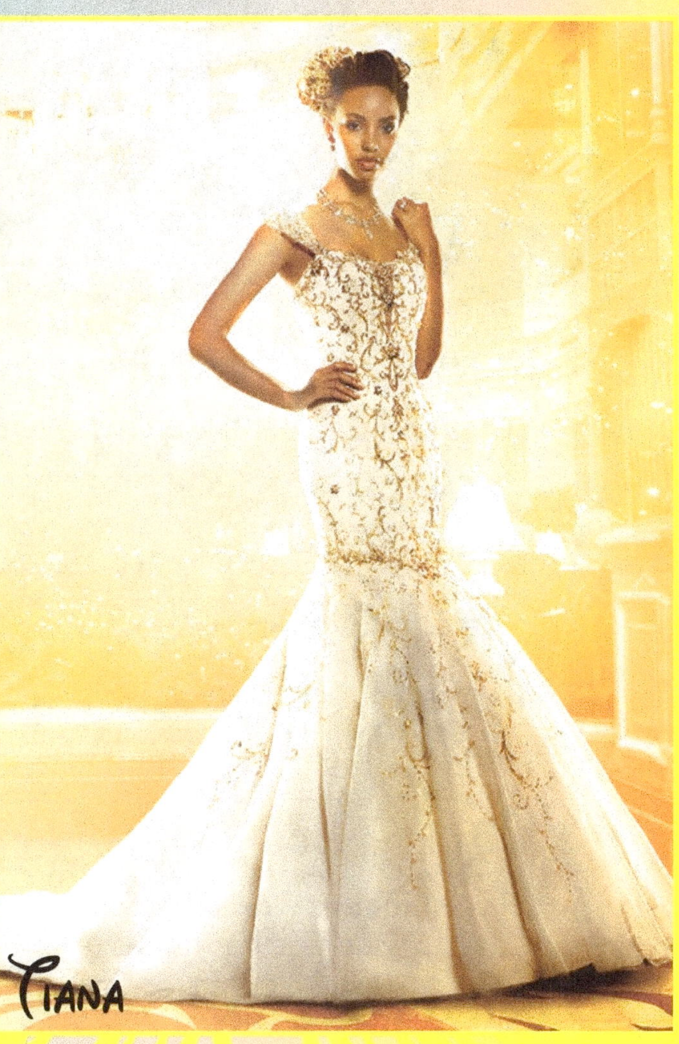

Also there are bridesmaid and flower girl dresses. These too are inspired by the princesses; though not explicitly said, it's obvious which princess the dress is reminiscent of. While the wedding dresses come in whites and ivories, the bridesmaid dresses are available in many pretty colors like purple and black. I quite like that. I bet that Belle dress would be even better in black or plum, right?

With all these options, there is a dress for every bride to feel like a princess on their big day. Not only is there every princess to choose from, the sizes range from zero to twenty-six wide. A fit for many brides as well.

But let's talk price. What would you imagine these wedding dresses cost? Have your answer? Good.

Almost two thousand dollars, is the correct one.

The bridesmaid dresses, on the other hand, are in the two hundred dollar price range.

Taking into consideration the design, materials, overall quality, and beautiful end product; the dresses are so worth the price. Looking at the details, every little detail that invokes the spirit of each princess and truly embodies her. And the imagination and creativeness that went into designing such details and the dresses overall. It's clearly worth every penny.

The designers of Alfred Angelo have again done a wonderful job this year. Any bride wanting to be her favorite princess, Disney or otherwise, on her special day will not be disappointed. ∎

Swarovski crystals scattered through the dress. If you're wearing this dress, you've obviously accepted the beast's proposal, finally.

Snow White's dress has a forest feel to it, with a sweetheart neckline, tulle cap sleeves, and the whole thing is covered in appliques of embroidered lace, pearls, and beading. The dress also features a detachable overskirt, which is pretty nifty. And for your big day entertainment, your stepmother has a choreography routine prepared for you. I've heard it's some pretty hot stuff.

My favorite dress is Mulan's. The dress has a lace mandarin collar, sweetheart bodice with open back, and simple skirt; all covered in embroidered lace. Like all the other dresses in this collection, this dress has been designed to represent this warrior well.

As well as these princesses, there are also; Elsa, Aurora, Tiana, Jasmine, and Rapunzel. All with just as lovely and well-designed dresses.

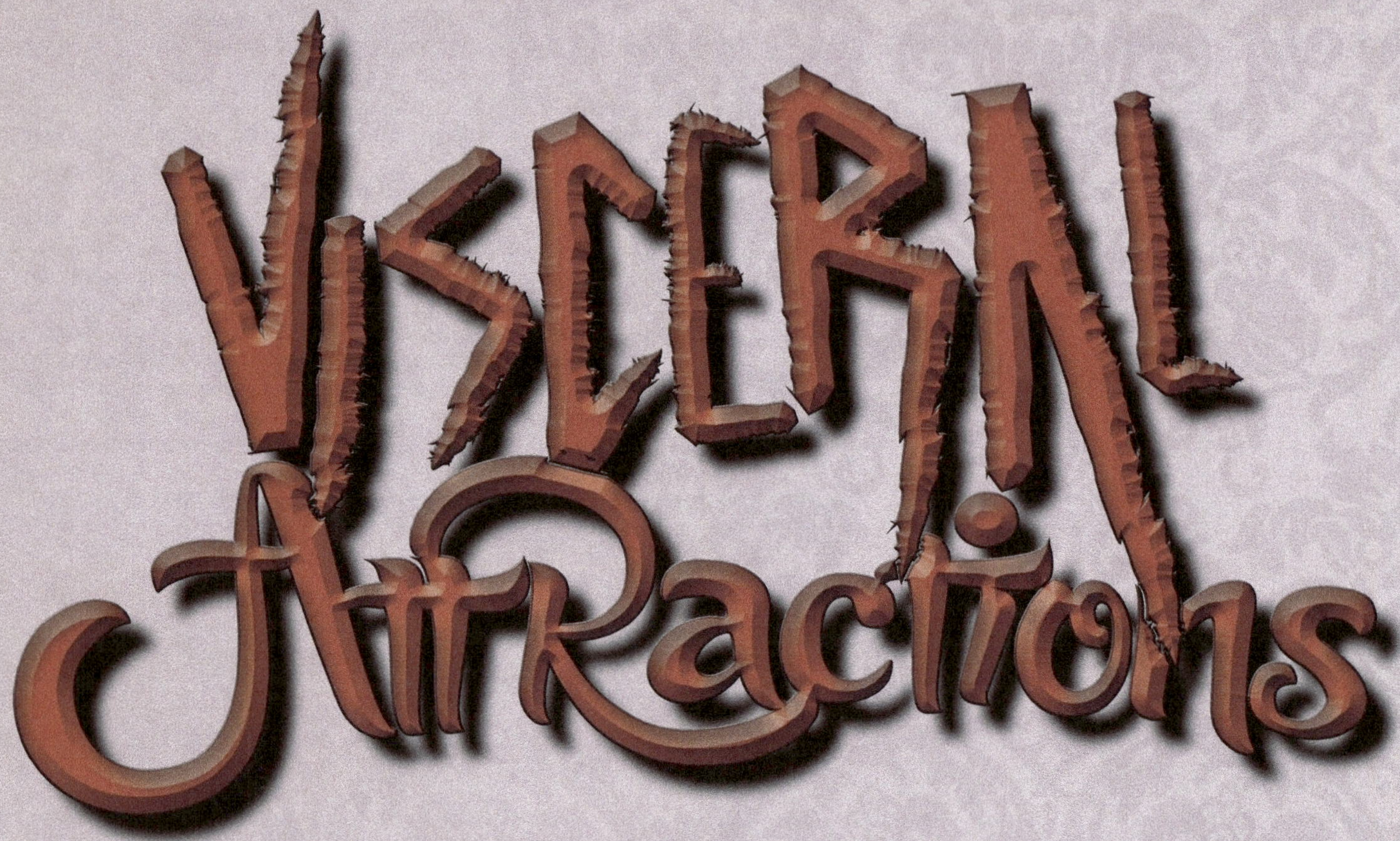

If you are a model, a photographer, a cosplayer or a designer and would like to have your work featured in Visceral Attractions, contact the editor at fashion@carpenocturne.net.

THEMES

WINTER - FANTASY
SPRING - SCI-FI
SUMMER - STEAMPUNK
FALL - GOTH

/VIS(ə)RəL/ -
coming from strong emotions;
not pertaining to logic or reason

Visceral Attractions is Carpe Nocturne's official Fashion insert, spotlighting the most unique and decadent counter-culture fashion designs out there.
Every quarterly issue features full page spreads of fashion, fetish and cosplay photographs to the theme of Goth, Fantasy, Sci-Fi, and Steampunk.

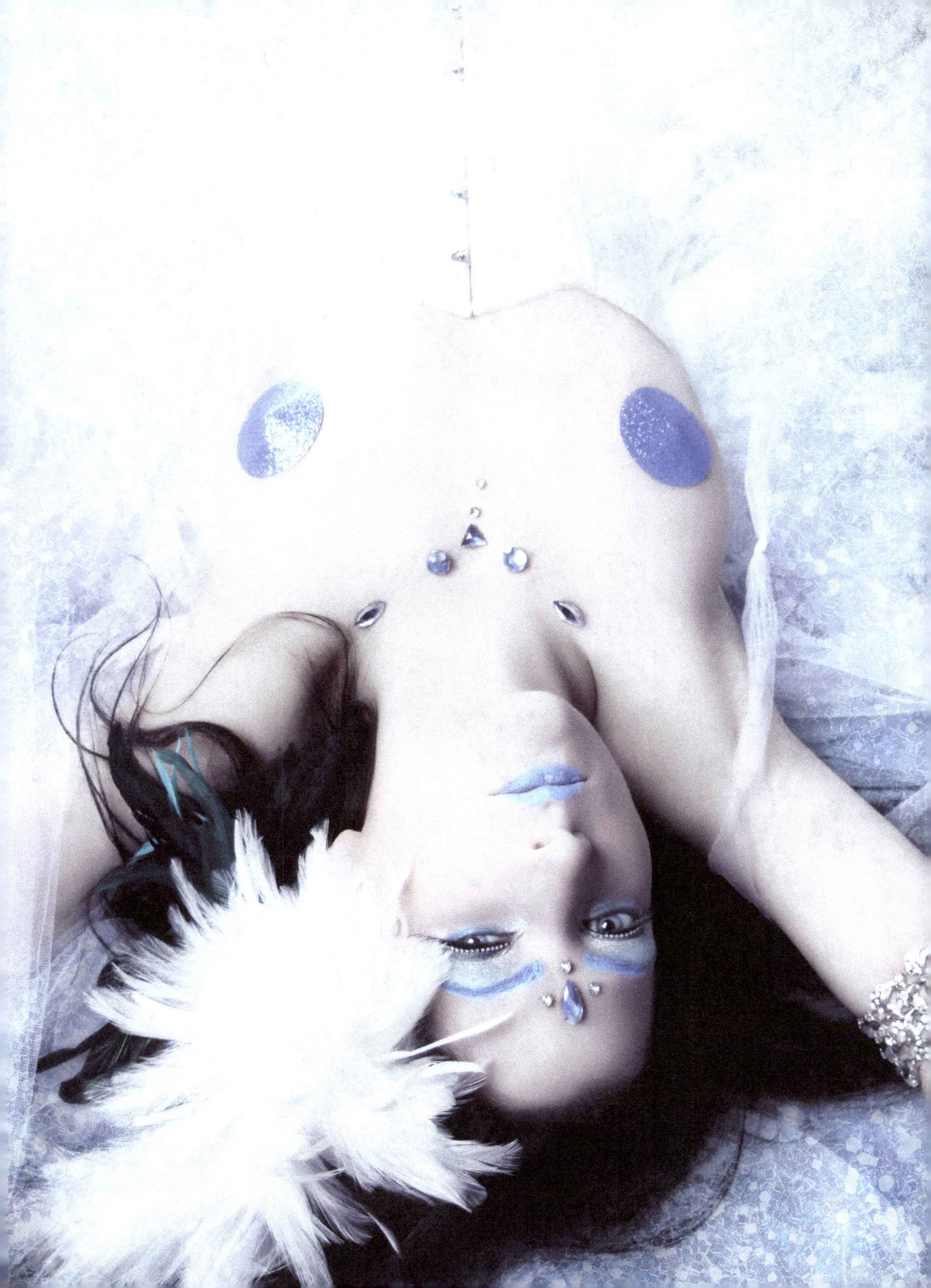

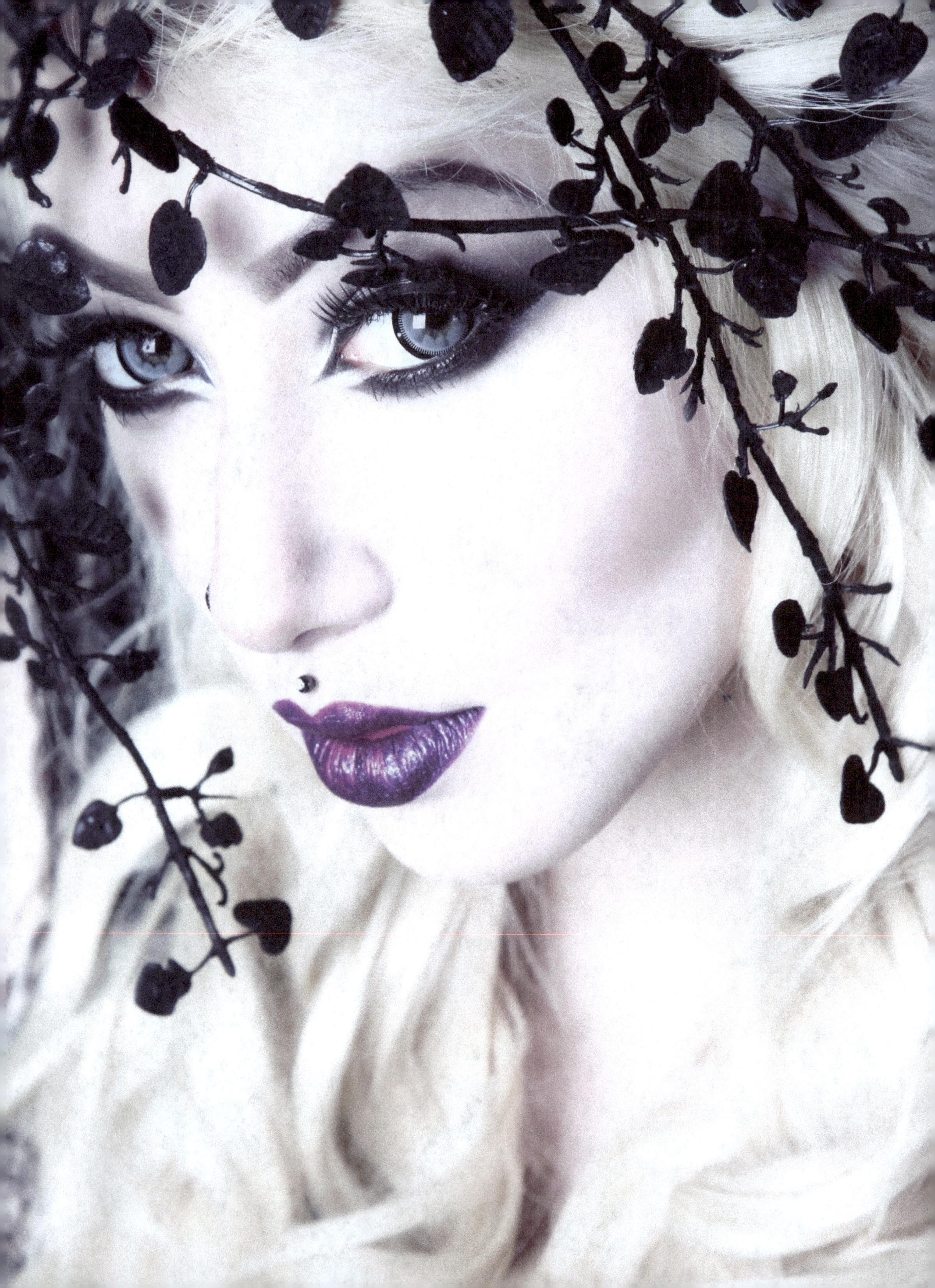

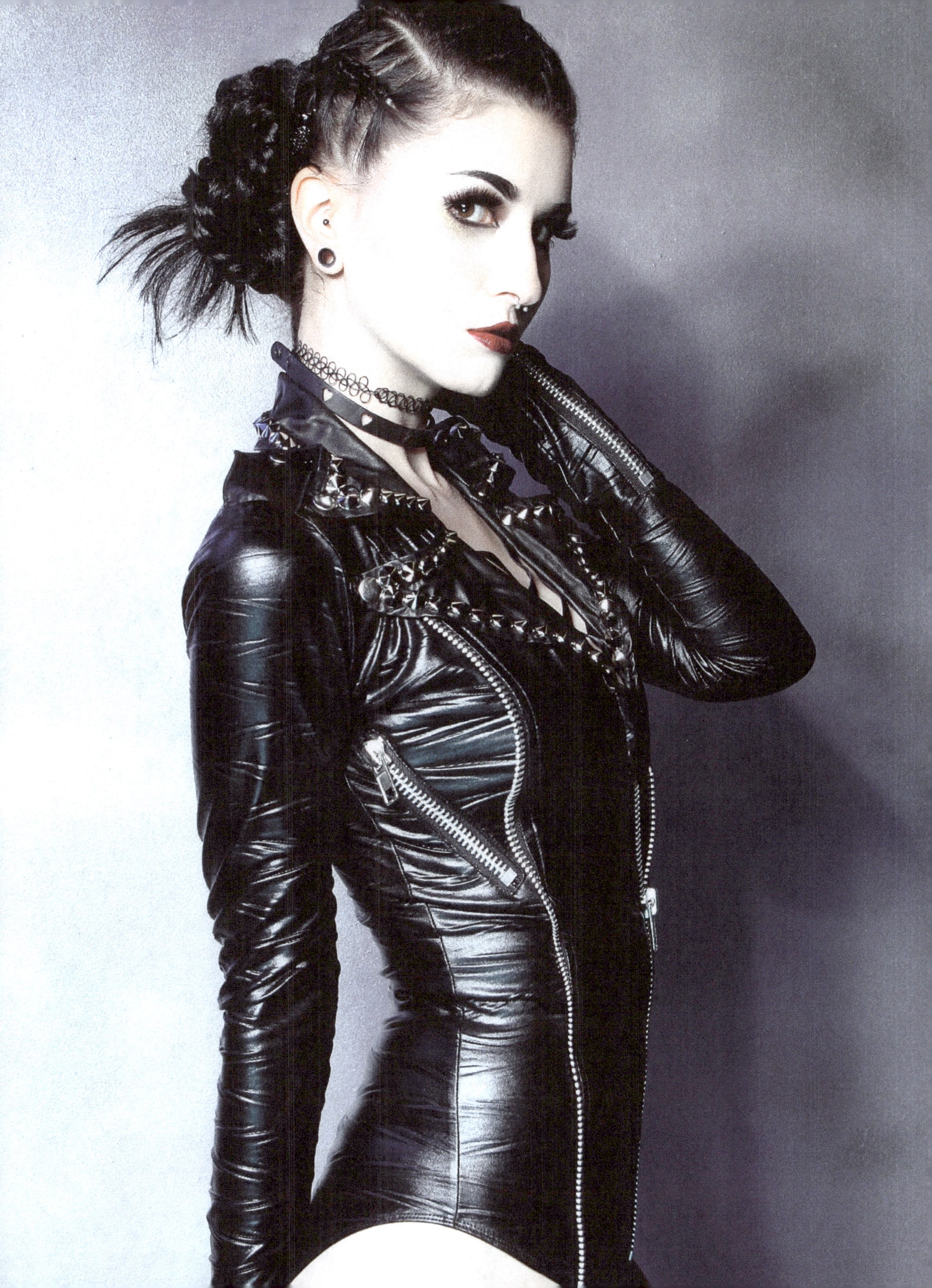

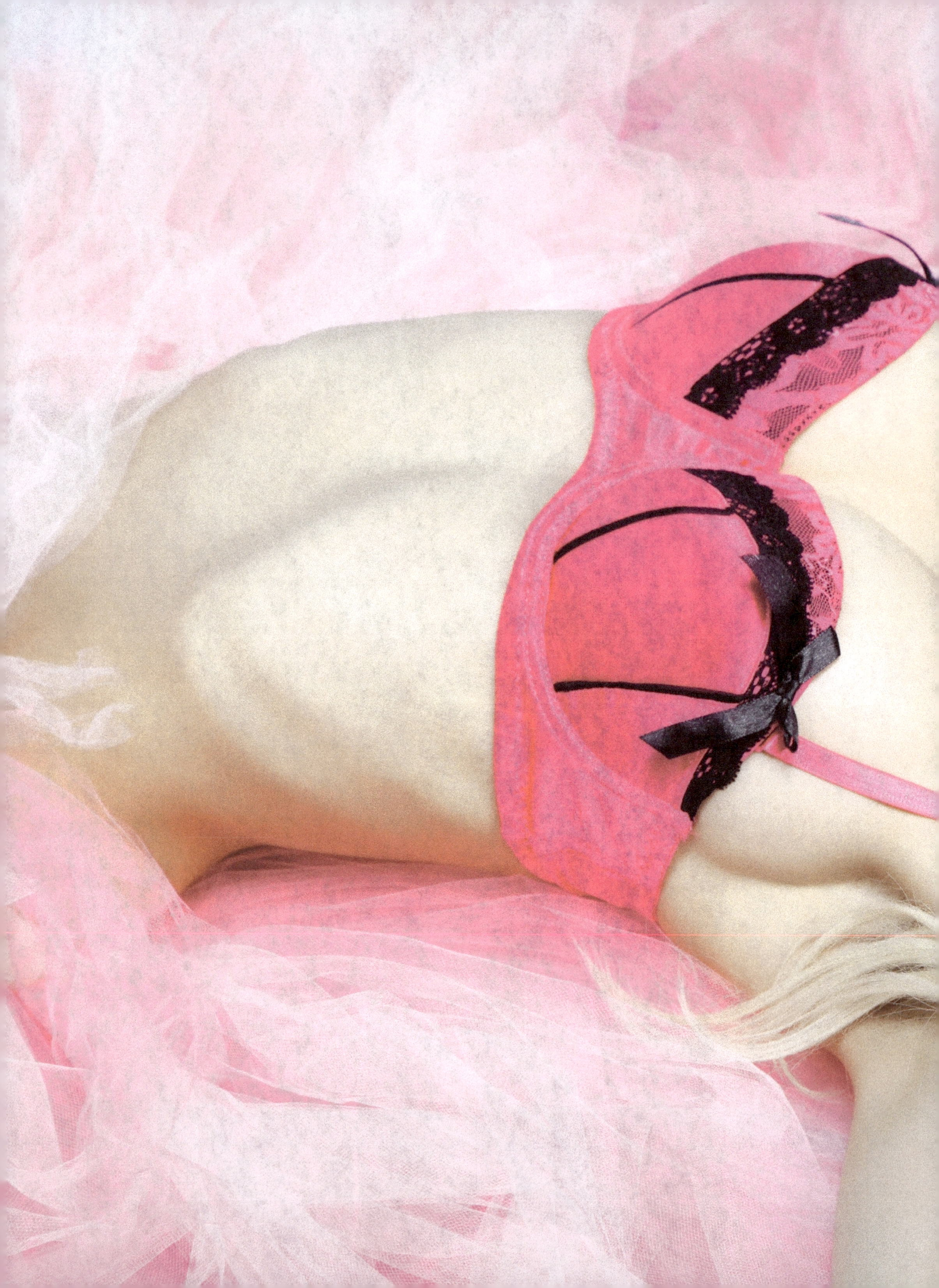

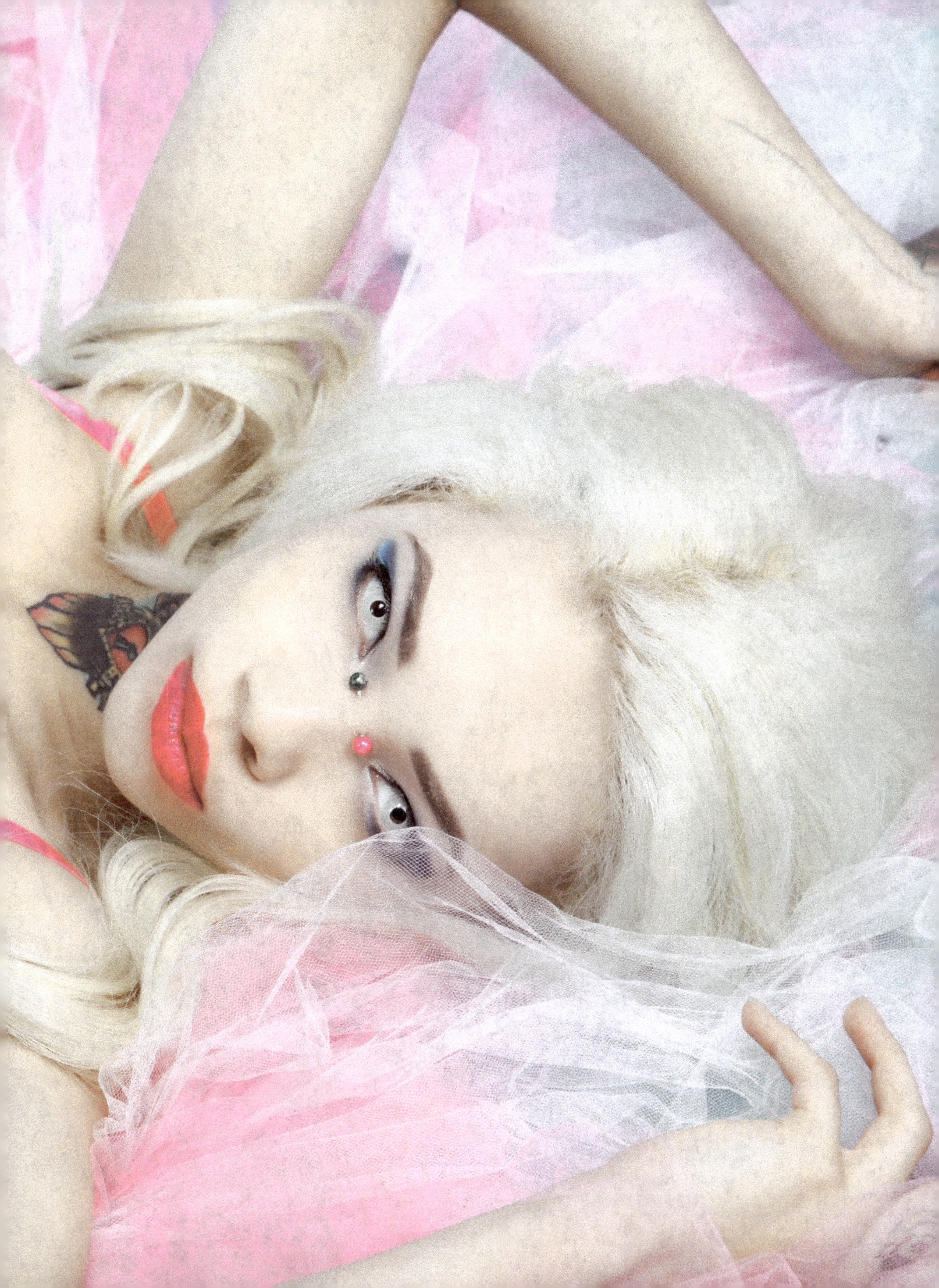

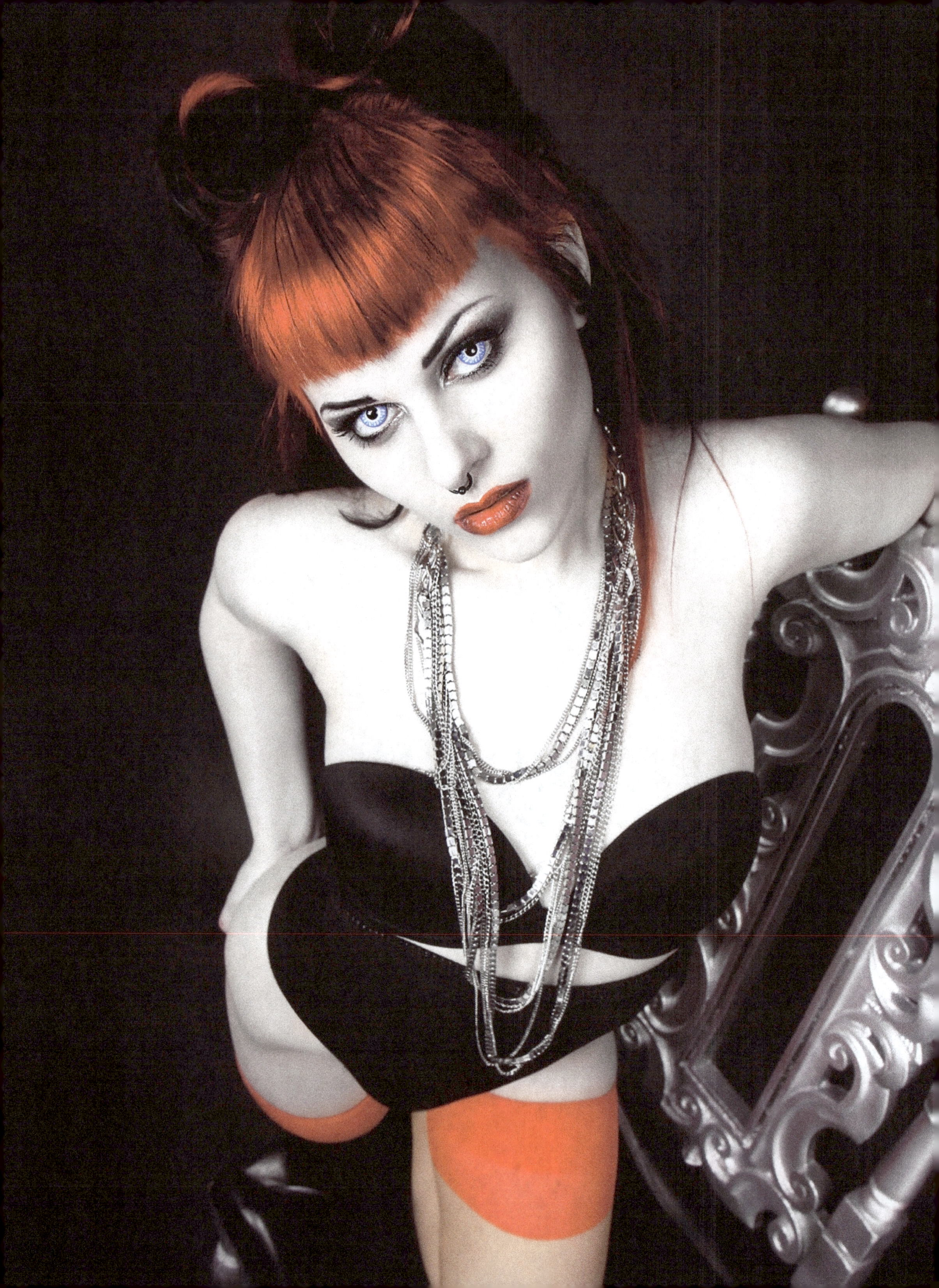

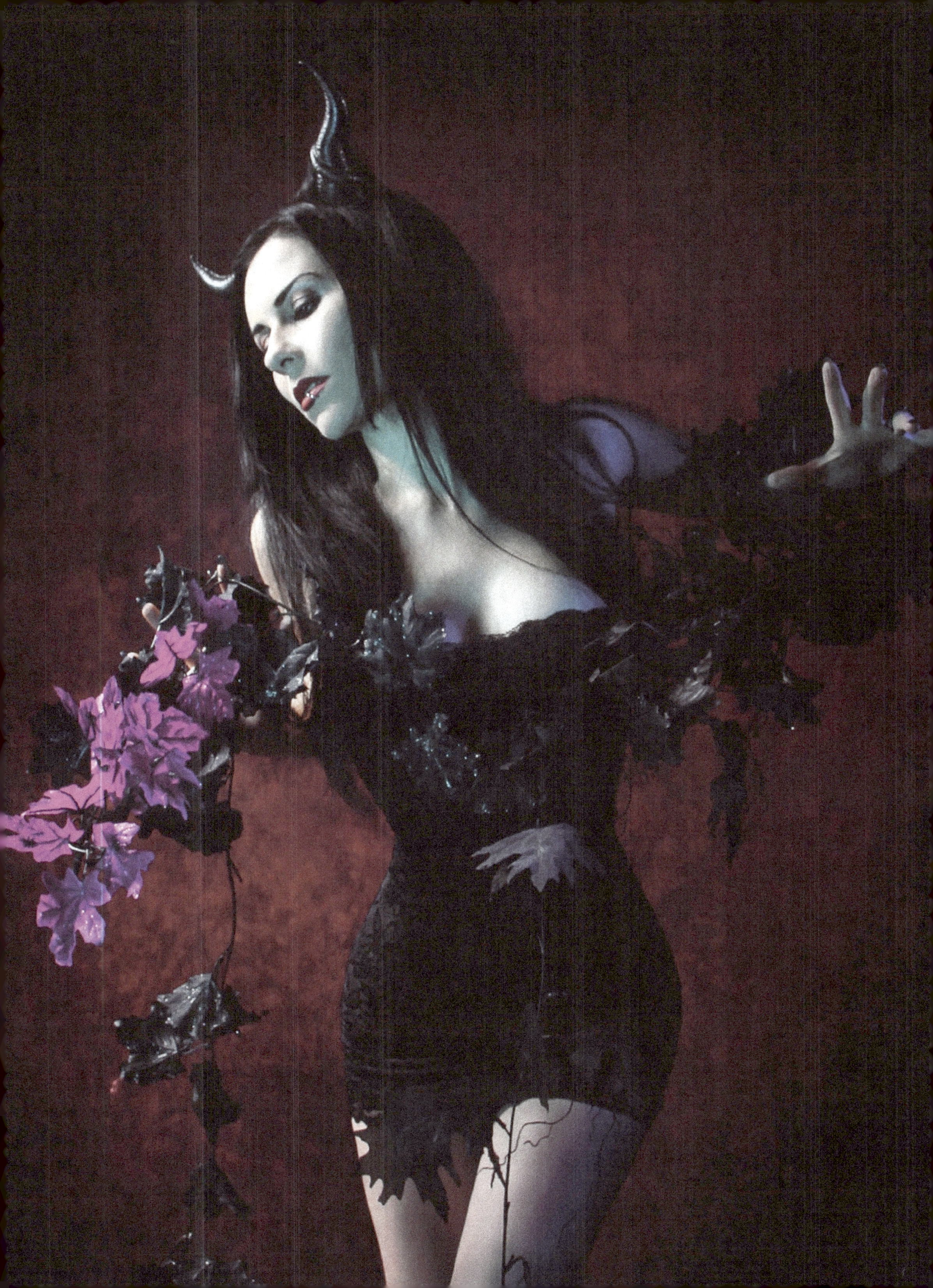

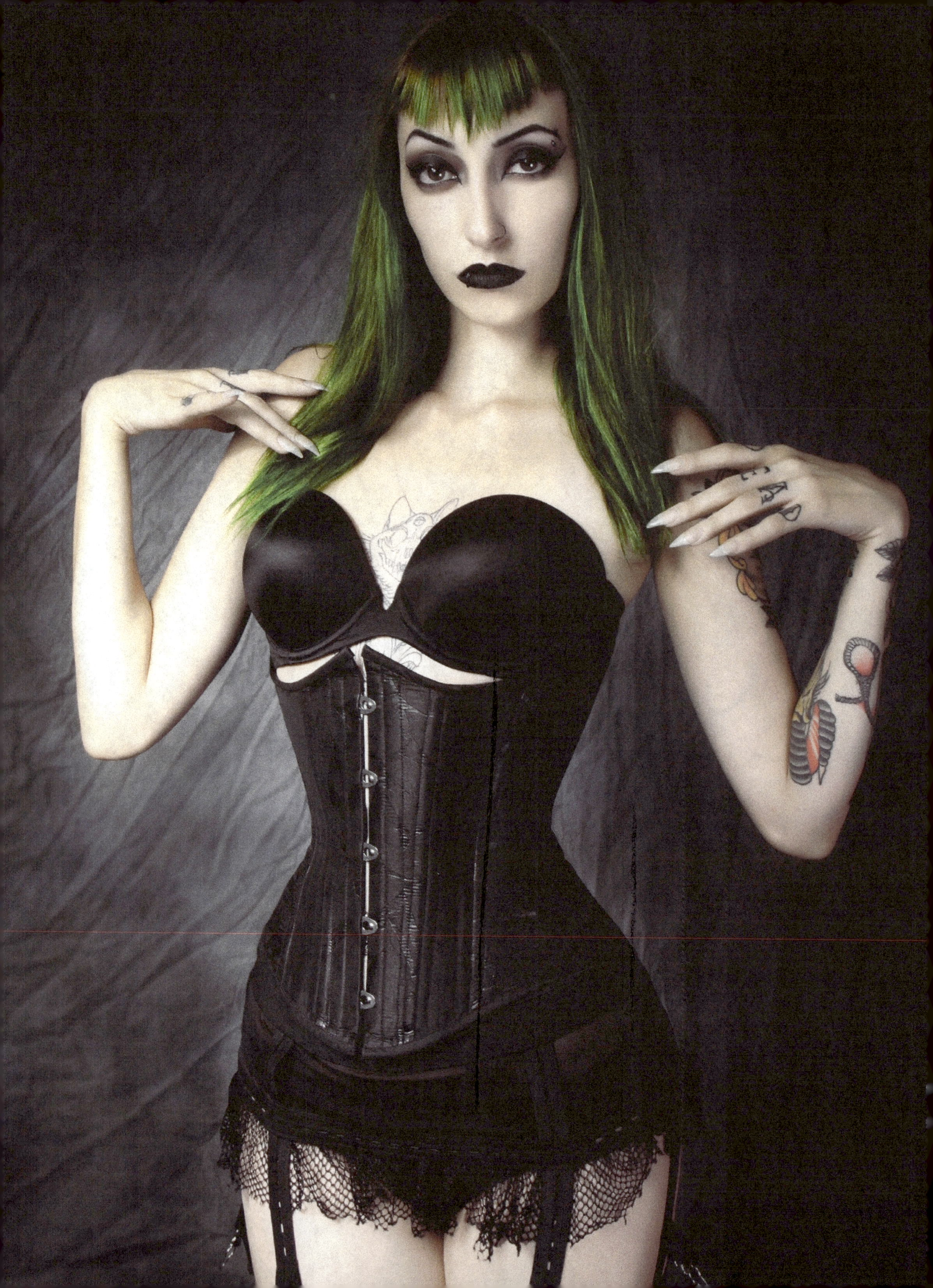

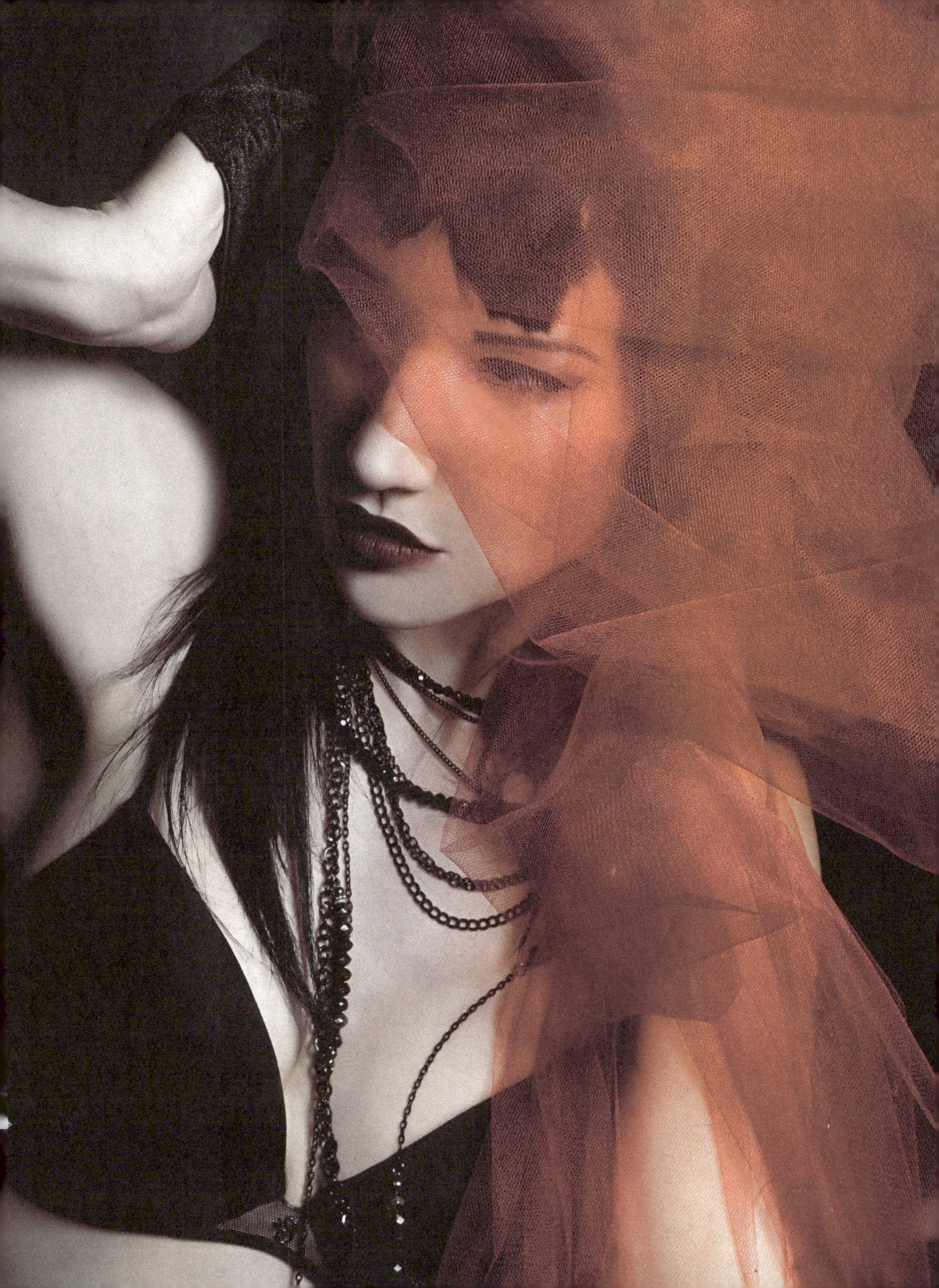

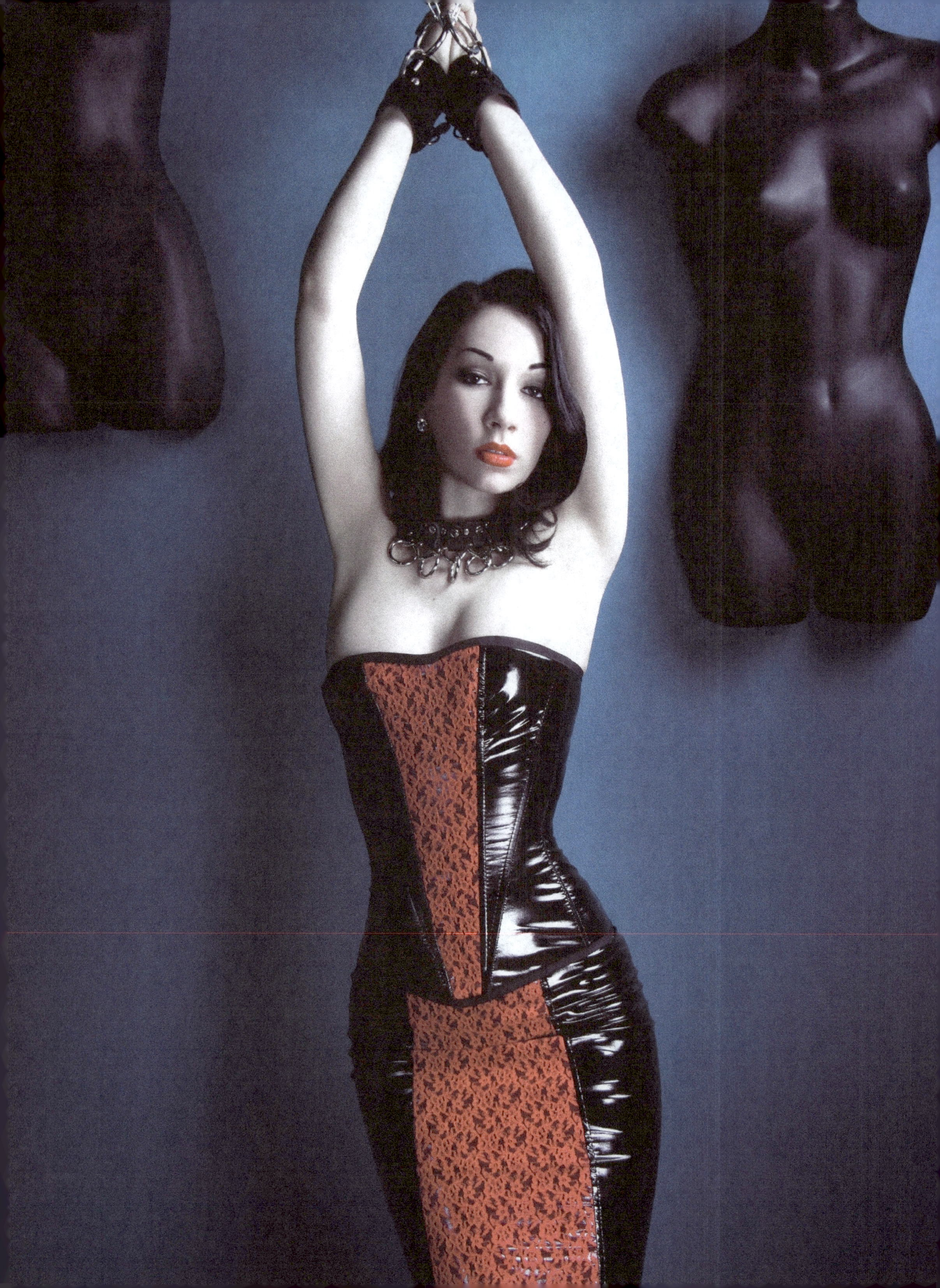

CREDITS:

If you are a model or a designer
and would like to have your photographs featured in
Visceral Attractions, contact the editor at
fashion@carpenocturne.net.

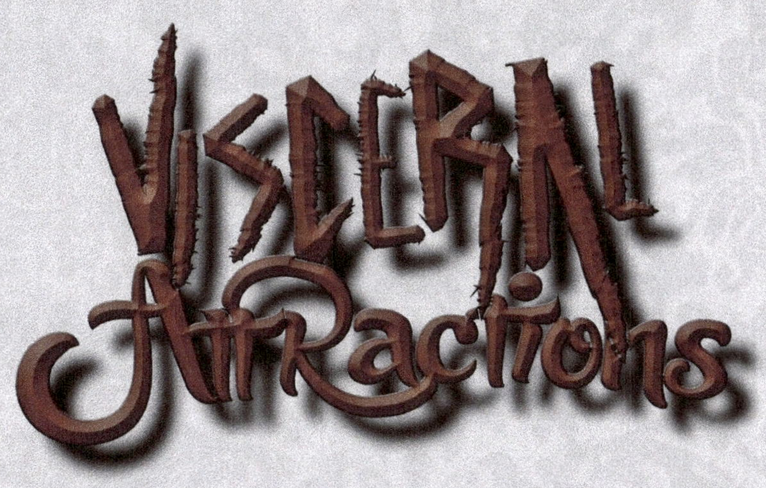

Page 37 - 46, Photographed by Candylust.

Page 37
Model Tiffany
MUA Gigi Rose

Page 38
Model and MUA - Dakota Alexandra

Page 39
Model Gigi Rose
Hair by Jess Parol

Page 40 - 41
Model Gena Tew

Page 42
Model and MUA - Alien Baby

Page 43
Model Onyx
MUA Candace Barbieri

Page 44
Model and Makeup Artist Cypress Bates

Page 45
Model and MUA - Valerie Abbey

Page 46
Model Marlo Marquise

Shuffling the Stars

Zodiac Tarot Predictions by Lexie

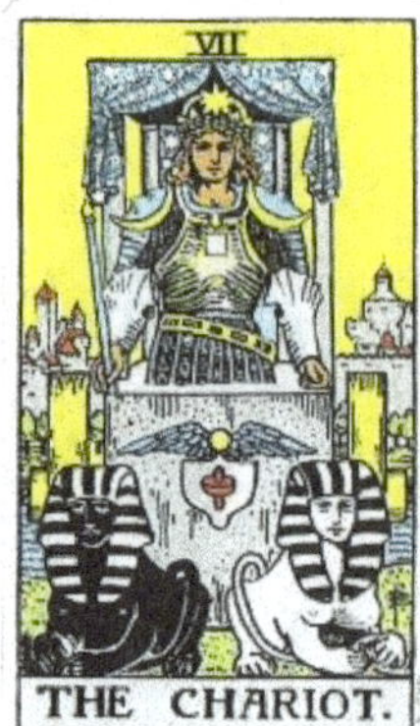

Aries the Ram (March 20-April 19)- Chariot: Okay, Aries. First off, happy Winter! Secondly, the card pulled for your sign was the Chariot. Take a look at the card. The chariot itself is being pulled by two different color figures, yet it is up to the charioteer to move them forward in the wanted direction. This is being asked of you now. This winter, you'll find that your needs, ambitions and desires come into conflict. One thing will pull you in one direction, while another pulls you in the opposite. At its best, this is annoying. At its worst, it leads to self-destruction. What to do? Use your intuition; it's particularly strong this season (pay attention to dreams). Pair it with your reason and this helps control those impulses (which we know can be a challenge for you at times) and with this combined, controlled effort of all your energies, your goals will be met.

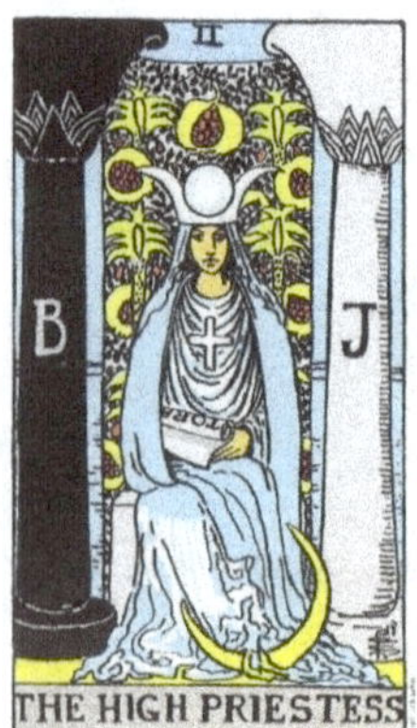

Taurus the Bull (April 20-May 20)- The High Priestess
One of the most psychic cards has just cropped up for you. Your intuition is so on point that it is a little scary. Peace, quiet and privacy are your best friends because of it, and you just may become the proverbial hibernating bear this winter. If friends find you cold, hey that's their problem. You're allowed to have an off-season. And speaking of off-seasons... the High Priestess represents a great deal of virgin deities. So, if your libido take a bit of hibernation (and I can't speak for all Tauruses as each person's birth chart is different) do not be surprised.

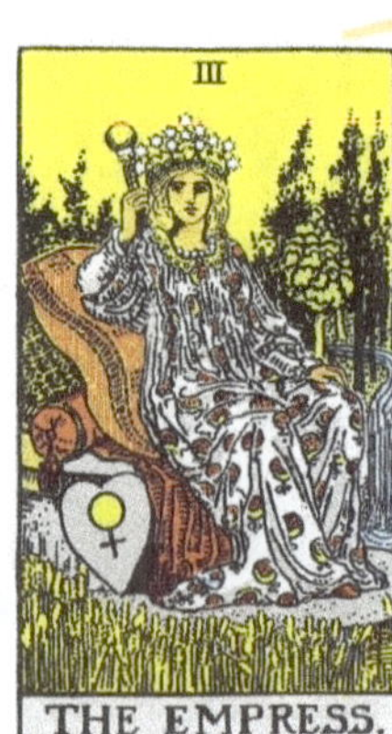

Gemini the Twins (May 21-June 20)- The Empress
Okay, the Empress is a messenger of physical bounties. Opportunities to indulge in physical desires are running rampant. Ideas and intuitive thought-forms more than help with business. Speaking of business, now is the perfect time to put a plan in motion. As this card is related to Venus, your romantic and social life will be on a high point this winter. On a warning note, try not to disintegrate your money. This card can warn of overindulgence and being a bit of a glutton at the mall or with online shopping, and the number of holidays and post-holiday sales don't make it easy on you.

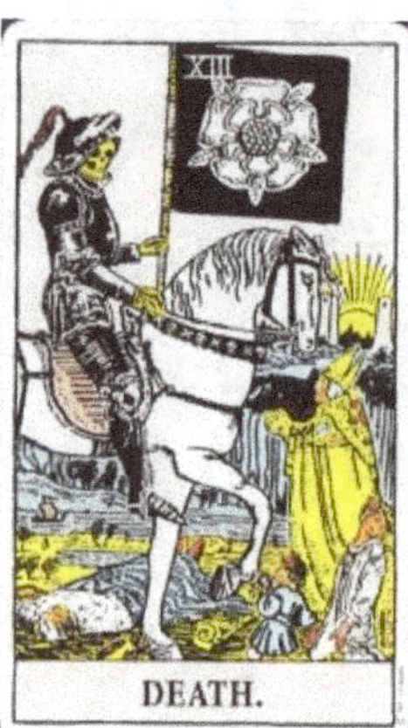

Cancer the Crab (June 21-July 22) Death
Okay, first of all, no freaking. I know this card is pretty scary, but please do not take it literally. Death is all about the ending of that which isn't needed, and the beginning of transformation. After the psychic flurry you underwent this autumn, now is the time of the aftermath. Consider this as 'cutting season.' You see things very clearly now, and know what and whom to cut from your life for your own growth and well being. It'll hurt, because your sign is known for hanging onto things. However, it's necessary and you'll be better for it.

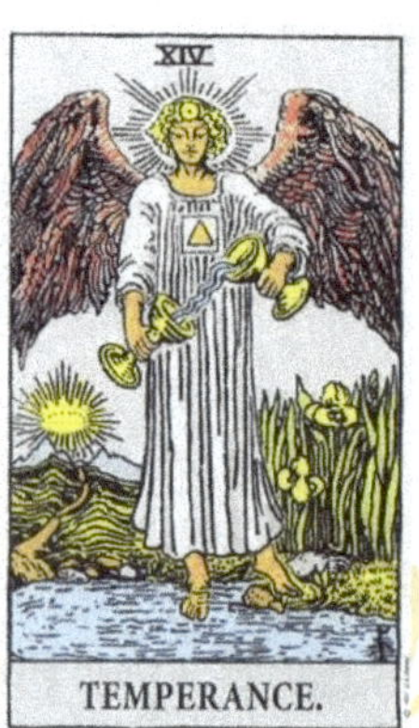

Leo the Lion (July 23- August 22) Temperance
This is the time to bring all things in your life into balance, and by that I mean your emotional, mental, and physical well being. Relationships that have seemed off, finances and the like are now fixable. Remember that high streak you were on? Well, as everything is a cycle, this card is leading you to the midway point of the wheel. On a mundane level, it asks you to keep your more extreme emotions in check. The winter, with all of its holidays, can be a trying time. Family may tap dance on your last nerve, but please, don't fly off the handle over the smallest thing.

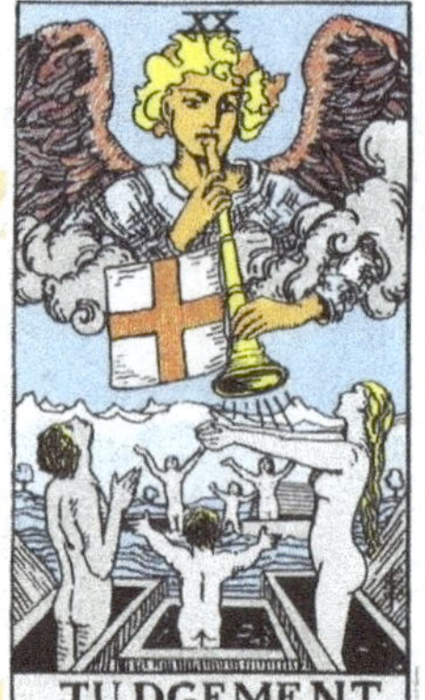

Virgo the Virgin (August 23-September 21) Judgment
As judgmental as Virgo can be at times, this card can cause a few tingles of anxiety. After all, no one is a harsher judge on you than yourself. But, don't worry. You know that proverbial "Aha!" instant, when you have that true Eureka moment? A wake up call? This is that card. Also, past issues are more than likely to crop back up for one last (annoying) rehashing before finally being laid to rest. Considering winter is just before the spring of new life, this is the perfect time to shake off the old, heavy snow.

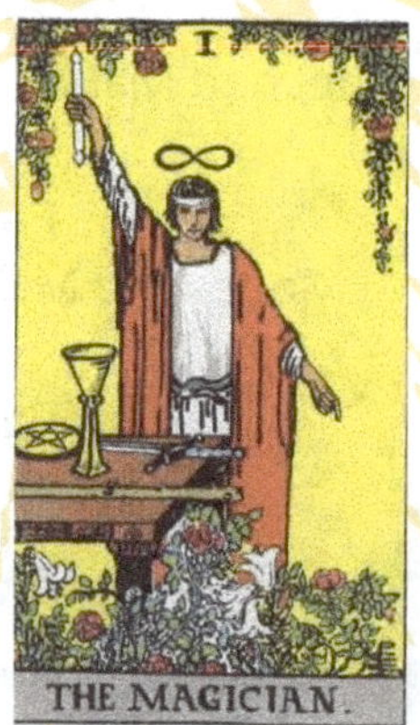

Libra the Scales (September 22- October 22) The Magician
This season, you'll find all aspects of yourself require a significant amount of attention. Others may accuse you of being needy, but this is not the case. Your will (wand) emotions (cup) mind (sword) and practical well being (pentacle) all need a certain amount of attention to stay balanced. Balance is all important for you, and if others cannot handle that, then you may need to reevaluate the amount of time spent with certain people if they are unwilling to compromise. In so doing, you'll find that things will come together to greater improve your own life.

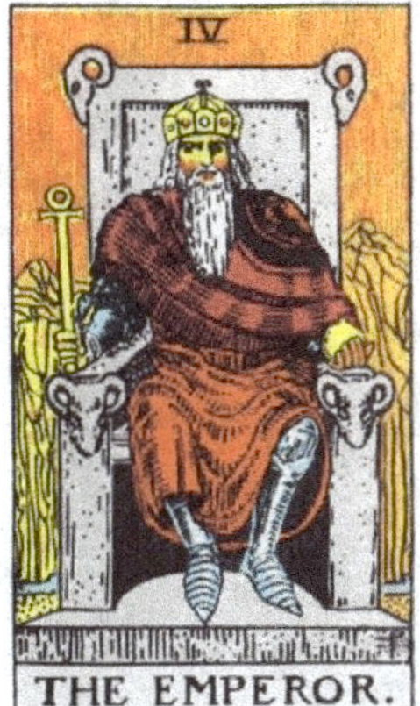

Scorpio the Scorpion (October 23-November 21) The Devil

The Devil tends to call up negative images, but don't worry. This card is about pure instincts. No, this is not just about sex (though it runs pretty high with this card). It is about looking out for number one. Your baser side is going to be on high. Indulging your physical side from time to time is a good thing, but becoming a slave to instincts can lead to nothing but bad. Another thing, this card warns against obsessions, addictions and unhealthy relationships. Are you holding onto something or someone when it'd be better if you just let it go?

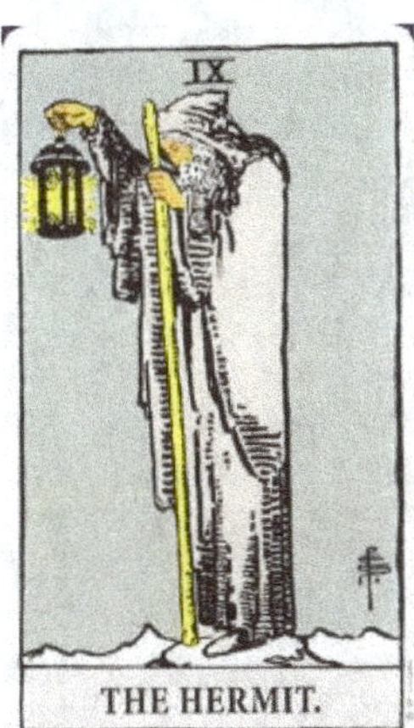

Sagittarius the Archer (November 22-December 21) The Emperor

The Emperor, the "Boss" card pops up here. After clearing out what hasn't served you this autumn, you now have room to assert yourselves and take control of your life. Also, as this card can have the meaning of a tyrant, take a look at yourself. Have you been overly domineering to someone, even without meaning to be? Is someone (irritating relative) doing the same to you? If it's the former, curb that impulse before it turns ugly. If it's the later, feel free to put that person in their place. But, regardless, this card also asks you to govern yourself and trust your instincts.

Capricorn the Goat (December 22- January 19) The Hermit

Okay, well, with the Hermit, the theme is that of introspection, solitude and truth seeking. Your curiosity is at its high point and you may find yourself questioning various things in your life. Things that you thought were a sure thing don't seem as such anymore, and it bothers you. That is perfectly fine. You may find yourself seeking out the guidance of an older and/or more experienced acquaintance for guidance. There's no shame in this. We all feel a bit lost at times, even if we like to think we know all the answers. Ask for help on business projects, in relationships, or with your own personal quest for enlightenment (if you have one). As great as self-education is, it can only get you so far at times.

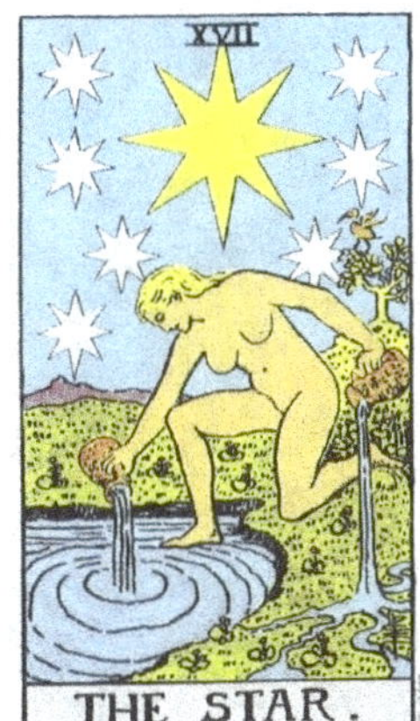

Aquarius the Water Bearer (January 20-February 18) The Star

The Star, the card related to your sign, offers hope for the future. The things you realized over the autumn are now within your reach, you just have to focus on them and not waver from the course, much like an explorer following the North Star. I know, I know, that sounds annoying and hokey, but Rome wasn't built in a day. Things take time. A business prospect, a new move, getting into the school you want...nothing's impossible, just perhaps improbable. That can be tweaked if you're determined enough. But, in other news, this card offers you to take your own natural optimism and altruism to aide those in need. Volunteering at a soup kitchen or animal shelter not only helps others, but also helps your own spirit as you work toward your own goals.

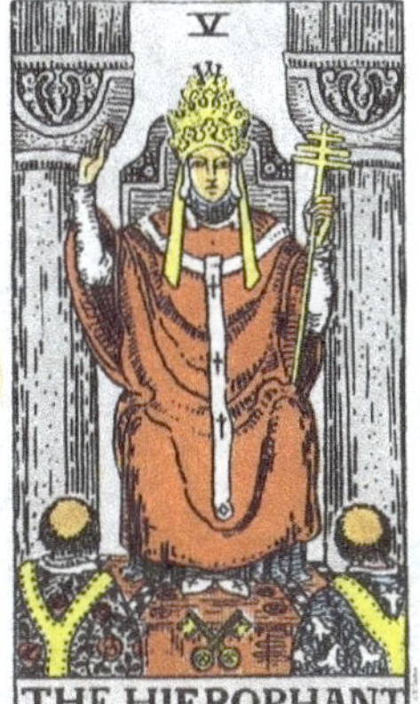

Pisces the Fish (February 19- March 20) The Hierophant

Oi, you're so not feeling it this season, are you? On the one hand, you feel the need to go with the current, and to not rock the boat. If this is something you've been doing your entire life, it is a hard habit to break. On the other hand, an urge to do your own thing has cropped up. Family may call your actions foolish and uninformed. The important question is do you think they are? You're your own person and as much as you love your family; you're the one who decides your own fate. You may find that a part of you LOVES being a bit defiant after all this time. Hey, it's cool. I know the feeling. Enjoy it when it's warranted, but don't let it go to your head. Agree to disagree and gloat in private.

The cards used in this reading are from the Rider-Waite tarot deck. ∎

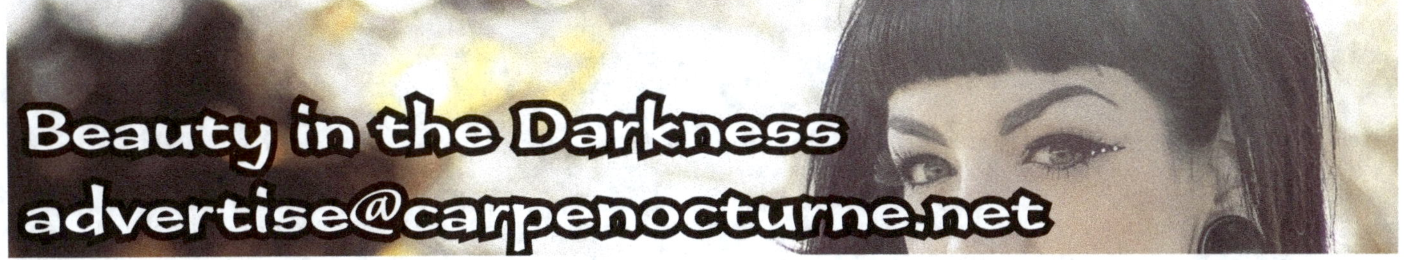

The Lasting Power Of Horror-Drama

by Bryan Akerley

Deep inside every Target and Wal-Mart in America, there lies a terrible secret. Pay the right price and you, too, could be the proprietor of this ancient secret as well. The secret: a portal to the other side, a line of communication with the dead, a piece of cardboard and a plastic planchette made in China. The price: somewhere around $20.

It is truly a feat of imagination to bring a Hasbro game to thrilling life, and a massive risk considering the disastrous *Battleship* (2012). It didn't work with *Ouija* (2014), but with a new cast, setting, and director in the brilliant Mike Flanagan, we have now an exciting entry in the trend of character-driven horror. And to think, it's based on a board game.

Taking place in 1967, the story centers on recent widow Alice and her daughters Lina, the rebellious teenager, and nine-year-old Doris. Alice acts as a medium—'acts' being the key word—about to incorporate a Ouija board into her performance. The board, of course, comes with rules like "don't play alone" and "always say goodbye"—rules that are broken early on as Alice attempts to communicate with her deceased husband Roger. Doris inadvertently gets herself possessed by malevolent spirits in what I call a reverse-Jumanji: yep, the game gets sucked into her.

The story only suffers in trying to connect with its predecessor. It takes place in modern day, but frustratingly for the writers of *Origin of Evil*, sets up a backstory that becomes this prequel's ending. Despite having to stick to this narrative, Flanagan actually manages to create a deeply affecting human story that is also really scary.

The Conjuring, and especially its sequel earlier this year, both take a classically ambitious approach to horror where the characters and story come first, and the paranormal elements come second. It's a method perfected by *The Shining* and *The Exorcist*—regarded as some of the best movies of any genre of all time.

It's difficult to place them in a genre box, but they are drama first— the ghost story is integral to the drama and often truly terrifying, but it doesn't necessarily form the backbone. Those films are only about ghosts and possessions the same way *Jaws* is about a shark, and *Ouija* is no exception.

Instead, Ouija burns slow at first, giving us time to like Alice for her undying love of her children and late husband, as well as witness her vices—a complicated relationship with the local priest, a strained relationship with her oldest daughter, the ethical dilemma of her business practice. Their decisions drive the story, such as the family's desperation to reach Roger through the board.

The movie also raises the stakes for us as the audience; for her innocence and longing for her father, we don't want to see Doris harmed. It's a powerful tool that ultimately manipulates us once she, in effect, becomes the villain through possession.

All movies are more powerful with empathy, but horror movies can traverse genres, making the stories unforgettable and the scares more personal. What we end up with is a truly visceral experience, the best compliment a horror movie can receive. ■

The Grotesquerie of Beauty

In Nicolas Winding Refn's "The Neon Demon", Beauty gets really ugly.

By James Donnelly

In the opening moments of "The Neon Demon", we see a beautiful young woman in a beautiful dress laying back on a sofa in a pool of blood that seems to come from her neck. That beautiful young woman is Jesse (Elle Fanning) and this gruesome scene is not a murder, but actually part of a modeling test photo shoot. Right out of the gate, co-writer and director Nicolas Winding Refn establishes the mood and style that will permeate every moment of the film from beginning to end; a blend of bloody dread and hyper-stylized pretentiousness.

Jesse has come to Los Angeles to become a model. At the outset, she strikes up a friendship with Ruby (Jena Malone), a makeup artist for models (as well as corpses) and a potential romance with test photographer Dean (Karl Glusman). She also meets her competition in slightly older models Gigi (Bella Heathcote) and Sarah (Abbey Lee) who are instantly jealous of Jesse's natural beauty and suspicious of her innocence. She signs with a modeling agent (Christina Hendricks) who insists she lies about her age (she's told to tell people she's 19 when she has actually just turned 16) in order to work in the field. During a professional shoot, the photographer Jack (Desmond Harrington) closes the set and decides to shoot her nude with gold body paint he applies with his hands. She continues to ascend as both she and Sarah are considered for the same runway show for a famous designer (Alessandro Nivola) and while he doesn't even look at Sarah, he is fully entranced by Jesse. Not long after this success, Jesse begins acting differently. She's totally self-consumed and self-obsessed with little to no regard to other's feelings, and here's where things start to get weird. And very, very bloody.

Coming from the director of "Valhalla Rising", "Bronson" and "Only God Forgives", one should never expect a straight-forward film from the Danish filmmaker. While he also directed the moderately conventional "Drive" (which was a triumph of both style and substance), he's gone back to a similar tone that he set for "Only God Forgives" which is one of bloody violence, hauntingly gorgeous visuals and not a whole lot else. He and co-writers Polly Stenham and Mary Laws give a modicum of plot, his performers give little more than two dimensions, and as a director, Refn concentrates all of his efforts on showing an almost David Lynch-esque blend of strong and often breathtaking visuals mixed with moments that escalate in their surrealism. For example, there's a moment where Jesse comes back to her run-down motel and believes an intruder is in her room. She goes to her uber-sleazy landlord (a super creepy Keanu Reeves) to assist with the situation, and when the door is opened, it turns out the intruder is a wildcat that snuck in the room. It begins a motif of carnivorous beasts that carries throughout the film, but it's certainly not a new commentary on the nature of the competitive nature of modeling. In all honesty, the film doesn't have anything new to say about the subject since there have been scores of films about this subject already ("Blow-Up", "The Eyes of Laura Mars", "Looker", hell, even "Zoolander"), but

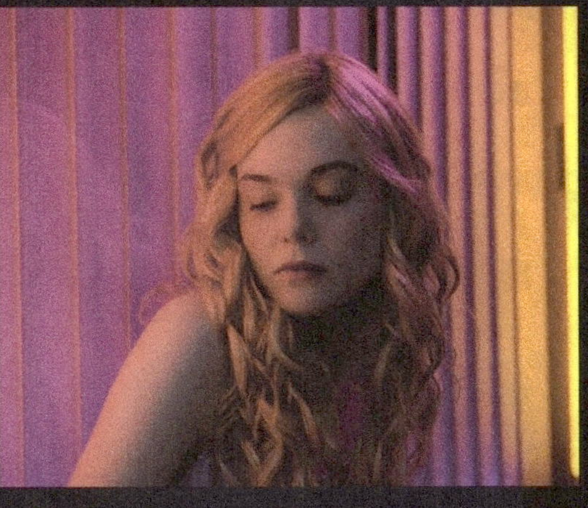

it's the way that Refn shows it that looks and feels unique. As the film descends further into madness and horror, the look and feel of the film cements itself as something intended to be more experiential than deeply thoughtful.

I once watched the Dario Argento giallo classic "Tenebre", which was one of my friend's favorite films, and once all was said and done, I called my friend and asked him why he loved it because I thought none of it made any sense. He went on to tell me that this was a film that isn't intended to make sense per se, but rather make you feel and make you react to what you're seeing. And after hearing that, I started looking at certain horror films through that lens and they started to work for me when they otherwise might never have. "The Neon Demon" is an experience like that. The performances aren't really significant, and the script is perfunctory, but this isn't a film about performance or script; it's about Refn's abilities as a visual filmmaker and how he crafts the film from moment to moment, no matter what may or may not make sense from a storytelling point of view.

And like the audience at Cannes, you will either give "The Neon Demon" a standing ovation or a very loud boo. Personally, I stood and clapped. ∎

Comics Fandom, Online Harassment, and the Toxicity of the "Gatekeeper" Mentality

by James Donnelly

Back in 2011, Marvel introduced a new Spider-Man to the world. It was Miles Morales, a creation of writer Brian Michael Bendis, who was half-African American, half-Latino teenager who gets spider-powers and becomes the new Spider-Man. This garnered national attention, and while a lot of it was accurately reported and greeted with high hopes, the ones that attracted the most attention were Fox News and Breitbart.com. Fox News had a conniption fit over the fact that Marvel was "replacing" Peter Parker with a biracial youngster. Breitbart gave it an even worse working-over when they mirrored Fox News's assessment but also added that Miles Morales was also going to be bisexual. The conservative white male hand wringing began in earnest soon after these reports.

Of course, what neither Fox nor Breitbart had revealed was more telling about them as outlets of information. While it was true that Morales was biracial, he was not bisexual (which in my opinion would have been interesting), and while he was "replacing" Peter Parker, this was not being done in the main Marvel Universe (or Earth-616 to fans), but in the Ultimates Universe, where that Earth's Peter Parker gave his life to defeat that Earth's Green Goblin and save the lives of everyone he cared about. Fox's "reporting" implied that Peter Parker was being replaced by a half-Black/half-Latino and they freaked out. To them, it was simply a matter of liberal bias and/or affirmative action that they replaced an iconic white character with a minority. But of course, if you really read between the lines, it's a fear of minorities being as highly regarded as whites. And apparently it felt necessary for Breitbart to add the bisexual claim as a fear-mongering tactic to scare hetero conservative white males as well; just as conservative news outlets did with Earth-2's openly gay Green Lantern.

To me, this was a clarion call that not only was racism and homophobia alive and well in the United States, but it was also a deep signifier that comics had entered the part of popular culture it never expected, which was the arena of the so-called social and political "culture wars".

In 1989, Tim Burton's "Batman" became the biggest film of the year, and Bat-mania swept the world. More people were coming into comic shops, more people were wearing comic book T-shirts and while it seemed like the culture at large was more accepting of the geeks, that wasn't quite the case yet. But as the years went on, geek culture rose and Hollywood became more accepting of these misfits, particularly when it came to the cash cows of 2000's "X-Men" and 2002's "Spider-Man". Soon, you couldn't escape Wolverine and Spidey T-shirts being sold in Wal-Mart and Target, and an entire sub-culture came out of the dark, ready to be fully accepted by those who once scorned them and kept them in the shadows. But that had a price that many weren't ready to pay yet, and maybe still aren't.

In just the past few weeks of October, we've had two significant

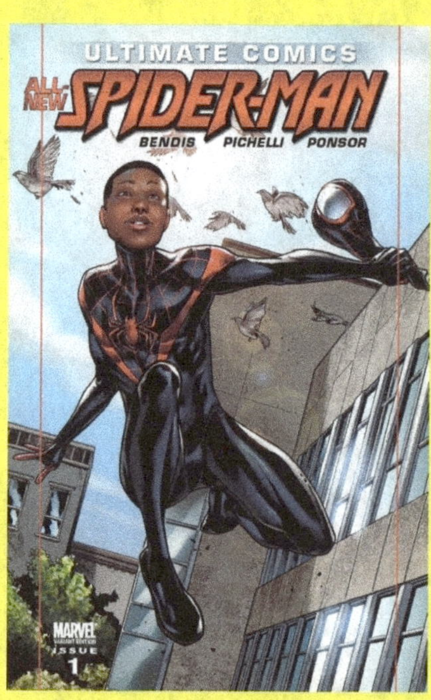

Miles Morales, Spider-Man

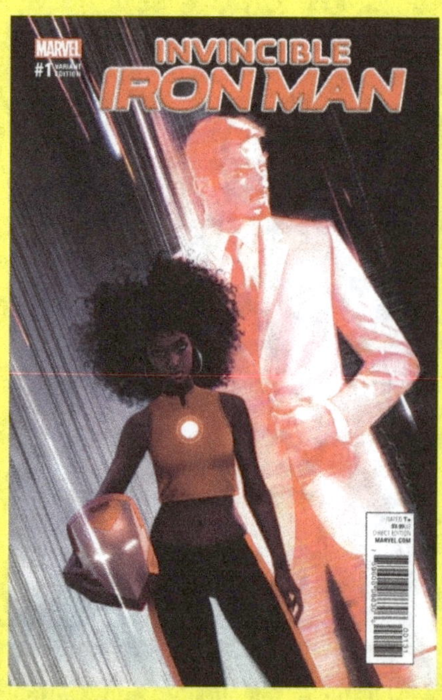

Riri Williams, Ironheart

comics-based controversies: first, there was a kerfuffle over a variant cover for an upcoming issue of "Invincible Iron Man" by popular artist J. Scott Campbell which shows Riri Williams, the 15-year-old African-American girl genius who will become the armored hero Ironheart. The cover was controversial due to it showing this teen girl in a sexualized pose. Online-generated backlash quickly mounted, and also spawned the hashtag #TeensThatLookLikeTeens and led Marvel to pull the cover from sale. Defenders of the cover state that the pose wasn't sexualized and they're just defending comics from "puritanical" beliefs or "pro-censorship" stances where people in favor of the cover being pulled stated that they're tired of seeing artists constantly going to a default of over-sexualizing young women and also that it didn't fit the character. Second, and far more egregious, was the reaction to the cover of "Mockingbird" #8, the final issue of the comic, which, despite overwhelmingly positive reviews, couldn't connect with the comic buyer and was being cancelled due to poor sales. On the cover, the character of Bobbi Morse is wearing a T-shirt that reads, "Ask me about my feminist agenda". This was apparently offensive to those who still see feminism as a threat, or a response to a "non-existent problem" of gender equality, and that somehow, writer Chelsea Cain was trying to force a sociopolitical agenda on the reader. This led to a sad dog pile of angry, insulting, demeaning tweets fired at Cain who, after several hundred of these happened, stated that she was leaving Twitter. Ironically, this led the first "Mockingbird" trade to skyrocket to the #1 spot on Amazon's graphic novel sales chart.

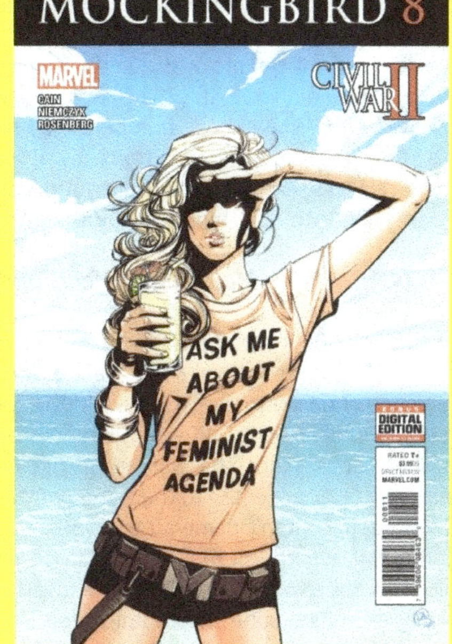

Bobbi Morse, Mockingbird

So the question that I found myself asking was the following:

If comics have been such a traditionally inclusive culture, why does it seem like it's becoming increasingly toxic? I came to a series of possible conclusions, some more depressing than the rest:

Conclusion #1 – *The mainstream has invaded the traditional fandom, and nerds are angry about it.*

Before the film versions of "X-Men" and "Spider-Man", comic conventions were still about comics. It was a showcase for writers, artists, creators, and editors. Once comic book and superhero films became a significant driving force in the market, mass media started to invade these havens for comic fans. This led to pop culture starting to dominate the major conventions, and that was disheartening to longtime fans. I went to Chicago Comicon back in 1989 (the year Burton's "Batman" was released) and you couldn't escape comics and toys and VHS bootlegs of old cartoons.

In 2014 and 2015, I went to the Phoenix Comicon. The big draws were people like Adam West, Stephen Amell, Alyson Hannigan, Karl Urban, Katee Sackhoff, Jason Momoa, David Morrissey and John Barrowman. When it came to comic books, you could find maybe six or seven booths with comics. The rest of the booths were dedicated to toys, memorabilia, costumes, and other various pop culture distractions. There were a few famous names in Artist Alley such as Jim Steranko, or Brian Pulido, but the rest of the con was all about the celebs, and that's just in Phoenix. San Diego Comic Con is when they have panels filled with mega-stars promoting their new films and TV shows to thousands of fans.

Some of the old guard sees this infection of mainstream popularity as an affront to their hobby, and that's made them angry. In their anger, they'll lash out at people that represent new ideas.

Conclusion #2 – *The audience has changed.*

For the vast majority of comic book history, comics were aimed at boys and young men. There were outliers as far as romance comics were concerned, but it didn't change the key demographic. Generations of comic readers saw a male-dominated demographic. Books were written, drawn, inked, lettered and edited by white males. Men who grew up reading comics went into the industry and the status quo was upheld. By the end of the 1980's, though, things started to change. The major publishers were trying different things that would appeal to more mature readers. Manga was also emerging in the United States. It suddenly wasn't just for kids anymore, and it also wasn't just for guys anymore. Women started to return to comics.

Since there isn't really a strong aggregate for sales breakdowns based on gender, publishers started to look at social media as a way to find out who was liking what. And what they saw was that, while the majority of people who liked comics and comic-related pages on social media were still male, females were strongly represented by over 40%. While those numbers may not reflect to actual sales, it's still a very big difference from how it was. When confronted with facts like this, exclusionary groups tend to puff up their proverbial bodies and lash out, thinking they're being attacked by outsiders.

Conclusion #3 – *Male fandom feels under attack by women.*

In the late 90's, I dated a girl who worked part-time at a comic book shop I frequented who would relate the most disgusting stories of men coming into the store asking if she could name the secret identities of several different superheroes, including some very obscure ones. Since she was an attractive young woman, she was automatically subjected to the notion of the "fake geek girl". Now she, like myself, couldn't name all of them, but she could, unlike me, tell you about everything that was going on in "Sandman" or "Preacher" or any number of Vertigo titles. She loved comics, but didn't love (or really even like) superhero comics. You know what? That's perfectly fine. But men who have read comics for years and years sometimes feel and act like they're the gatekeepers of comicdom; if you can't pass through their gates of knowledge of comic facts, you're not allowed in the doors. I've been a comic fan almost literally my whole life. My earliest memories of reading are of reading comics, but no one, and I mean no one has ever asked me if I could tell you what planet Superman is from or what Peter Parker's superhero identity was and that's largely because I'm a guy. Comic fandom has largely consisted of men, and some of those men have taken it upon themselves to "protect" comics from certain kinds of people. One of the tweets (written by a man) directed not specifically at Chelsea Cain but about her and the controversy, stated the following: "Comics are NOT for everyone. Certain people should not be able to read or create comics."
If that's not indicative of not only a lack of inclusivity but also a gatekeeper entitlement, I don't know what is.

Conclusion #4 – *The Internet can just be a horrible, awful place.* *

For the better part of a century, comics have been a male-dominated industry in terms of readership and creators and that has created negativity towards female readers, but also a brick ceiling as far as women in the industry are concerned. And when women finally get a voice in comics, that small but extremely vocal community of self-appointed gatekeepers begin to exhibit their toxicity and things get ugly. But that's only part of the mindset.

The geeks and nerds of the planet espouse the virtue of inclusivity, but there's always that one group of hive-minded souls that believe that the sanctity of comics can only be preserved by keeping everyone else out saying, "This is mine and no Johnny-come-latelies or bandwagon-jumpers are allowed on board". I don't want to be a total hypocrite and say I've never felt that the same impulse, but I've tempered it with the understanding that not everything is made just for my demographic as well as the compassion that people don't deserve to be attacked based on their gender, religion, race or sexual identity. You know who helped teach me that compassion?

My mom. ∎

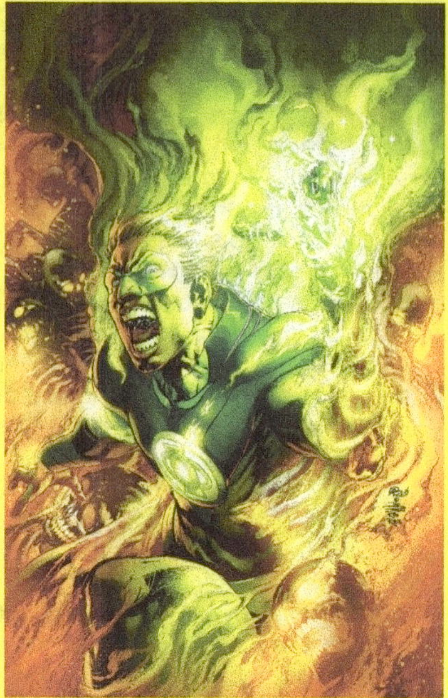

Alan Scott, Green Lantern

** This doesn't really require further exploration. I realize that this negativity and harassment still only represents an extremely small proportion of the comic community, but it's not something that can be dismissed out of hand.*

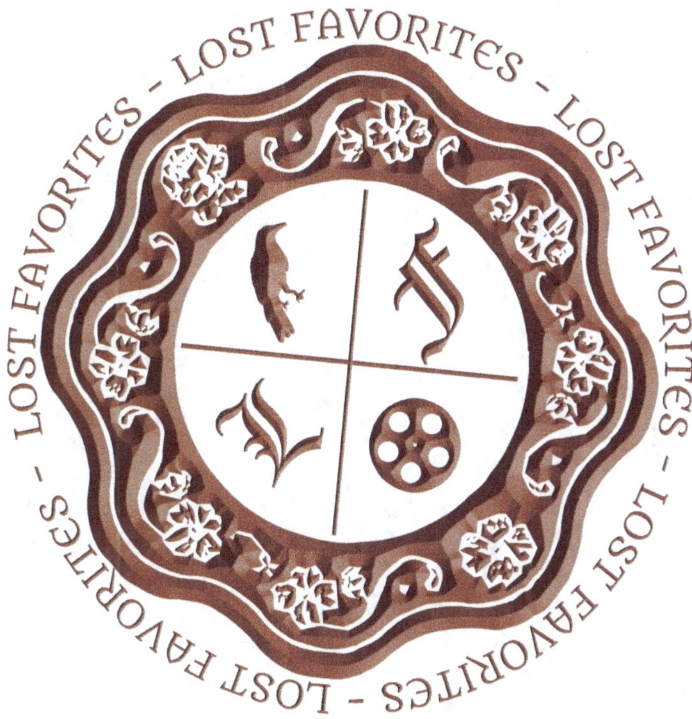

by Xxx Zombieboy xxX

FLESHEATER

"...This evil which will take flesh and blood from thee and turn all ye unto evil..."

Flesheater is one of those films that you fully acknowledge is pretty terrible overall. But, for some reason that you cannot quite put your finger on, you just LOVE IT! That may not sound too promising as reviews go, but bear with me. This awful film is a treasure! It's one that I watch up to three or four times every October.

Flesheater (aka Revenge of the Zombies, Zombie Nosh, Revenge of the Living Dead, and Revenge of the Living Zombies depending on the release) follows a typical group of horny and drunk teens (played as usual by actors and actresses much too old to be teens) as they take a hayride into the woods in what looks like rural Pennsylvania. They gather to drink and have sex. Meanwhile, the farmer that owns the land is pulling a stump out of the woods (for no discernable reason). Beneath is a block of cement with a Pentacle Star. Beneath this slab is a coffin with a wax seal bearing the warning quoted above. The farmer of course ignores the warning and OUT POPS THE LATE AND GREAT BILL HINZMAN!!! Yes, the Cemetery Zombie from Night of the Living Dead! STILL DRESSED AS THAT ZOMBIE! He rips the farmer's throat out and wanders off. Shortly after, the farmer sits up, now also a zombie.

The rest is pretty predictable. As the "teens" separate to have sex, one by one they fall prey to the flesh eaters. Each one that dies gets up to stalk the others. Eventually, they catch on to what is happening, try to lock themselves into a farmhouse against the growing number of the dead, fight amongst themselves, make more dumb decisions, and get et'. They even brought back Vince from Night of the Living Dead

to accidentally kill the last survivors with friendly fire. He even jokes that he is getting pretty good at this.

The acting is terrible. The sound is clunky and often badly timed. Zombies now have superhuman strength and use melee weapons. I mean, there is so much not going for this film that I should hate it. So why do I love it so much? It is utterly charming! It comes off as that student horror film you just love! There is some pretty decent gore for one thing, brought to us by Gerry Gergely who worked on Tom Savini's Night of the Living Dead. The setting in autumn woods is atmospheric and reminiscent of Romero's better moments, and the acting actually picks up a bit when the fit hits the shan. The film is really kind of a side story to Night of the Living Dead, even if it is never stated. The score is a nice little (highly repetitive) theme that is creepy and tragic. And we get to see Bill Hinzman going around eating people again. I met Bill before his death at Spooky Empire in Orlando and got him to sign my copy, and we talked about the film together. It turns out it was his baby, and he felt much the same way about it. It was a low budget joy ride that never tries to be more than what it is. And therein lies its magic. He even eats his real life daughter which is oddly um... touching!

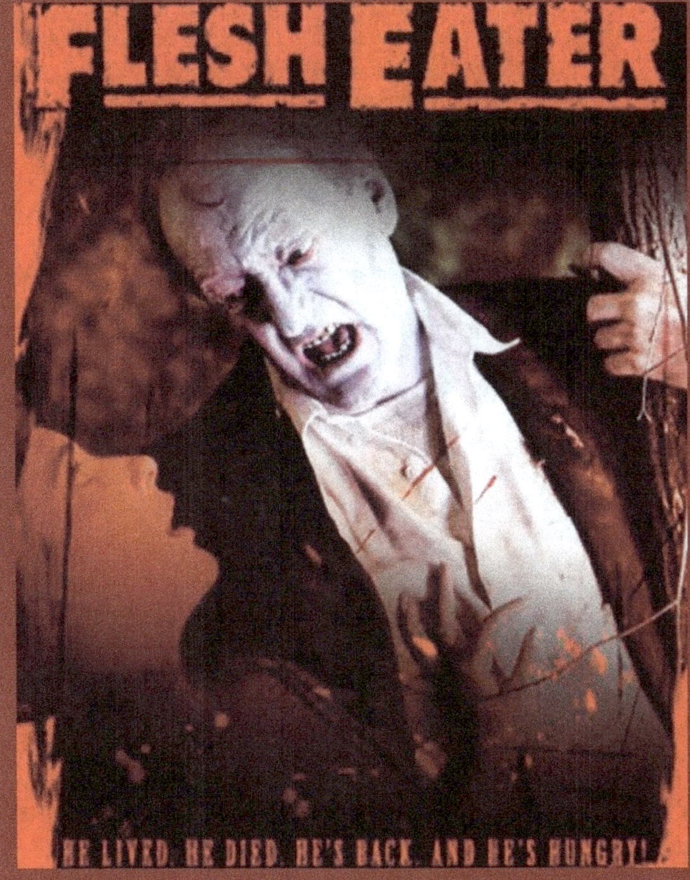

The Shriek Show DVD release also comes with some nice extras. The menu of falling autumn leaves is lovely. The extras include a nice little featurette called Back Into The Woods, a pizza commercial featuring Bill as a zombie and the soundtrack. This is a wonderful film to invite your friends to watch, eat popcorn and drink cheap beer, and make fun of the whole time. For those that love B-Horror, this is a MUST to add to your collection! ∎

ROGUE ONE
A Political Story

By Cosmic

2016 was a weird year, and it seems Star Wars could not escape it. The divisive election of one Donald J. Trump happened to coincide closely with the release of *Rogue One: A Star Wars Story*, and political outrage and speculation still hung thick in the air as a film mainly about battling the

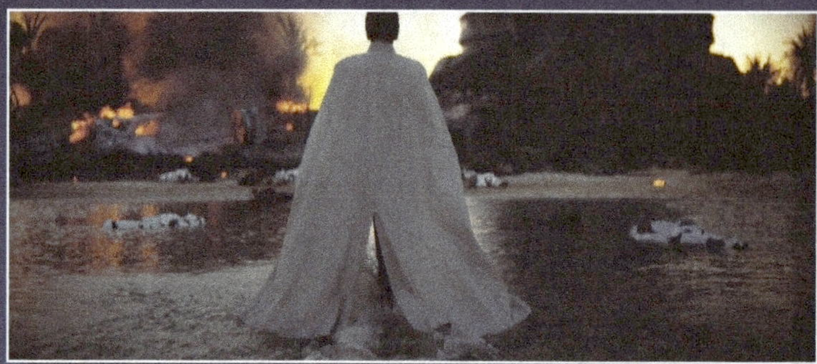

oppressive forces of fascism hit theaters exactly one weekend before the Electoral College was set to vote on whether a man who might turn out to be an actual fascist should be allowed to lead a global superpower. As of this writing, the word is still out on who the Electoral College actually chose. By the time of Carpe Nocturne's winter release in 2017 - the time of this article's printing - the controversy surrounding Star Wars might seem meaningless compared with what awaits us after the Presidential Inauguration in January.

And yet, it might also serve as precedent for how we can expect big film franchises such as Star Wars to be received in this new era of cultural and socioeconomic uncertainty. The same disgruntled fervor that seemed to poison any excitement for the Ghostbusters reboot/remake (I guess Sony will never tell us for sure which one it is) also managed to slip its slimy tendrils around Rogue One. Not that those tentacles managed to do much damage to Disney or Lucasfilm. Despite endless complaints of the film having a "feminist agenda," Rogue One still netted $290 million on opening weekend worldwide.

Make no mistake, though. Star Wars is political, no matter what Disney CEO Bob Iger tells you. At the film premiere for Rogue One he told the Hollywood Reporter, "Frankly, this is a film that the world should enjoy. It is not a film that is, in any way, a political film." He added, "There are no political statements in it, at all." To be fair, he had been asked to respond to #DumpStarWars, an online movement whose supporters claimed the film had been reshot to undermine the President-elect. Iger's job as CEO is to protect Disney's interests, of course, in attempting to downplay any political fervor surrounding the film, Iger actually managed to do the opposite by going for such an extreme viewpoint. Really, Bob? Is it truly so terrible to have a political message in your film?

More importantly, when did it become obligatory for film creators to sanitize their works of any cultural or political viewpoints? The Star Wars films are just that: they're films. Films are always going to reflect the inspirations and thoughts of their creators, just like any art form. They can be interpreted in different ways, but the common retort to any sort of in-depth analysis to a blockbuster film is often, "Ugh, it's just a movie. Just shut up and have fun!" Sure, Star Wars is fun, but are we necessarily required to turn our brains off with every fun endeavor? Does fun have to equate to vapid, every single time, forever and always? Star Wars has been a cultural icon since 1977, and it is engraved into our collective psyche. If there is any franchise worthy of artistic critique it is certainly that of a galaxy Far, Far, Away.

That being said, Star Wars was a political story from the get-go. A group of rebels desperately attempts to destroy a weapon of mass destruction that is in the hands of an oppressive Empire. Said Empire calls its feared soldiers "Stormtroopers," which is a direct reference to the

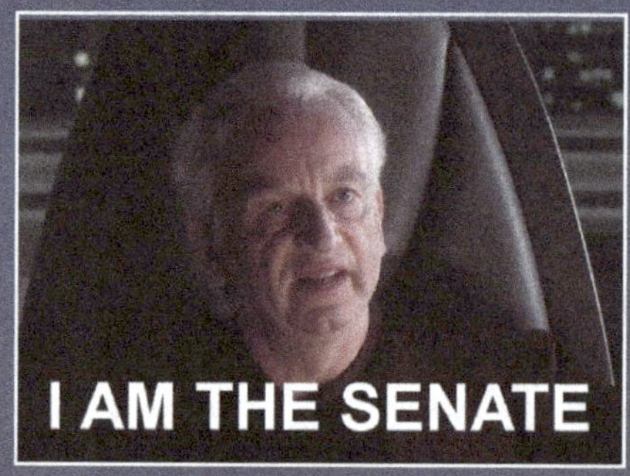

Pictured: Dialogue from a previous Star Wars film

soldiers of the same name in the time of Nazi Germany. Much is made of the Stormtroopers' ruthless execution of innocent moisture farmers and scavenging Jawas. There is also the matter of Darth Vader and his Machievellian Sith master, Emperor Palpatine, who managed to convince the entire galaxy to give him absolute power - and he did this by manipulating the outdated and corrupt innerworkings of the Republic and orchestrating an unpopular war to destroy his enemies.

Sound familiar?

"It is not a film that is, in any way, a political film." - Bob Iger

It would be a disservice not to recognize the political story in Star Wars. It is a story inherently concerned with corruption; not just corruption of government bodies, but of the human spirit. After all, how much screen time has been devoted to the seductive quality of the Dark Side of the Force and its penchant for bringing suffering and death everywhere it goes? Star Wars, like many Science-Fiction and Fantasy stories, is as much a cautionary tale as much as it is a fun romp through outer space. There are meaningful lessons and philosophies that can be gleaned from it, and while they may seem childish on the surface, these are stories that have brought hope and inspiration to fans for generations. And despite what the voices behind #DumpStarWars may claim, those generations were not exclusively white and male. Including more women and people of color in the newer films may seem like a "feminist agenda" (whatever that means), but from Disney's point of view it would be bad business to ignore half the planet as a potential source of revenue.

However, even if you disregard the capitalistic aims of Disney and Lucasfilm, the story of Star Wars tells you everything you need to know about what is at the heart of this so-called debate. In *Return of the Jedi*, Master Yoda gave Luke Skywalker one last instruction before passing away and becoming one with the Force. Specifically, he stated, "pass on what you have learned." That message did not include, "but not anyone who doesn't look like you, a blonde-haired blue-eyed human male." For as flawed as the prequel films may have been, the Jedi Order that existed before Darth Vader destroyed it was large and diverse, and it included people of many skin colors, cultures and even different alien species. The fact that it was summarily destroyed and then replaced by a totalitarian regime of mostly white men should make it obvious to #DumpStarWars (and to Bob Iger for that matter), that the story has always been pretty clear in its stance on fascism and systemic racism. It should come to no surprise to anyone that the lead writers of Rogue One tweeted the symbol of the Rebel Alliance with a safety pin attached to it following the election in November. The safety pin has been a symbol of solidarity with persecuted minorities since the Brexit vote, and it has been adopted by many Americans in response to Donald Trump becoming the President-elect. Perhaps it is this, then, that has protestors of the film so riled up. For the first time, a portion of audiences are forced to face the music:

Star Wars does not belong to just an elite few. ◼

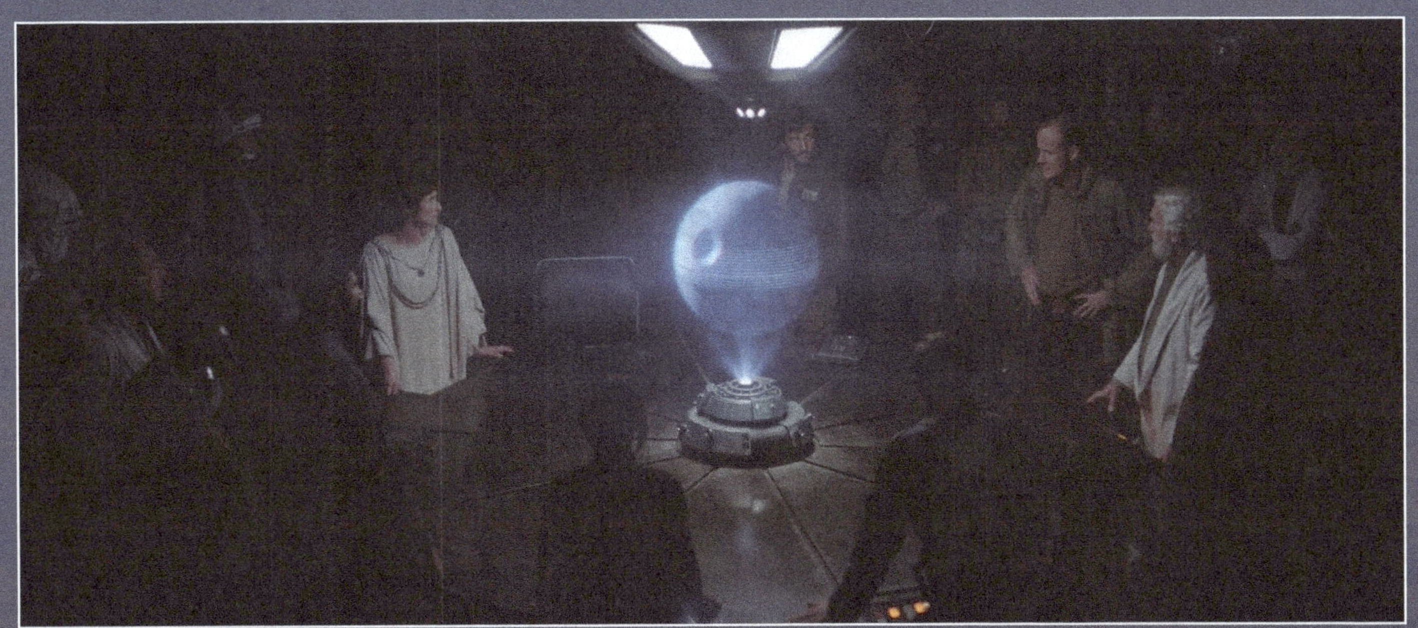

TORN CURTAIN

by Sergio Manghina

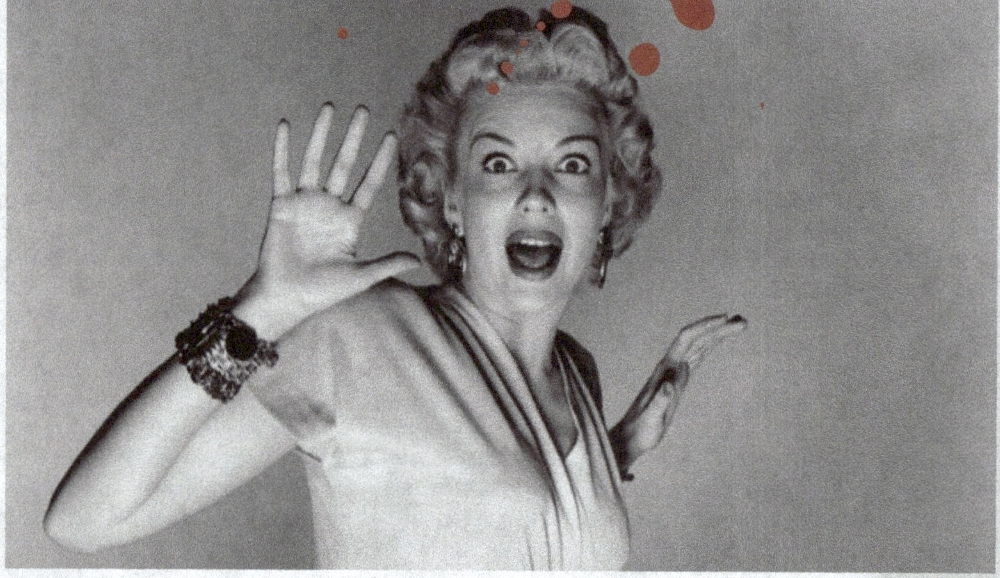

IT CAME FROM OUTER SPACE
Directed by: Jack Arnold
Studio: Universal 1953
DVD: Universal 2002

Point one: Mathematically, Jack Arnold is to science-fiction as Alfred Hitchcock is to thriller. All differences considered, of course.

Point two: The aliens of Jack Arnold are not the usual extraterrestrials. Also, their spaceship, in this movie, looks very different, being similar to a luminescent crystal.

Point three: Unlike other directors, his films introduce the point of view of the visitors from another planet.

Yes, because the strangers (from another Country or a remote galaxy) are not always hostiles or malicious, but (who knows) perhaps only castaways! It is certainly also a true fact: those guys from the deep space are not saints, that's for sure. Indeed, they have the bad habit to replace the unwitting inhabitants with perfect copies of them. This story happens in one of those small towns – Sand Rock - lost in the Arizona desert. In effect, the UFO crew is victim of a crash on planet Earth, facing the risk of serious consequences. Hence, they are a little bit disappointed, and frankly, this is understandable. Anyway, at the bottom, they are not so bad, but the town sheriff chooses the hard way. Fortunately, an astronomer, helped by his sweetheart, tries a peaceful encounter with those entities, so avoiding some major trouble for Sand Rock and probably the whole Earth!

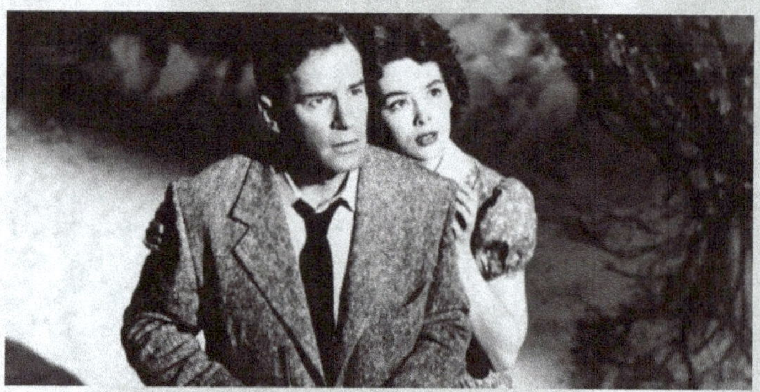

"It Came From Outer Space" was the first 3D movie from the Universal Studios, and the first with stereophonic sound. Inevitably, it is a classic plot of this genre, however enriched by significant messages and juicy gimmicks. The telepathy-screen used by aliens for shifting humans is a perfect example.

Arnold shoots Westerns masked by sci-fi-horror: "Tarantula" or "The Space Children," just to name a few. In parallel, he captures some true Westerns such as "Man in the Shadows" and "No Name in the Bullet" and does it with a certain style and originality. His typical location is the desert that becomes - in his skilled hands - a nowhere land, a place of mind, a metaphor. It is definitely a blank page to fill. ∎

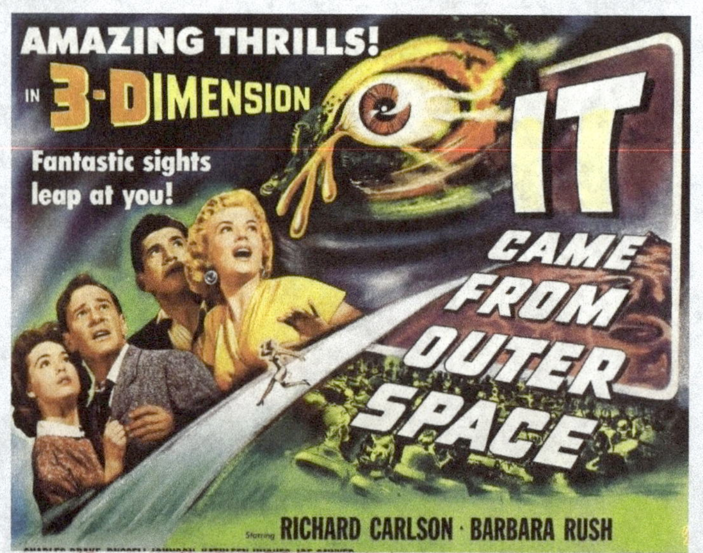

DARK CORNERS

~From the darkest corners of our imaginations, soar the most beautiful creations....

Crystal Nymph
by Zahara's Tangled Web

Frolicking in the foamy swells, a Sea Nymph
longs to test her spells.

She spirals through the salty veneer
comprised of all Earth's bitter tears,
and floats upon a briny wave, without a care
if she'll be saved.

Her skin caressing the silky sea, longing for a
change in scenery,
beseeching with her conjuring eyes, she
beckons a waterspout to the skies.

The depths attempt to drag her down and
chain her to a darker crown,
yet gentle, rocking, buoyant lifts propel her
upward to the mists.

Encircling restless energy, it entices with airy
serenity,
and dissipating in newer waters, the spout
releases the Ocean's daughter.

Touching down along the reeds, she's trapped
by chills that this place breeds.

Colder temperatures suspend all life... and
Nymph becomes Old Winter's wife.

Unable to swim or move at all, she's painfully
aware her voice cannot call!

Eyes and hair now shimmering Divine,
reflecting all the pearly moonshine,

She's encased by tiny crystal masses... frozen,
while Winter slowly passes.

Dusk of Devil
by Asylum Attendant

Office grind and a big salary
Don't appeal to me.
Predictability and morning coffee
Just depress me.

Settling on a ready-made blueprint of a life,
Complete with a stepford wife,
Is not a part of my reality.

Freedom from routine and complacency
Is where I want to be.
Imagination and creativity
Will never come second.

Inner truth is always right,
While outside opinions can take flight.
My life is not yours to take
And no life path is the same.

Keep your upgrades and business trips,
I'll stop and smell the tulips.
The moment is worth more than money can buy
And happiness cannot be penciled in.
A one-size fits all life
Only leads to boredom and strife.
Individuality is the golden key
Unlocking all my possibilities.

Off The Clock
by Einsam Vuk

In the dusk of the night.
The restless silence terrifies.
Clockwise walk slowly.
The drops fall over and over again.
I can hear it, I can feel it.

Everything around me is moving very fast.
My body trembles and my eyes disappear.
For a moment, all is darker inside me.
I can hear it, I can feel it.

This dominates me, this invades my soul.
It is waging a great inner fight.
But this devil has become in me.
Pray for salvation and run away from me.
I'm ready for my eternal damnation
and this world will be my new hell.

To Sleep, Perchance to Dream

by Jezibell Anat

They called me Sleeping Beauty,
Lying serene and lovely
Within my wall of sheltering thorns.
Perpetual repose, they thought,
The fools who pitied me.

I was hardly immobile.
That stillness of my body
Released my spirit from the material world
Into other realms of reverie and wisdom.
I toured the deep unconscious,
Transcending flesh and passion.
No hunger or thirst or pain for me.
I could travel lighter and longer
And quicker and quieter
Than any embodied being.

Mingled with elemental energy,
My soul explored the universe,
Shifting smoothly from earth to water, air to fire.
Unbound by space or shape,
I crumbled with thunder and melted into mist.
Spun sand across deserts and flowered in jungles.
I flew with the fairies and swam with the undines,
Witnessing the mysteries of earth and sky
At the crossroads of creation.

Then, penetrating my dreams, an evil vision -
A man with a sword of steel,
Cutting through my thorns
And forcing my breath with his kiss.
They called him a hero,
The fools,
Thinking he restored me to life.

I awakened to a prison.

**Think your poetry is good enough to be published
in Carpe Nocturne?**
**Send submissions to mj@carpenocturne.net
subject line "Poetry."**
**All submissions must be under 250 words, and will
be judged by Managing Editor Michael Jack and
Assistant Managing Editor Zahara.**
**The best entries will be featured in our next issue
along side of our very talented staff.** ∎

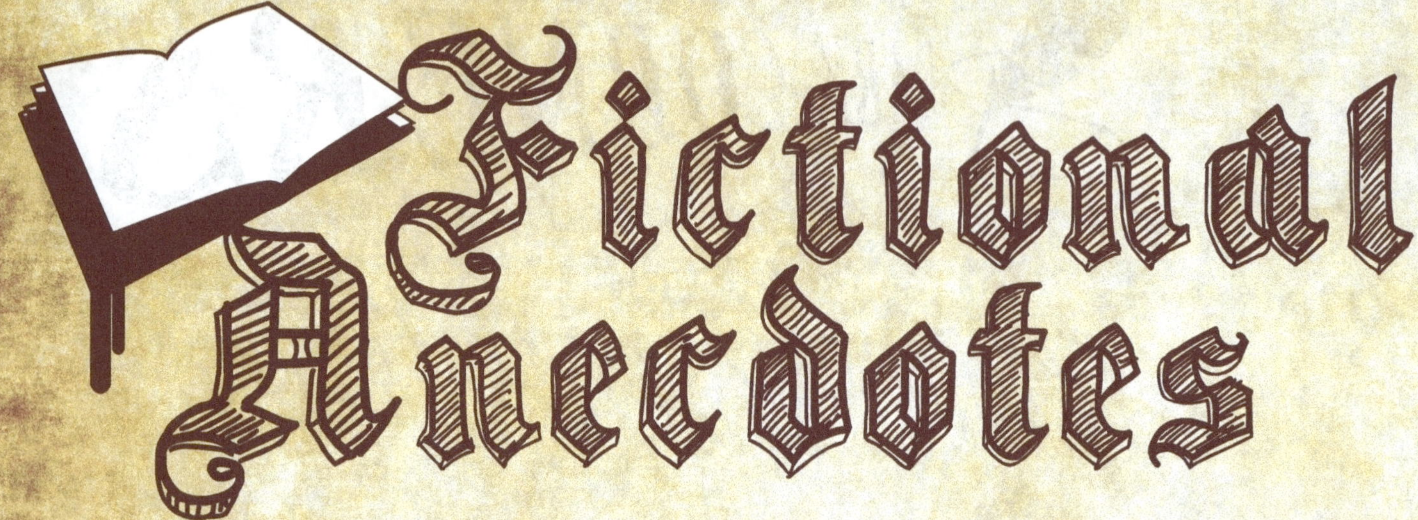

The Vainest Maiden

by Jesse Orr

Once, in the kingdom of Lanshire, there lived a maiden, the most beautiful and the vainest in all the land. All up and down the wide but steadily narrowing canyon, men spoke of her fair skin, her smooth curves, and what it would feel like to tighten their grip upon her light blonde hair.

These words were spoken by the race of men, and were heard before long by the other inhabitants of the valley. Men were overheard by dwarves, who told the gnomes, and everybody knows gnomes are notorious for spreading gossip. They told the wood elves the very same day, and so the word spread up and down the valley of the fair maiden and later, nobody remembered (or would admit) who told the dragon.

Ilda Graves was born to Catherine the Gentle, a mother as beautiful as Ilda herself would become. She had revolutionized healing in the kingdom, and was regarded as a saintly figure by the commonfolk. By contrast, Sir Brannon Graves was a raven-haired giant, whose booming laugh delighted his daughter Ilda, and whose broadsword was legendary on the battlefield.

On the final day of Ilda's thirteenth autumn, the air was cold and it was near twilight with a howling wind and spitting snow. Sir Graves returned, exhausted, from a long and bloody campaign against the goblins in the North Mountains. Instead of being greeted by his wife's cries of joy as she rushed into his arms, he was informed by the castle major-domo that his wife had perished in her sleep a fortnight ago. Just after his daughter Ilda's thirteenth birthday.

The major-domo had a sneaking suspicion that the young lady might know more about the affair than she was letting on. Her lack of surprise and disingenuous tears led him to believe that she may in fact know more about it than the kingdom could stand. That, and the grief Sir Graves was exhibiting, made him reconsider sharing his suspicions, but he never forgot them.

The truth, that Ilda had crept into her mother's room that night, and smothered her with a pillow, was too unthinkable, even for the major-domo. No one could know that Ilda, who was growing up to surpass her mother's beauty, had come to hate her mother for her flawless grace and natural loveliness. Ilda loathed her mother for the way all heads turned when she entered the room, and how all eyes followed the curves of her body as she exited. Ilda coveted those eyes moving over her, coveting her as they did her mother, for her mother was the most beautiful woman in the valley. There could be no room for Ilda while her mother held claim to that title.

Sir Graves mourned his wife's death, the major-domo held his silence, and the kingdom moved on. Ilda grew to be a stunning woman, an almost carbon copy of Catherine the Good. On occasion, Ilda would catch a glimpse of her mother in the looking glass, seeming to stare at her with an accusing look, but a blink of her own eyes always erased her mother's.

When she finally married, it was to one of the sons of her father's questing partners. Not yet knighted, Adam Danning was nonetheless a fearsome fighter and a good provider for the daughter of Sir Graves, which was what her father had planned for her all along. Ilda became pregnant, and watched in horror as her body swelled and distorted before going back to very near its former state with the birth of her first child, but she was not the same. She loved her son, but privately mourned her own loss. In spite of anything she could do, she became pregnant again. It was less horrifying, but the damage was more severe. She could see lines beginning to form on her face, and her figure was not what it had been.

There had been no magician in the kingdom for hundreds of years, and those who lived in Lanshire had become adept at dwelling without magic. It was said, normally by those in their cups, that the last remnant of magic dwelt at the base of the mountain, where the

"Time!" Ilda said, and her voice echoed in the chamber. "Time is taking away what I was! Can you stop it?"

valley ended. There was a huge chamber, they said, over which the mountain crouched like a stronghold, sheltering the dragon, which had been there since the beginning of time, it was said. There had never been a time the beast had not dwelt there, and if anything in the valley had ever seen magic, it would be the dragon.

Ilda Graves set out for the dragon's lair, to ask it if there was any cure, any remedy that it might have learned in its long years. She was prepared to pay any price. She could feel herself aging, and hastened her steps. There wasn't a moment to lose.

The dragon lay in the sun on its back, basking in the rays. One clawed foot twitched as it dozed, greenish scales rustling against the boulders. One hundred meters from wingtip to wingtip, the air coming from its nostrils scorched the very rock beneath them. Its long forked tongue hung out, waving between fangs the size of her arm.

Still, she wasn't afraid. The dragon had been within walking distance, so to speak, of the kingdom for generations without ever showing even the slightest interest in menacing its inhabitants. She cleared her throat. The beast's eyes snapped open and it looked at her. It grinned. Upside down, it looked grotesque.

"Lady Ilda," the dragon said, its voice like rocks rolling down a hill. "Welcome."

"I bid you good tidings," Ilda called in what she thought was a calm, rational voice.

With surprising speed, considering its bulk, the dragon pushed itself upright and looked at her, elongating its neck until they were eye to eye.

"And the same," it rumbled, ruffling Ilda's hair as it scented her with its hot breath. Ilda smelled burnt campfire and saw one of the threads on her dress was singeing.

"You want something," it said, and withdrew its head. It circled, pawing at boulders, then lay back down, this time right side up.

"Well, yes," Ilda said, her knees weak and wondering if she could go through with it. She thought of the lines on her face, the toll

gravity was taking, the crushing, inexorable progression of time's decay on her features, and her resolve strengthened.

The dragon chuckled, and the very ground seemed to shake with its thunder. "This should be good."

"Time!" Ilda said, and her voice echoed in the chamber. "Time is taking away what I was! Can you stop it?"

"No one can stop time, fool," the dragon said, its voice scornful. "Can you stop the sun's set?"

"No one in Lanshire can!" cried Ilda in frustration. "There hasn't been magic there for hundreds of years, not since the last magician--"

"Flagg," the dragon said, and ran its tongue out. "I ate him."

"You—er—yes," Ilda had lost track of her thoughts amid sudden images of the creature before her eating another human being, and remembering exactly how close to her its teeth had come.

"Spare me your words," the dragon said. "You seek a wizard's method of stopping time's work upon your body." Its scorn was evident as it chuckled. "Your race never ceases to disgust me. If you are desperate enough, I will share the secret with you."

"What must I do?" Ilda asked, coming closer. "What token will you accept for your assistance? There is nothing I will not undertake."

The dragon brought its head closer. Ilda took an inadvertent step backward. Its head stopped less than meter from hers. Its eyes were larger than her head.

"To know this you must give it your whole heart," it said, its voice crackling. "This is impossible while your heart belongs to others. Bring their hearts to me, and I will spare you from death's slow march."

It took a moment for this to sink in. Then the faces of her family swam before her eyes. Her children's. Her husband's.

Then her own face. She beheld it sagging, her smile warping into a grimace as her flesh fell off her skull in large chunks. She gasped, staggering back from the dragon's face. It ran its tongue out, tasting her suffering, and sighed with apparent pleasure, a deep sound from the depths of its chest.

Ilda somehow found herself in a tub later that night, the water dyed red as she attempted to scrub the blood from her hair. She did not weep, for her tears had already been shed. She watched the water lapping the edges of the tub, red with the blood of her children and husband, and her mind with great force jerked itself back to the vision of her face falling off. They died for a good cause, she told herself. They would have wanted me to be beautiful forever.

It had been even easier to smother her children than her mother. The elder of the two put up a little resistance but she doubted he had even woken up. The youngest never made a sound. Her husband, she knew, would wake up and undoubtedly throw her off if she tried smothering him with a pillow. Taking his dagger from its scabbard where it hung over the bedpost, she placed its keen edge against his throat and sliced, opening his throat nearly to his spine. After some gasping and flailing, it was all over. All but the harvesting, which was somehow the easiest. She almost enjoyed it, except for the cleaning.

Placing her precious cargo in her husband's battered leather satchel, she tied her skirts about herself and swung onto his horse. Twining her fingers into the horse's mane, she nudged it with her knees, sending them down the moonlit path. As they neared the base of the mountain, the horse grew skittish. Though invisible to her, Ilda knew the horse was picking up the fiery scent of dragon, and urged it forward until it would go no further. Continuing foot, she made her way down into the chamber, which glowed with an angry red light from some unseen source.

The dragon was waiting for her, its eyes fixed unblinkingly on the entrance to the cave. Her shadow fell across its threshold before she crossed it, and its jaws spread open in a nightmare of a smile. Its head

It took a moment for this to sink in. Then the faces of her family swam before her eyes.

The dragon chuckled, and the very ground seemed to shake with its thunder.

moved across the cavern to sit on the ground before her. "Lady Ilda Graves, I welcome your return," it said. "I welcome what you bear more eagerly still." Its tongue ran out and nearly caressed her.

Hiding a shudder, Ilda took a heart from the bag. It was clearly one of her children's, by its size, and as the dragon watched, blood dripped from one of the severed veins. Its tongue, lighting quick, flicked out and caught the drop before it reached the ground. The tongue then wrapped itself around the heart in Ilda's hand, lifting the organ into its mouth. It closed its eyes, savoring the taste for a long moment.

"Exquisite," the dragon said, its eyes snapping open. It nudged the bag she carried with its nose. "You have more. Another child, and a man."

"Yes," Ilda said, not looking at the beast. She turned the bag over and both hearts fell out. The dragon's head snapped forward, plucking the two hearts out of the air. Its pleasure at their flavor was evident in the way its scales quivered as it devoured them.

"So prime, so prime," it said, its tongue snaking in between its fangs, seeking remaining chunks. "A pity they don't grow larger."

"Now honor your word, and tell me how to stop the aging," Ilda said, an edge of hysteria in her voice. "I implore you!"

The dragon snorted, sending a puff of smoke toward the roof of the cavern. "Oh, that." It nodded at the bag she still clutched. "You have already performed the service for your family. That is the only way to stop the aging."

Ilda stared, not understanding. "You said..."

"I have just told you," it said, and now its voice was colder than she had heard it. "Your family will remain as they were when you killed them, ageless for eternity. The passage of time cannot be stopped. Only by ending yourself where you are now, can you hope to achieve any measure of immortality."

Ilda understood then, and a great rage rose within her. "My family... I killed them all... why?" She was screaming. "How could you let me do that?" She picked up a rock and threw it at the dragon.

Before she knew what happened, she had been knocked on her back by the dragon's head crashing into her and sending her sprawling. It stood over her, pinning her to the ground with a single claw.

"Fool!" it hissed, pressing down. Ilda felt the claw pierce her chest. "You come to me seeking advice on how to cheat death, time, and nature itself, so desperate for these things that you think nothing of slaughtering those closest to you." A rib cracked, and she screamed. The dragon grinned. "You will suffer now, but take comfort in the fact that once I eat your heart, you will be reunited with your family."

Another claw sunk into Ilda's chest. As she was torn open and watched her heart plucked from within her by the dragon's claws, her last thought flashed through her mind.

"Now I will die beautiful." ∎

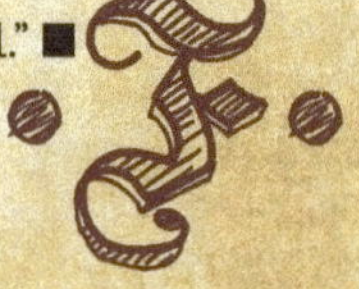

The Lovely Burn of "Girl on Fire"

By Zahara

"It's not a matter of if you'll get burned - it's when, and how bad..."

Cherie Dawn Haas (Cincinnati, Ohio) is a fire eater, dancer, and artist. Her first novel ("Girl on Fire") offers an intimate glimpse into the world of tribal belly dance and fire arts. Cherie Dawn's real-life experience as a local entertainer came in handy when creating this fictional story. Following heroine Summer on her brave quest for artistic expression, we witness the moment she takes her first belly dance class, as well as the many twists and turns of her blazing trail as a fire

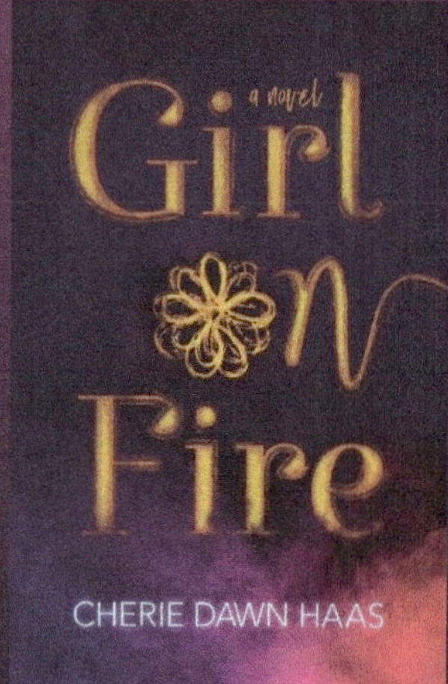

artist. Struggling to leave a painful part of her past behind, Summer immerses herself in this new world. She meets several colorful characters along the way and strives to enjoy life on her own terms.

Told in a very down-to-earth manner, the story reveals not only Summer's motivations and aspirations, but those of her tribe mates (Rhiannon, Adrian, Morgan, Rosie and Phoenix), as well. There are lessons to be learned along the way, some more painfully than others... and not just when dancing with flames! What does it mean to be beautiful? What is acceptance? Who are the important people in my life? How do I move forward? These are questions we've all asked ourselves, and "Girl on Fire" perfectly illustrates how different people answer those questions while conquering betrayals, temptations, and egos. Even if you're not a belly dancer or fire artist, you're sure to find parts of this novel that resonate with you.

The book can be purchased on Amazon at http://bit.ly/p20GirlOnFire. For more information about Cherie Dawn, visit cheriedawnlovesfire.com (no www) or follow her on Twitter (@CherieKre8s). ∎

The Collective Works of xxx ZombieBoy xxx

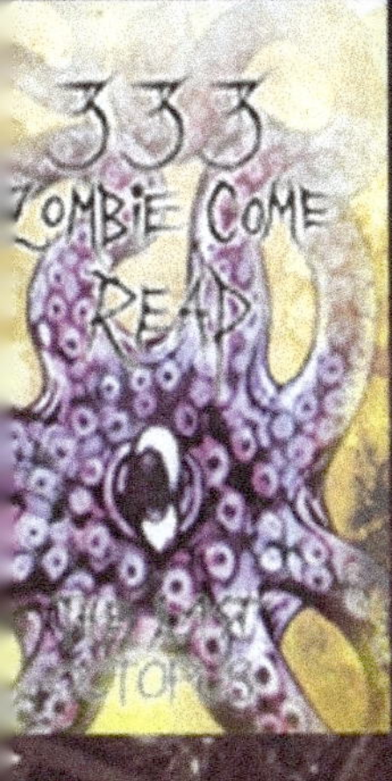

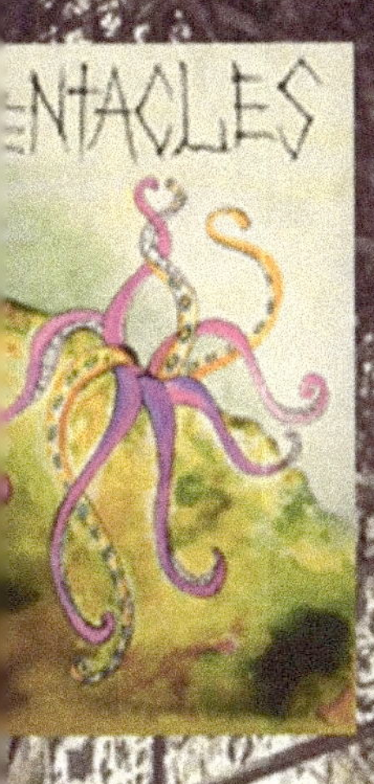

AVAILABLE ON AMAZON

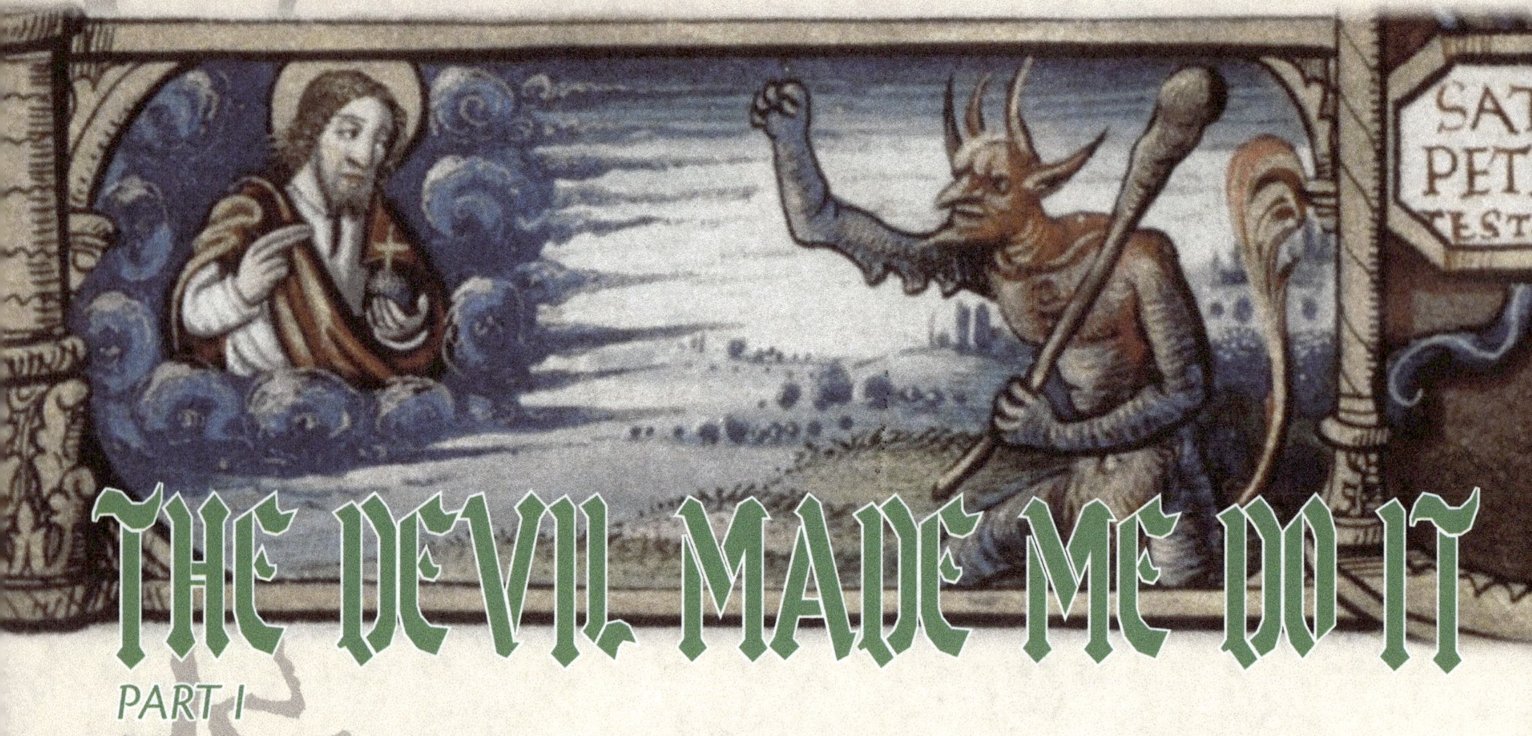

THE DEVIL MADE ME DO IT

PART I

By Joseph A. Zuchowski

He's a rebel and he's never ever, very good, he's a rebel and he never ever does what he should.

The Crystals 1962, "He's a Rebel"

Black robed figures chant softly and slowly around a stone altar covered by a black cloth with occult symbols upon it. Lit only by black candles, a nubile, struggling female lies upon the cloth, naked except for her bonds and gag, her eyes wide with fear at the man whose head is covered by a goat-headed mask. In his upraised hand is an ornate but vicious dagger.

Yes, that is a scene out of a 1970's Hammer horror film, or any number of grade B occult films. At the last moment, the brawny hero comes in, guns ablaze, rescues the fair maid, and we can guess the rest.

This is the stock view of the religion of Satanism, that it is a path of carnal indulgence, of wantonness, of dark secrets to obtain power over others. Actually, Satan is an intrinsic part of Western Christianity, the religion of 80% of this country. According to Anton LeVey, founder of the recognized Church of Satan, "Satan is the best friend the church ever had. He's kept it in business all this time."

It is time to give the devil his due. The name Satan derives from the Hebrew word *Shaytan* meaning an adversary or opponent. Satan figures much more in the Christian (New) Testament than in the Hebrew (Old) Testament, where Satan does not appear until Numbers, the fourth book of the Torah. Here he has King David challenge God's authority by holding a census, something that God had forbidden. This surprises many people as they assume Satan has been in there from Genesis on.

As children, most of us are taught that Satan took the form of a talking serpent to tempt Eve to eat the fruit from the Tree of Knowledge. However, Satan is never mentioned either directly or indirectly, and that distortion is simply a later reinterpretation. Look at the actual story - God lied by saying that Adam and Eve would die if they ate the fruit, but the serpent spoke the truth by telling them that they would gain knowledge.

So they eat, their eyes are opened, and they see they are naked. Then God gets very upset. "Behold, now that man has eaten from the Tree of Knowledge and knows of good and evil, what if he should put forth his hand and eat from the Tree of Life and become immortal like us?" (Gen. 3:22) It is never made clear who the "us" is in what is supposedly a monotheistic religion; humanity is simply expelled from Eden.

Satan features as a major player in only two books, Job and Revelations, which were written around four hundred years apart. These books reveal a major shift in view from the Hebrew to the Christian one. Job refers to Satan as *Ha Shaytan* (The Satan) a member of

God's celestial court. Here Satan is not the adversary of God but of God's creation, humanity. Satan tests or punishes mankind according to God's direction. Job, a good and righteous man, who has been God's favorite and showered with material blessings, becomes a plaything between God and Satan, a view that becomes intrinsic to the Abrahamic viewpoint.

Biblical scholar Bart D. Erhmann explains in his book *God's Problem* that human suffering is all a part of God's plan. This is the problem with monotheism. How can you propose an entirely benevolent, omniscient, omnipotent god without a valid interpretation of why there is suffering? Evil can only exist because God wills it in some way.

The Hebrews were not the only ancient peoples who viewed suffering as divine will, but a polytheistic world view presents a plethora of forces at interplay. In monotheism, evil is ultimately the result of the will of the one god instead of resulting from conflicts between multiple divine entities.

In Persia around the 8th century BCE, a religious reformer called Zoroaster or Zarathustra claimed to have had a divine encounter that led him found a new religion which was essentially a streamlined polytheism. Zoroastrianism states that the world consists of two opposing powers, Ahura Mazda, the force of good, symbolized as a radiant sun being, and his brother and arch-enemy Ahriman, a force of corruption and chaos, symbolized as a snake.

This conflict results finally in a glorious war between the Sons of Light and the Sons of Darkness, where evil is finally purged and an eternal perfect heavenly order is universally established. Sound familiar to anyone? Zoroastrianism had a great influence on Judaism, Christianity, and Islam, and it still survives today in Iran, with about two million adherents.

Satanism never was an organized religion prior to the twentieth century. Pagan religions usually included dark deities who represented the forces of destruction, rage, chaos, and death in the context of a pantheon that was more amoral than moralistic. Zoroastrianism provided the template for the dualistic struggle between good and evil.

Zoroastrianism inspired the Yazidi religion of the Kurds, still practiced in parts of Syria and Turkey. In their theology, God placed the world under the care of Melek Taus, the Peacock Angel, who bestowed both blessings and misfortunes upon humanity. The Yaziidis, are often called devil worshippers by their Jewish, Christian, and Muslim neighbors, though they are far from any view of Satanism, as we know it. In Syria Daesh (ISIL) has a program of genocide against them.

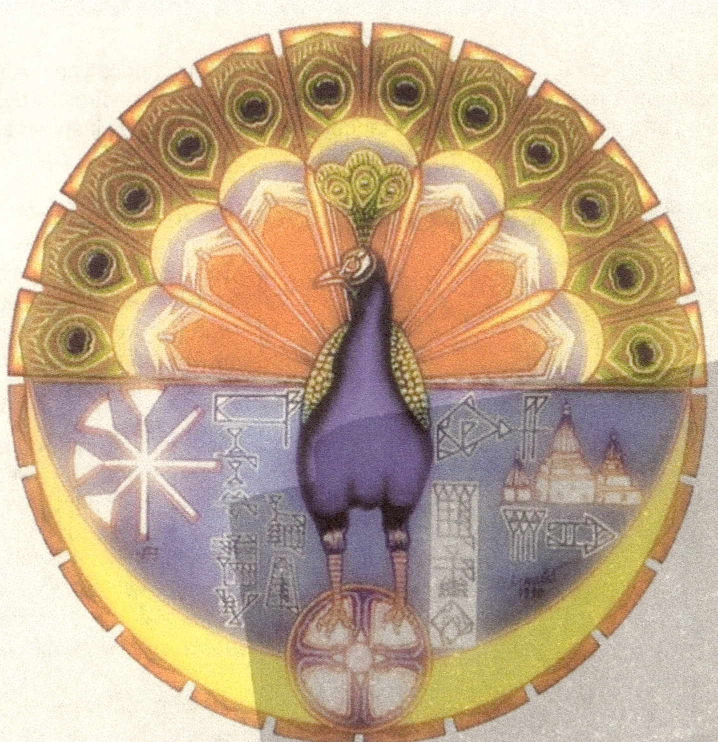

So how did the concept of Satan develop in Christianity? Christianity began as an oral tradition but by around 100 CE, a fledgling body of literature centered around their founder. In the Gospel of Mark (c. 70-75 CE) Christ foretells the destruction of the temple and the "end of days," marked "by wars and rumors of wars."

This theme was the focus of Revelations, the final book of the New Testament, written by a banished leader of the church named John. Revelations is a violent, bloody book that is as controversial today as it is when it was written, seventy years after the crucifixion. By then, Jesus' generation was either very old or already dead, and, since he had not returned, many Christians were questioning their faith and all that they had given up for their salvation.

To them, John wrote a book full of admonitions and warnings of what was to befall those who either opposed or left the "True Faith." Revelations presents Jesus as an avenging conqueror, inspiring "The Battle Hymn of the Republic" where God releases his wrath upon the Confederacy. Revelations also condemns Rome with all its "abominations," meaning all the different religions that were practiced within the Roman Empire.

While this book claims to have been revealed in a series of visions, it was more likely influenced by mortal sources.   For example, the Book of Daniel described a dream of strange and horrific monsters very similar to those in Revelations, and includes a vision of a messianic figure.

Revelations presented the concept of a world ruler, called the The Great Beast by Christians, who demanded utmost submission and required his followers bear his mark. It was common in those times to brand slaves, which continued up to the 19th century. Even in the Harry Potter series, Voldemort's followers bore the dark mark.

In Revelations, Satan and his armies are ultimately defeated in the great battle of Armegeddon, a site ("Tel Megiddo") which had been the site of major battles in the ancient world. The defeated Forces of Darkness are then thrown into a Lake of fire to burn forever. (Interestingly, the origin of the lake of fire is in the Egyptian Book of the Dead.)   At last, the "New Jerusalem" descends from heaven and the eternal kingdom is restored. Revelations inspired "The Left Behind "series of novels and movies which have become very popular among evangelical Christians.

The belief that 666 is the number of the Beast derives from gematria, a system of numerology in which the Greek letters had a numeric value. 666 was a code allegedly referring to Nero, the emperor who executed the apostles Peter and Paul and ordered some of the worse Christian persecutions.

Revelations also inspired Charles Manson to convince his cult ("the family") to go out and commit some of the most infamous crimes in history, the Tate /LaBianca murders. Manson used the Book of Revelation to validate that he was both Christ and Satan united in one being.

Concepts presented in Revelations still affect our worldview today, especially the term apocalypse. Apocalypse in Greek means literally to uncover. The looser Latin translation is revelation. Today it has come to indicate a destroyed dystopic future where the survivors struggle vainly against overwhelming and desperate odds. Often tagged with zombies, it has inspired shows such as The Walking Dead, Z Nation, and many horror films.

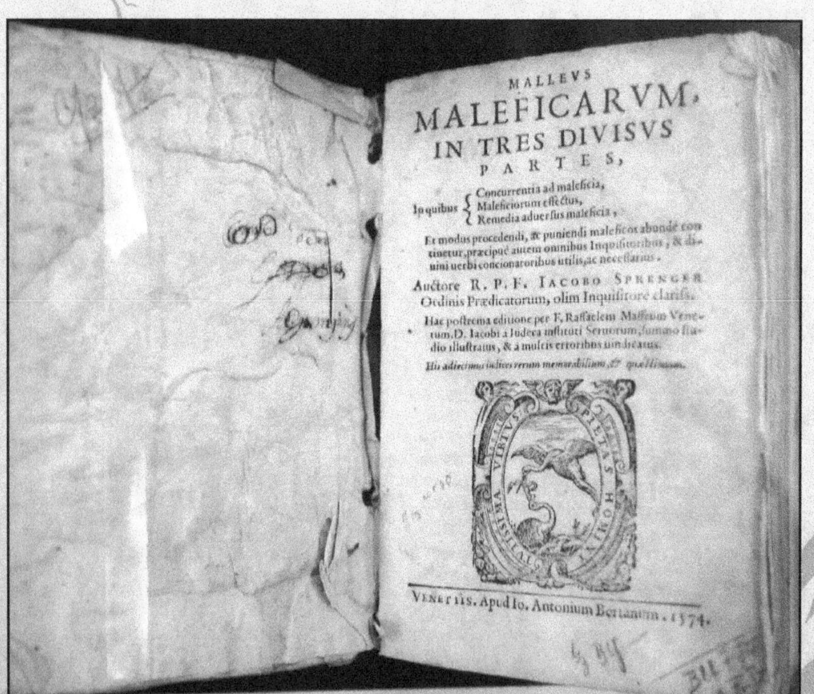

As Christianity grew from a cult into a state-sponsored religion, other faiths were outlawed or severely restricted. Their gods were considered devils. Early Christians saw Judaism as a flawed and incomplete precursor - those who followed Christ became the "good Jews," the sheep to his shepherd. Christ described those who did not follow him as "goats."

Goat was an old term for a iconoclast or a conformist. Unlike sheep, who will easily follow a leader, goats have a lusty and independent nature, The Greek word for goat is *kapri*, the origin of our word capricious. The emperor Tiberius, had a resort palace on the island of Capri which was basically was a private bordello. Goats were associated with the pastoral god Pan, who was in turn associated with Satan.

Pan himself was a relatively minor deity. A son of Hermes, he was the leader of the satyrs, nature spirits who were randy, amoral, and earthy. He shared some similarities with Dionysos, god of the vine. Pan and Dionysos were both troublemakers and liberators, the rebels standing up to the status quo, an attitude which would be adopted by Satanist of later centuries.

By the end of the Middle Ages Christianity had become the predominant religion in Europe. In 1486 the *Malleus Maleficarum*, a manual of how to discover and punish witches, was written by two Dominican priests, Heinrich Kramer and Jakob Spengler. This book claims that witches made a pact with Satan to gain the power to do maleficent magic, establishing the link between witches and the Devil that has fueled many horror stories and films. The *Malleus Maleficarum* concluded that witchcraft existed because Satan exists.

This book described an inversion of the Catholic Mass called the Black Mass which was supposedly celebrated during the witches' Sabbat. It also told the Inquisitors what questions to ask and what tortures to apply, and allowed the acceptance of testimony from children, the insane and known perjurers. The Protestants also used this manual, and by 1639 it was the most widely read book in ecclesiastical circles next to the Bible in the West.

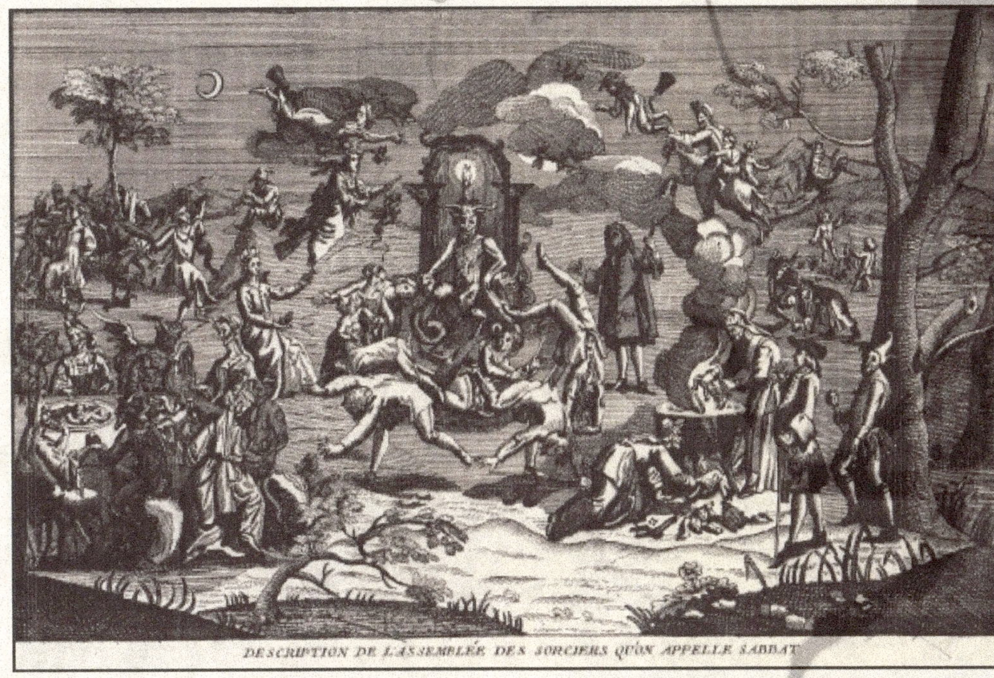

By the seventeenth century, the witchcraze had reached epidemic proportions in both Catholic and Protestant countries. When an accused witch was convicted, the victim's property was divided in thirds between the accuser, the Church, and the state. The major targets were herbalists, midwives, gypsies, homosexuals and the insane, and the most striking fact is that 85% of those killed were women.

In Auldearne, Scotland, the confessions of Isobel Gowdie (c.1662) both terrified and titillated her neighbors and judges. Gowdie claimed that she had been made a witch by the devil who took the form of a man dressed in gray. He had baptized her in an abandoned church with her own blood and marked her as his own. She claimed that she and twelve other women would fly to deserted areas around Auldearne, engage in wild orgiastic Sabbaths, and perform spells to wreak havoc on the local people. Her tale keep the hysteria going. There is no recorded of what happened to her, but it is commonly assumed that she was burned along with the other "witches" in Auldearne.

However, among the jaded French aristocracy, dabbling in the occult became a pastime. In the late seventeenth century, during the reign of the Sun King Louis XIV, a fashion of attending an eroticized "Black Mass" arose. One of the main organizers was the fortuneteller Catherine

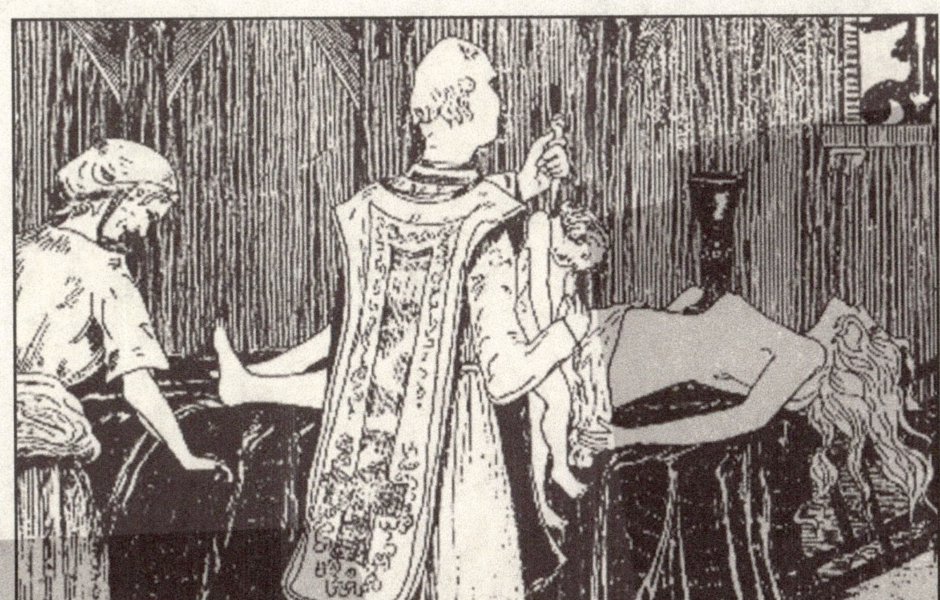

Deshayes, known as "La Voisin," using the services of defrocked cleric Abbé Guibourg. The sensational stories of murdered babies at these Masses probably refer to the ritual employment of the products of LaVoisin's other trade as an abortionist. Widespread accounts of poisoning among the nobility led to police investigations from 1679-1682 and uncovered evidence that the king's mistress, the Marquise de Montespan, had sought LaVoisin's services to keep Louis' attention. As a result, Louis covered the scandal, exiled the nobles, executed the commoners, banned fortunetellers, and declared witchcraft to be a superstition.

The witch trials finally ended as the Enlightenment spread through Europe, bringing the idea that the universe was simply a vast machine, mechanical and impervious. But, Satan did not disappear - more about him in Part II. ■

From the very beginning, the life of the woman known as Mata Hari alternated between luxurious fantasy and brutal reality.

Eye of the Day

The Legend of Mata Hari

by Jezibell Anat

From the very beginning, the life of the woman known as Mata Hari alternated between luxurious fantasy and brutal reality. She was born Margaretha Geertruida Zelle (variously nicknamed M'Greet, Griete, Gresha, and Gretha) on August 7, 1876, in the town of Leeuwarden in the Netherlands. Her father Adam Zelle was handsome and elegant, with a successful haberdashery business, and he spoiled his only daughter. He sent her to an exclusive girls' school where she excelled in languages, learning French, English, and German.

She was beautiful and remained her father's favorite even though she had three younger brothers. He gave her gifts such as a red velvet dress and an exquisite miniature carriage pulled by goats, gifts which the neighbors thought were far too extravagant for a little girl. But Gretha delighted in driving her friends around the neighborhood. One of her schoolmates described her as an orchid in a field of dandelions.

This storybook childhood crashed to an end in 1889 when her father went bankrupt through oil speculation. He left the family and scandalized the town by filing for a legal separation and living openly with another woman. Then Gretha's mother died in 1891. Her brothers went to live with their father and his new wife, but she was sent to an uncle.

Gretha felt heartbroken, angry and betrayed, and she was probably a difficult charge. In 1892 her uncle sent her to a boarding school run by a friend of his, a well-respected educator named Wybrandus Haanstra. She was to train to be a kindergarten teacher even though she had no interest in children, and she became involved sexually with the married, fifty-one year old Haanstra.

Today this would be considered exploitation of a minor, but in the conservative Netherlands it was Gretha who received the blame for her lack of morals. She was expelled in disgrace. Haanstra continued his career successfully until his death, while Gretha was sent off to relatives in The Hague.

The Hague was a much more cosmopolitan city than Leeuwarden, and it was filled with people returning from the colonies, including soldiers on leave. Because Gretha's prospects were not great, she answered a newspaper ad for a wife placed by Rudolf MacLeod, a hard-living soldier of Scottish descent on medical leave who was twenty years her senior. After an initial infatuation, they were married in 1895.

Rudolf was a soldier who had lived a soldier's life, and within weeks he was drinking and carousing and overspending. But the marriage provided some social standing for a girl whose life had been marred by scandal, and they had a son. In 1897, they set sail for the Dutch East Indies.

What a contrast to the dull, staid bourgeoisie of the Netherlands! Indonesia was a place of brilliant color and sensual delight, of hot golden sun and lush vegetation, flowers, fruits, and spices. All the colonials were changed by their experiences there. Often women shed their corsets in the tropical climate and wore looser, lightweight fabric. The MacLeods lived like royalty, with servants and a grand house, and they had a second child, a daughter.

Here Gretha could leave her children with their nurses while she explored the island, and she discovered a splendid and dramatic style of dance. Some sources say she even joined a local dance troupe. Indonesia has over 3,000 dance forms, most of which originated in ritual. One component was that Hindu stories were incorporated into lavish dance-dramas, with graceful, elegant movements, meaningful hand gestures, and elaborate headdresses. From encountering this rich dance culture, Gresha would draw the inspiration to become Mata-Hari.

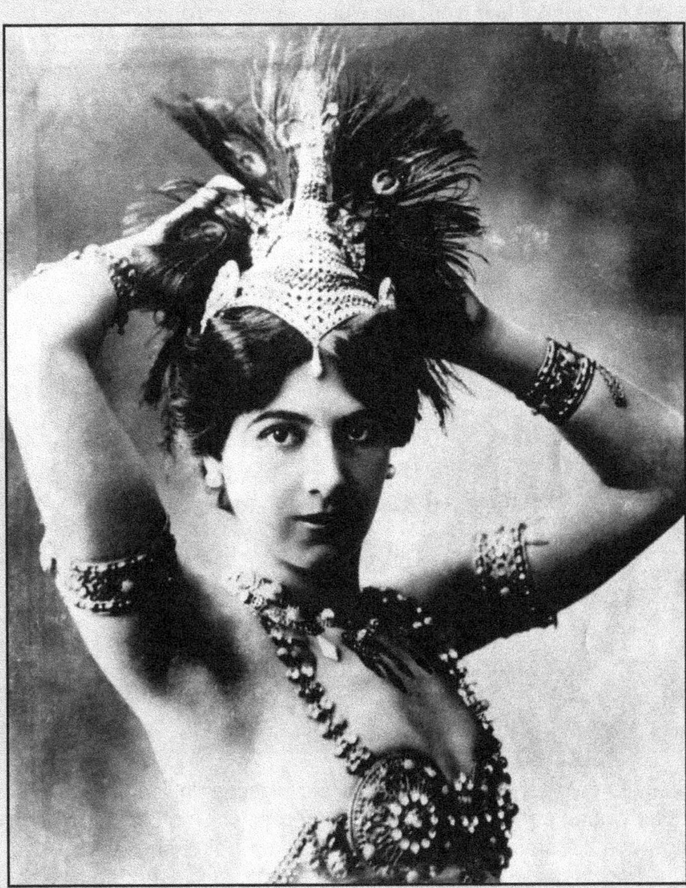

As an officer's wife, Greta's status was high, and her beauty drew attention in colonial society. But her marriage was on the rocks. Rudolf became jealous of her popularity, and they quarreled frequently. He also kept a native concubine. Their son died in 1899, and Rudolf was devastated. His drinking increased, and he began to beat her.

In 1902, they returned to the Netherlands and separated; Rudolf took their daughter. Lost and unhappy, Gretha stayed with several relatives and tried to make money modeling and acting with little success. Finally she went to Paris. When asked why Paris, she said "I thought all women who ran away from their husbands went to Paris." In chic, sophisticated Paris, the worldly city of art and intellect, she found her calling. When she got a job with an equestrian circus, the owner recommended that she become a dancer and introduced her to some influential society ladies.

In a magnificent feat of self re-invention, she became Mata Hari. In the Malay language, Mata Hari is usually translated as sunrise but literally means "eye of the day." The World's Fair of 1889 had sparked the fashion for Orientalism, and her experience in the Indies gave her the inspiration to present "sacred dances." She had been condemned for her sexuality and beauty; now she turned these into assets.

Paris was used to the ballet and cancan. Modern dancer Isidora Duncan had caused a scandal by dancing without a corset, but no one could combine the exotic and the erotic like Mata Hari. She introduced herself by stating "My dance is a sacred poem in which each movement is a word and whose every word is underlined by music."

Her presentation created a mood of luxurious splendor. She wore flowers, jewels, a casque of gold upon her head, a jeweled bra, and swathed her body in sheer veils. She used some of the postures and body articulations of Javanese dance, but her style

between Mata Hari being both a renowned dancer and an expert courtesan, and she took full advantage of her charisma and fame. The upper classes in Paris lived sumptuously, and powerful men openly paraded their mistresses in society. She later admitted, "I never could dance well. People came to see me because I was the first who dared to show myself naked to the public."

Mata Hari's rising star drew the attention of her separated husband Rudolf, who filed for divorce on the grounds of immoral behavior and adultery. She knew that a court of law would take a dim view of her performances, so she decided not to contest the divorce nor ask for custody of her child. She never saw her daughter again.

After her first triumphant years, sustaining her success became a challenge. She had been nearly thirty when she began her career, and she was not a trained dancer. Meanwhile, "Oriental dancers"

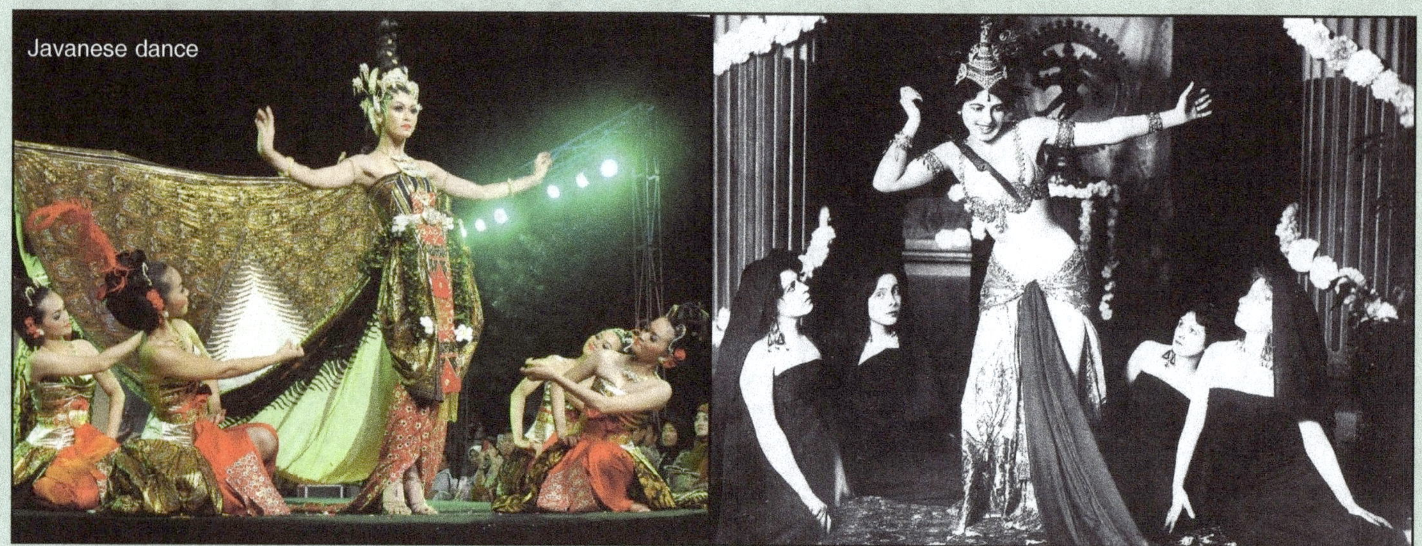

was her own - she removed her layers of fabric until she appeared to be wearing only her ornaments and bra, which she always kept on because she was self-conscious about being small-breasted. She did wear a skin-colored body stocking, but promoted the illusion of nudity.

The claim that she was performing ancient temple dances, often dedicated to Shiva or other Hindu deities, protected her from charges of indecency. Her audience was the aristocracy, the wealthy art lovers, women as well as men. She made her debut at fashionable salons hosted by respectable ladies, and performed at the Musee Guimet, a museum of Oriental art. She immediately became a celebrity, and she relished her success.

Reporters were eager to talk to her, and she spun them fantastic stories of her past, sometimes claiming to have been a temple dancer, born in India or the Indies. The publicity continued to shape her mystique. She began to get bookings in larger venues, theatres and upper-class music halls, and even a role in the opera. The *New Vienna* Journal claimed "Isadora Duncan is dead! Long live Mata Hari!"

Her performances attracted wealthy admirers, and she became the mistress of several influential gentlemen. In this glamorous era, later designated the Belle Epoque, there was no discrepancy

in abbreviated costumes were appearing all over the music halls. Maud Allan had gained fame by dancing the role of Salome in Richard Strauss' opera, a part which Mata Hari craved but never received. Mata Hari had begun to gain weight, and Ballet Russe impresario Sergei Diaghalev would not allow her to dance in his productions. Her last performance was in 1915.

Times and trends had changed with the arrival of World War I in 1914. In the glittering pre-war society, she had been a free-spirited bohemian artist. With the continent ravaged by battle, she was viewed as wanton and dangerous. She was used to traveling freely through Europe, which she could do legally because she was a citizen of the Netherlands, a neutral country. But in wartime a woman traveling alone aroused suspicion.

In 1916 she fell in love with a Russian officer, Vladimir ("Vadime") de Masloff, fifteen years her junior. With her profligate lifestyle, she was always short of funds, and she wanted to earn enough money to set up a household with Vadime, who became blind in one eye at the front. Mata Hari continued her career as a courtesan with clients of several nationalities.

The stories about her alleged espionage are confusing. She was accused of being a spy, or even a double agent, However, Mata

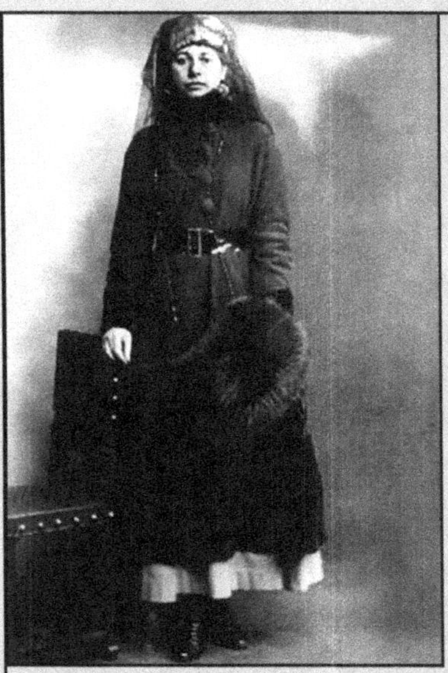

Hari was a visible celebrity who drew attention to herself, not the type of person who makes an effective operative. But by 1917, France had suffered heavy losses at the bloody battle of Verdun and needed a scapegoat. Mata Hari was arrested in February by the French police and charged with being a spy for Germany. She was put on trial in July.

She had spent her life fabricating stories about herself, and, under interrogation, the slightest discrepancies were seized upon. She admitted to being divorced and to being a courtesan; she even admitted to taking money from the Germans but insisted that she gave them nothing, saying "A courtesan, I admit it. A spy, never! I have always lived for love and pleasure." Her interrogators did not believe her, and she was sentenced to death.

On October 15, 2017, she was executed by a firing squad. She faced her end with dignity and courage. She refused to be blindfolded or tied to the stake, and she even blew a kiss to the firing squad before they shot her. Thirty years after her death, one of her prosecutors admitted that "there wasn't enough evidence to flog a cat."

Mata Hari's life has been portrayed on film with Greta Garbo (*Mata Hari* 1931) and Sylvia Kristel (*Mata Hari* 1985), and ashe was the first sexual encounter for young Indiana Jones in the TV series. Pat Shipman's *Femme Fatale: Love, Lies, and the Unknown Life of Mata Hari* is an excellent and readable biography. There is a documentary on youtube https://www.youtube.com/watch?v=SWvk00RbMcM ∎

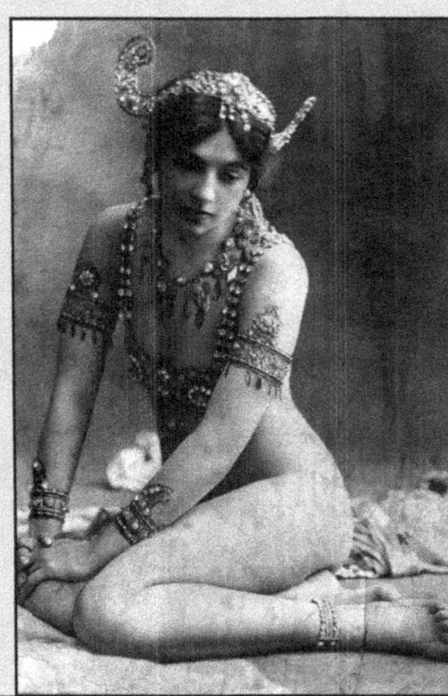

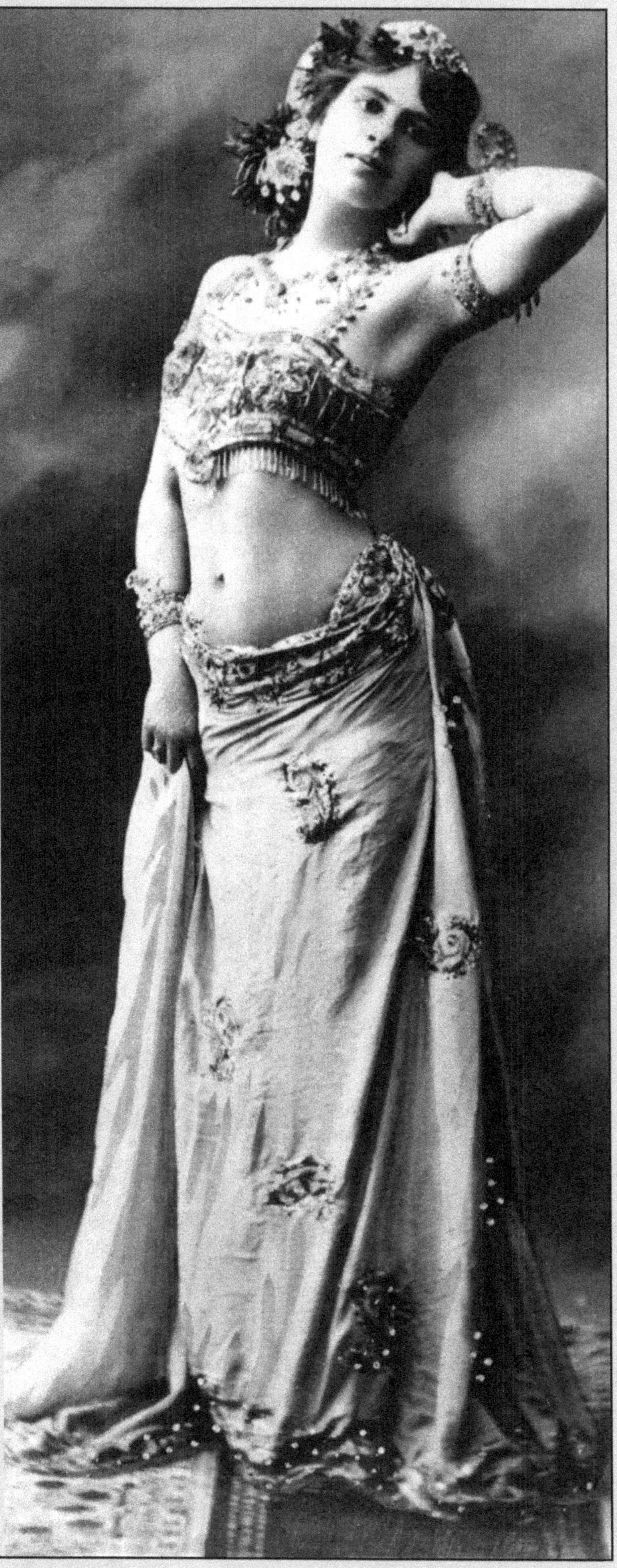

Saidi
Flavor of Egypt

by Jezibell Anat

Gothic, tribal, fusion and other alternative forms of belly dance have brought innovation and creativity into this ancient art form. Contemporary styles emphasize on technique, including intricate isolations and postures that expand the body's range of movement. They have also sparked the development of unique and sophisticated combinations. Dancers today present elaborate choreographies and spectacular costumes.

But sometimes this focus on proficiency comes at the expense of authenticity. I don't mean authenticity in terms of style but of content. Dance is more than just a showcase of athleticism and flexibility. Dancers express and interpret the music through their bodies.

This is where knowledge of traditional dance can deepen a dancer's range and repertoire, even if s/he is not planning to perform folkloric styles. These regional dances are grounding and centering, and they provide a genuine integration of body and spirit.

One great style to explore is Saidi traditionally, known as Raqs Saidi. (Raqs means dance in Arabic.) This dance originated in the Said, the rural area around Luxor and Aswan in Upper Egypt, which is actually the southern part of the country. (Remember, the Nile flows north, so Lower Egypt is the area below the Mediterranean Sea, and Upper Egypt borders on the Sudan.)

The Said region has a rich culture and history, as it is a site of ancient temples, tombs, and palaces. The men used walking sticks to develop a fighting art known as tahtib, which dates back to Pharaonic times; the tahtib was part of the training for Egyptian soldiers. We don't know exactly when or how the dance style known as Saidi developed, but it does incorporate movements of tahtib. When women dance Saidi, they are mimicking the men.

"I got bitten by the Saidi bug about 20 years ago, and I never looked back!!" Says Vanessa, a dancer, teacher and choreographer who has lived in Cairo since 2008. She performs at five-star hotels, teaches at the Nile Group Festival, and produces folkloric shows; she is probably the first and only American woman to start a production company in Egypt.

Vanessa elaborates on the modern development of the Saidi dance. "Mahmoud Reda, founder of the first Egyptian Folklore dance company, the Reda Troupe, travelled to the Said to take ideas and inspiration from the everyday culture. It is because of Mahmoud Reda's research that we have this specific style. Modern Saidi is a theatricalization of tahtib and general Egyptian folkloric steps."

The Saidi music has a distinctive drum beat (dum tek dum-dum tek) which is very strong and earthy. Traditional instruments include the rababa, nicknamed the Arabic fiddle, a stringed instrument that dates to the 8th century, and the mizmar, a reed instrument with a loud powerful sound similar to a bagpipe, which you can hear in both folkloric and tribal fusion music. Saidi sections often appear in Egyptian pop songs as well.

Vanessa adores the music. "The wailing of the mizmar, the almost melancholy tones of the rababa, the heavy drums and percussion....it gives me chills ... the heavy saiidi rhythm is EVERYTHING!!! It's like listening to rock and roll .... you hear it, and you can't help but follow the pulse. The music tells you what to do. Feet to the beat, baby!"

In Raqs Saidi, the body is erect, with a lot of upper torso movements including chest pops and shoulder shimmies. Footwork includes hops and prancing "horse steps" that mimic the gait of the dancing horses of the region. Interestingly, Saidi is not the only dance form that imitates the movements of a horse; classical ballet also has its own pas de cheval (horse step) that involves a pointed foot articulation.

The characteristic feeling of Saidi is grounded, proud, fun, and slightly aggressive. Movements such as the large hip circle and big shimmies are dynamic and very powerful, and this style can be particularly freeing for dancers who usually focus on small intricate motions.

The tahtib element comes in with the stick or hooked cane known as assaya, but the style is far different from the showy cane manipulations of Fred Astaire. Tahtib is a martial art, and stick fighting is basic to many cultures.

However, the assaya itself has an even deeper meaning. Gamila el-Masri, star of Manhattan's legendary Egyptian era of dance and former choreographer for the Egyptian American Folkloric Group, says "The assaya is literally the 'staff of life' in the pastoral environment, used for walking, plowing, herding animals and other daily tasks. It becomes an extension of the people themselves, used naturally and organically in the daily process of their lives." This organic feeling infuses the dance, making the assaya much more than a gimmicky prop.

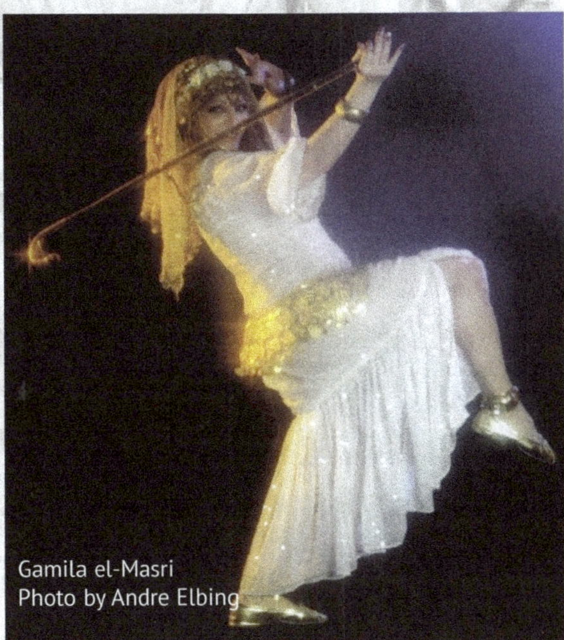
Gamila el-Masri
Photo by Andre Elbing

Some of the most fun steps are twirling the cane forward, backwards, and overhead, coordinating your body movement with the twirling cycle. Vanessa adds, "Swinging a stick around and whacking it on the floor is quite therapeutic!"

One very traditional move is the tawalla. This is an athletic step, which Gamila describes as "standing on one leg with the other lifted and bent right angle at the knee and propelling oneself forward keeping that position." The cane is held in the right hand, resting on the right shoulder.

Sometimes a dancer uses two canes. A duet or group number may include tossing and catching each other's sticks or a mock battle. Dancers often balance it on their heads. Of all the balancing props, I think the cane is the most difficult because it's so thin and light. It can be also balanced on the hand, hip or thigh.

I love the Saidi dance because it's lively, proud and sassy, and the costume is comfortable. The regional attire is the gallabeya, a loose fitting robe with wide sleeves. Professional dancers usually wear a tighter, glitzier version of this traditional dress adorned with beads and sequins and usually with a side slit in the skirt to allow freedom of movement. In folkloric dance styles, the belly is not bared.

For performances with her group, Gamila created a white dress with an elaborate gold coinbelt and scarf for her "ma'ulema" role in the assaya; on farms where a woman was in charge (perhaps widowed) the "boss lady" wears a white gallabeya.

In cabaret performances, a dancer may perform a Saidi segment in her belly dance costume. One fun contemporary adaptation by American dancers is wearing a witch costume and dancing Saidi style with a broom for a Halloween shows, or using a red and white striped cane for a Christmas dance.

If you've never seen Saidi, there are lots of examples on youtube, and also check out the men's tahtib. Gamila has an excellent article online at Gilded Serpent, which is a great resource for information on all aspects of belly dance http://www.gildedserpent. com/art43/gamilaniledance1.htm For more about Vanessa's dancing, visit http://www.vanessaraqs.com. She just released a great DVD on Saidi technique and combinations through World Dance New York, which produces quality instructional in many styles of dance at https://worlddancenewyork.com/products/ saidi-dance-technique-and-combinations-with- vanessa-of-cairo.■

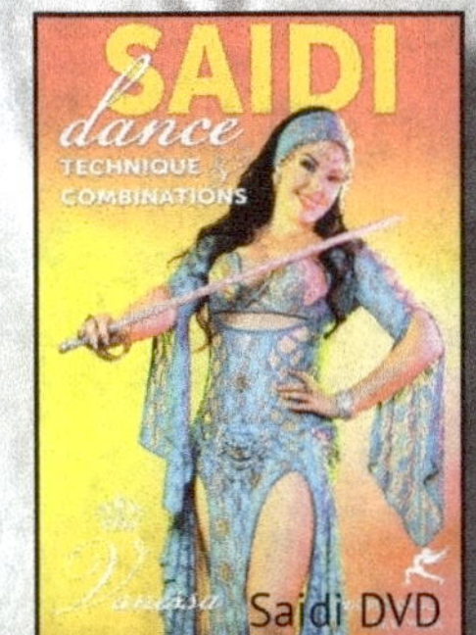

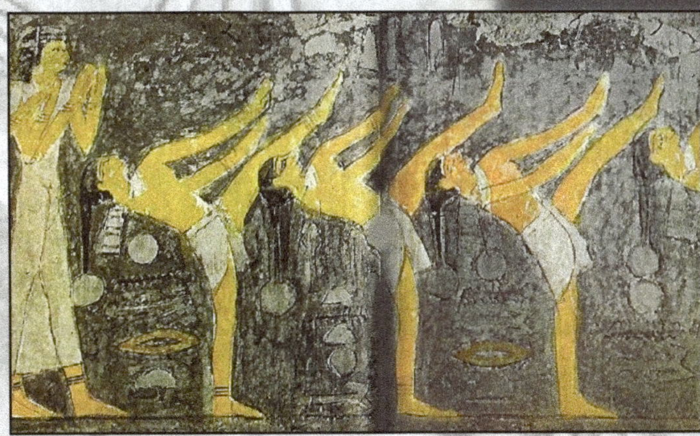

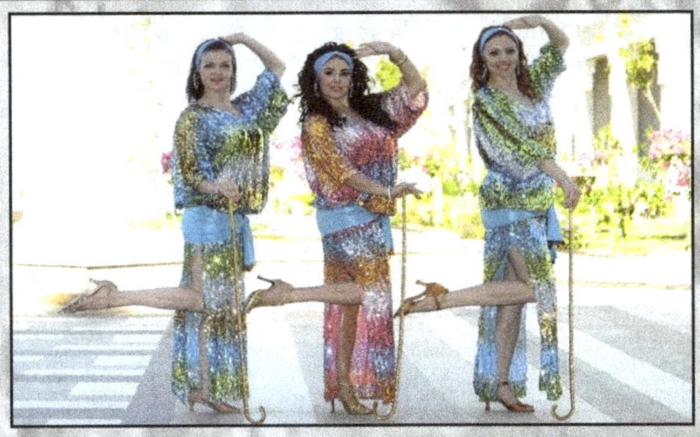

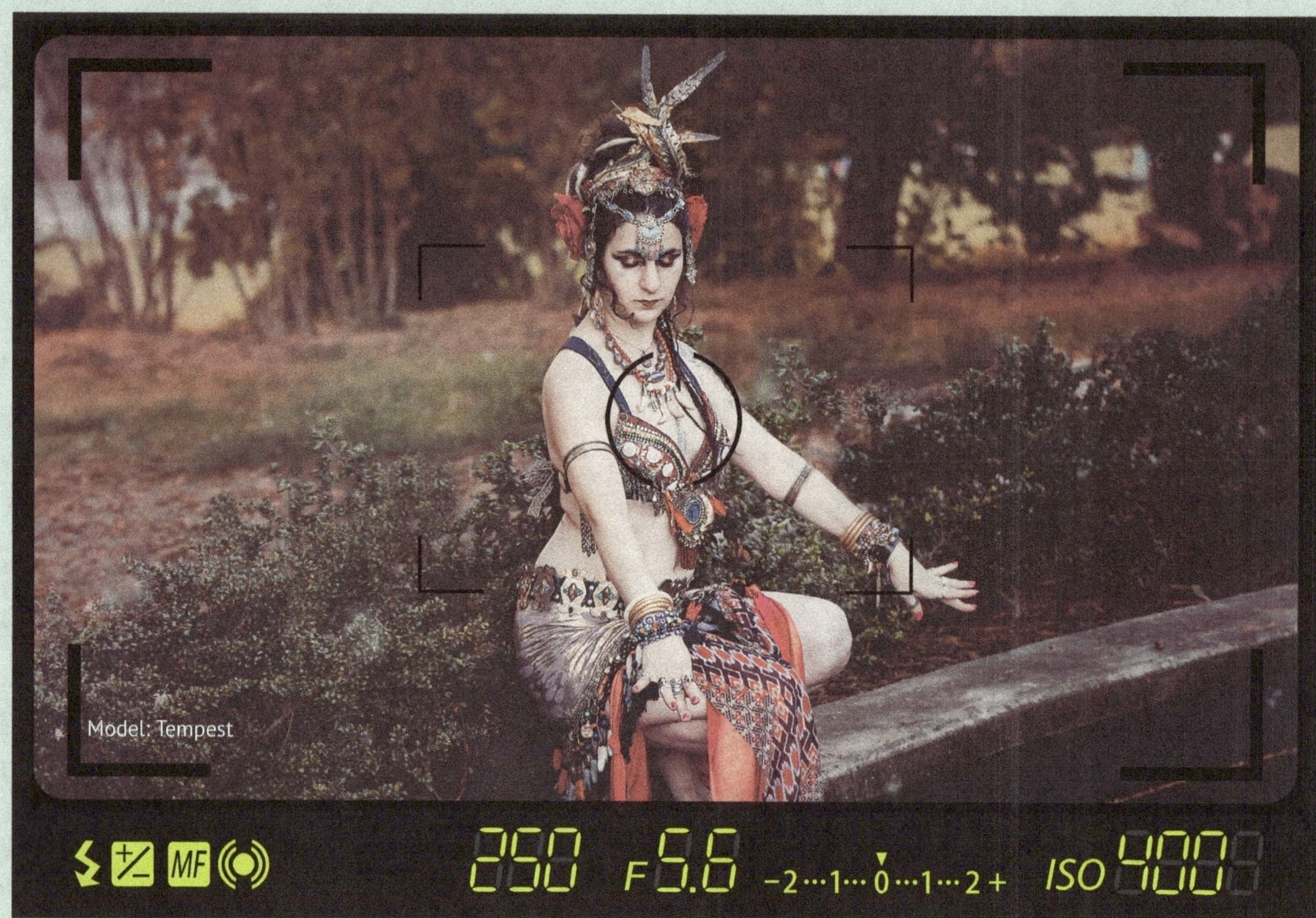

I Spy with The Dancer's Eye
Belly Dance Photography by Carrie Meyer

by Zahara's Tangled Web

As a professional belly dancer, I often work with photographers for promotional pictures. It can be difficult to capture just the right shot, due to the reflective surfaces on costumes and trying to incorporate movement into the photographs. I had my first sitting with Carrie Meyer in 2012, and it was a completely new experience for me in dance photography. Carrie is also a belly dancer, which is why her photo sessions are usually sold out during belly dance festivals around the country. Her honest suggestions before and during our photo shoot changed the way I see the art of dance photography.

Carrie began belly dancing in 2001. "At first, I sought it out as an alternate form of exercise to help me keep weight off, while not being tied to the gym. Little did I know at the time, this was just the beginning of a love affair with dance that has now spanned well over a decade." She's proficient in several belly dance styles, including Egyptian, American Tribal Style, and Fusion. Carrie has also been active in several St. Louis belly dance groups and currently performs in a duet called "Khepri". Her direct knowledge of the

costuming and movements for each style gives her an edge over other photographers, because she knows firsthand what clothing her dancer clients should wear to create the best possible pictures.

"When I started taking dance classes, I was almost immediately inspired to begin photographing dancers. I saw an opportunity to combine my love of belly dance with my love of photography. I realized that I could offer my dancer subjects a unique opportunity to work with an artist who truly understands the dance from the inside. I think being a dancer myself has given me a good perspective on how dancers see themselves, and also personal insight into how dancers want themselves to be portrayed." Performers want to be captured in the moment while still showcasing their best features and conveying a connection with the audience through the camera lens. Carrie coaches her subjects to make tiny physical adjustments while posing (or during dancing shots) to create her stunning belly dance portraits. Carrie's background in dance and theater influences much of her performance photography. "In addition to belly dance, I have photographed a wide variety of local, regional, national, and international burlesque dancers, pole dancers, fire performers, actors, and musicians."

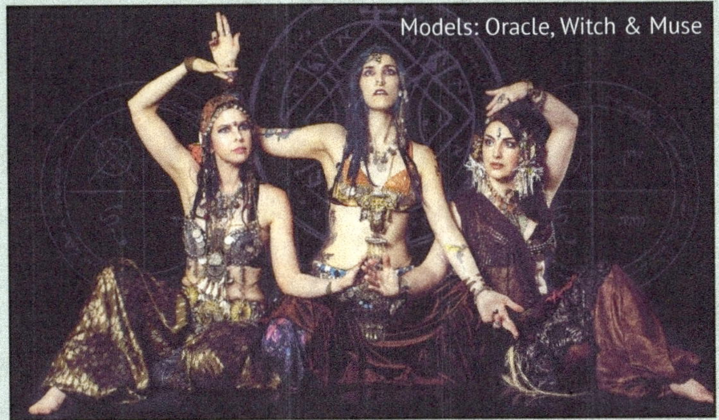
Models: Oracle, Witch & Muse

She began pursuing photography professionally in 2006, opening two studios in 2010. The Dancers Eye studio focuses on belly dance portraiture and live belly dance performance photography, while her Insomniac Studios caters to clients outside the belly dance industry. I asked Carrie if she has a preference between taking portraits or capturing performance shots, since she's so talented in each area. "I actually love both, but I really enjoy the portraiture. I make an effort to get to know my subjects whenever possible, in order to understand their strengths and what they seek in their photos. It is important to me that my clients feel at ease and free to be themselves. This is when some of the best photos are captured." I personally found it very comfortable working with Carrie because of her dance background, and I felt she understood the look I was trying to portray.

Carrie's photography has been featured on the covers and in the pages of many well-respected belly dance magazines, including Shimmy, Fuse, Jareeda, Zagareet, and Yalla. She's also displayed her photographs in local businesses and in juried art shows in St. Louis. Some of the juried art shows include those held at the Mad Art Gallery, Koken Art Factory, and Soulard Art Market. She was also a St. Louis RAW Artist in 2013.

Being a professional photographer isn't always as glamorous as it appears, and being self-employed can be especially grueling. Carrie works very long hours and rarely has time to herself, as she's constantly meeting tight deadlines. "The travel; the almost constant back and forth with clients and vendors; the planning and budgeting; and the long days, nights, and weekends of shooting are sometimes stressful." The bulk of editing, especially after large events, can be quite exhausting. "From the outside looking in, many people think my job is fun. And sometimes it is, because I do love the work. But it is also very hard work," she says.

Carrie does face certain obstacles as a traveling photographer. When it comes to live performances, one pet peeve stands out from the rest. "Bad or no lighting is absolutely number one on my hit list. If you don't have the proper lighting, it is almost impossible to make great photos – even with the fastest lenses." Tight performance spaces are also a concern, especially when trying to put up additional lighting or taking photographs without blocking the audience's view. "And events with too many photographers falling over each other often creates bad results for both the photographers and the performers."

Carrie is full of ideas and helpful suggestions for the performers who employ her. Here are her top three tips for belly dancers when booking a professional photography shoot.

1. "Plan ahead and talk to the photographer. I love it when people contact me before their session and say 'Hey, I want to do this!' You should feel like you and your photographer are a TEAM in crafting the concept for your shoot. Your dream photos will be more likely to come to life if you work with your photographer to conceptualize the themes and ideas you want to realize. If you don't know, or don't have ideas, or need help – say so! Brainstorming and conversation helps. If you clearly communicate what you are wanting, you are setting me (and inherently, US) up for success."

2. "Makeup tips... more is more! Just as if you were performing on stage, we need more makeup. We are going to want that same look for our photo shoot. Not unlike bright stage lights, a flash will wash out colors. So don't be scared off by that dramatic over-finished look – it won't photograph that way."

3. "Arrive on time. By arriving late, you've lost that time in front of the camera. Less time in front of the camera means less variety, and less options. Be respectful of the photographer's time and your time. Be on time or be early."

As an active member of her local belly dance community, Carrie is keenly aware of the reluctance some dancers have to being photographed. "Unfortunately, women usually aren't afraid to offer criticism about themselves. In fact, we're downright professionals at criticizing ourselves!" Typically, if a woman doesn't like having her photo taken, she usually tells Carrie when making the appointment. "At that point, I congratulate her on coming to the point of booking the session in the first place. That's a big step, and I appreciate her trust in ME! Upon the first conversation, I assure clients that having photographs taken by a professional is different, and if they have never done it before, they will love it in the end, and we will have fun." As always, she listens to their concerns and works with them to create the photographs they want. "And hey, we get on stage just like we are, so why not have professional photos of ourselves in our belly dance gear? We work long and hard for our art form and should be proud of it (and ourselves)!"

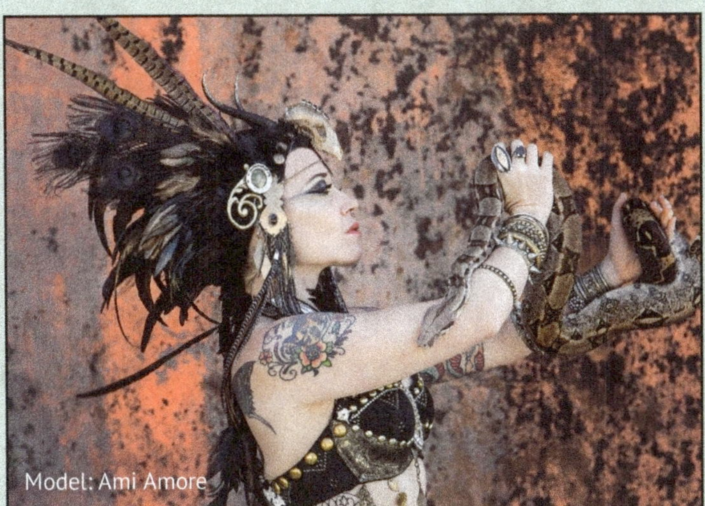
Model: Ami Amore

Carrie's website has a list of her photography workshops and photo sessions for belly dancers who are interested in booking her.
The Dancers Eye – Fine Art Belly Dance Photography – www.thedancerseye.com
Insomniac Studios – www.insomniacstudios.net
Facebook: Insomniac Studios - https://www.facebook.com/InsomniacStudiosLLC
The Dancers Eye - https://www.facebook.com/The-Dancers-Eye-Fine-Art-Bellydance-Photography-182196285164718/?fref=ts
Instagram: carriepph ∎

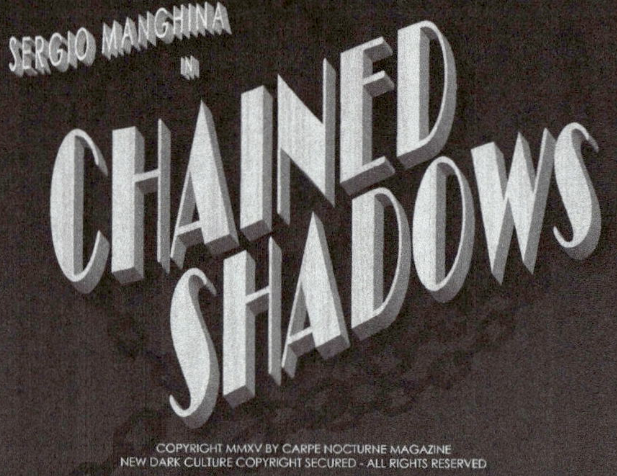

COPYRIGHT MMXV BY CARPE NOCTURNE MAGAZINE
NEW DARK CULTURE COPYRIGHT SECURED - ALL RIGHTS RESERVED

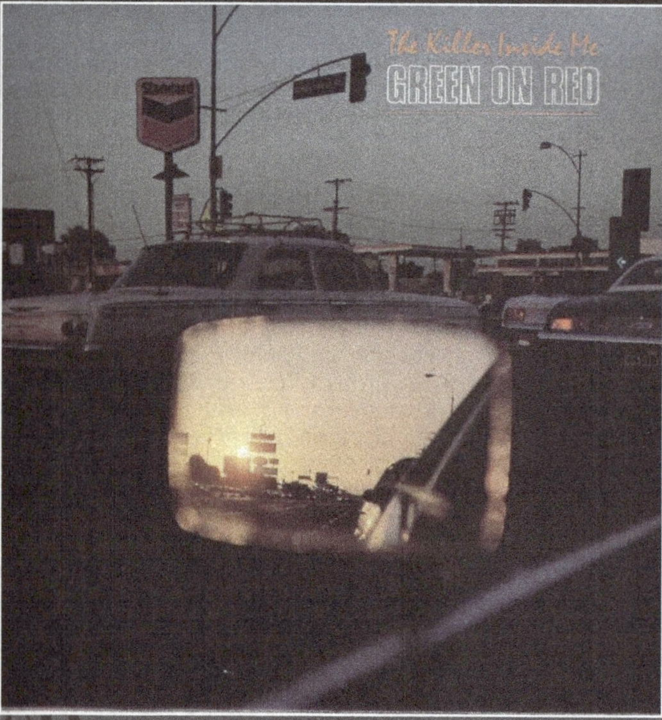

GREEN ON RED
THE KILLER INSIDE ME
Label: Mercury 1987

Paraphrasing an interview by John Doe (X frontman) to The Los Angeles Times in 2013, we could say that Jim Thompson is the bard of "the sordid stuff that could go on after the sun goes down, and before it comes up." His pages are sharp, even unpleasant, above all drawing the unflattering portrait of the deputy sheriff Lou Ford, the sociopath protagonist of "The Killer Inside Me."

An unbreakable thread connects this book to an album of the same title released in 1987 by Green On Red. Dan Stuart sews the pieces of an always more tottering group after certain remarkable episodes of psychedelic-garage splendor called "Gravity Talks" and "Gas Food Lodging." He admires Jim Thompson in the same way in which John Doe estimates Raymond Chandler and James M.Cain. There are electric ballads, heavily influenced by Neil Young, pretty bad, rough, and acuminated. Something smells of country-rock.

Everything is on the reverse side in this album, included an American Dream as a gift never received in time for the birthday. But reality is broken, a desperate trip in the company of disreputable people, directed to nowhere, beholding distant lights and shabby motels. Stuart has always been self-destructive and a regular visitor to the dark side of the street. A worthy friend of Jim Thompson, in short.

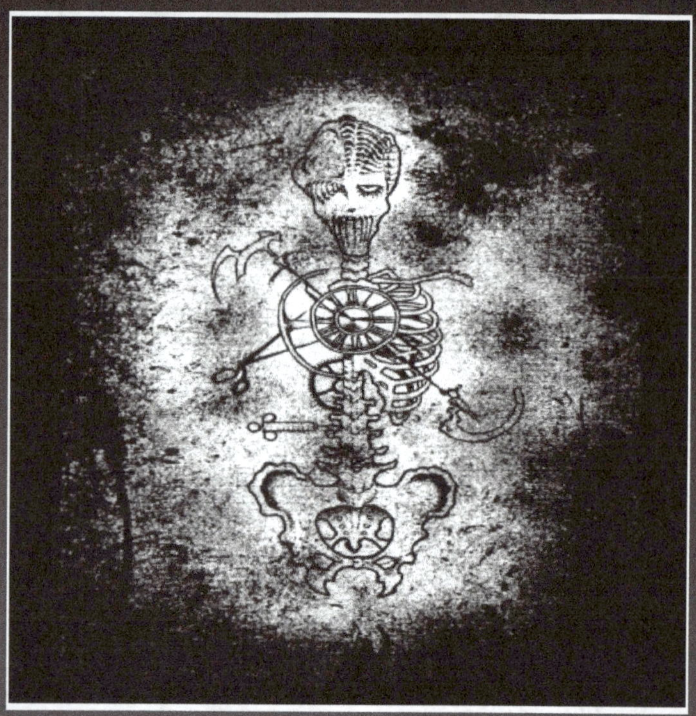

RODENTIA
THE BEST OF DARK ROOTS MUSIC VOL.1
Label: Devil's Ruin Records 2008

A poisonous flower with a thousand petals. This series of four impressive anthologies came out between 2008 and 2010 as a fairly complete document of the so called Gothic Country in many of its facets. Rodentia - the first act - is surely the more organic and accomplished of the lot. It is divided in two discs and ten chapters titled - to name a few - "Cloak of Darkness," "Descend Into Town," and "Diablerie." Here, there are 34 tracks and overall well selected, starting with the band Strawfoot from Missouri (with a superb ballad) followed by Dad Horse Experience, Uncle Sinner, Pinebox Serenade, Ghostwitch, Slackeye Slim, Lonesome Wyatt, Sons of Perdition, Those Poor Bastards...Folk and neo-folk, gospel, bluegrass, murder ballads, spaghetti western, and dark-cabaret. The compilation is roots music coated with a "dust and death" look. The songs have traditional accents of guitars, fiddles, harmonicas, banjos and so on, sometimes crossed by an aversive punk cloud or even a reckless experimental-noise digression. The following compilations - Rodentagogue, Rodenticide, Rodentum - add further artists and bands building a monumental collection that includes Muzza Monroe, Joe Munly, Liquorbox, Murder By Death, Strawman, JB Nelson and many others. Unfortunately, Devil's Ruin Records from Leo, Indiana, no longer exists, but its rich catalogue remains a precious mine for passionates and collectors of the Dark Roots. ■

DEARLY DEPARTED

By Cosmic

The expression that 2016 took a lot of people from us became a cliché before the year's end, but each tragic loss was no less painful. This quarterly column couldn't have possibly kept up with its own Dearly Departed, and yet all the same we at Carpe Nocturne Magazine would be remiss not to devote some space to the many souls which have brought us inspiration over the years. Most recently, Carrie Fisher, of Star Wars fame, and her mother Debbie Reynolds, who passed not twenty-four hours apart from one another. Both mother and daughter were talented actresses and cultural icons; Fisher most famous for her role as Princess Leia in the Star Wars franchise, and Reynolds for her role in *Singin' in the Rain*.

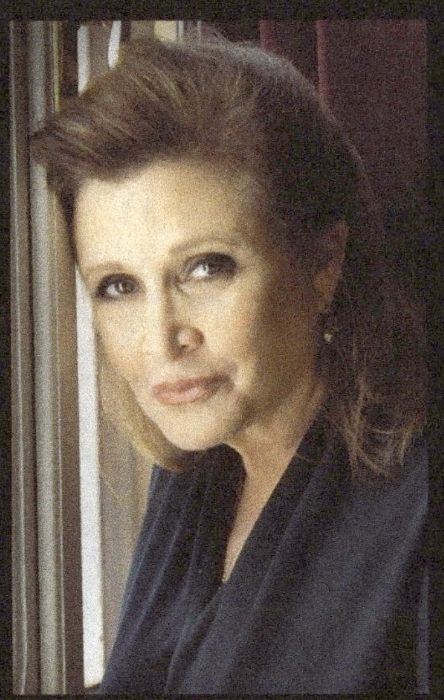

Carrie Fisher was rushed to the hospital after a severe heart attack on December 23, 2016 while on a flight to Los Angeles during the book tour for her latest memoir The Princess Diarist. Fisher was not only a role model and icon to generations of Star Wars fans, she was also a highly sought after script doctor, going uncredited for her work on films such as *Lethal Weapon 3* and *The Wedding Singer*. Carrie Fisher never shied away from speaking on her personal adversities regarding bipolar disorder and drug use. Along with her outspoken activism on addiction and mental illness came a resounding wit and sense of humor that continues to inspire. In her 2008 book *Wishful Drinking*, Fisher declared what she would have liked to have seen written in her obituary: "I want it reported that I drowned in moonlight, strangled by my own bra." At her burial the following January, her brother was photographed carrying an urn shaped like a giant Prozac pill, apparently another wish of Carrie's before she departed. She was buried side by side with her mother as thousands of online players of *Star Wars: The Old Republic* paid tribute to her on a virtual version of Princess Leia's homeworld of Alderaan.

Leia Organa was brought to life by this amazing and talented artist, and it was due to Carrie Fisher's efforts that millions of little girls all over the world and across generations were able to see themselves as more than the passive and submissive damsels of Disney tradition. Leia was a reflection of Carrie in many ways, and it showed in the character's bravery and willingness to face adversity head-on and unapologetically. We at Carpe Nocturne sense that the Force will be with her and her talented mother, always.

by Chirality

Leonard Cohen was a Canadian singer, songwriter, poet and novelist. His career spans generations and his focus was politics, sexuality, religion, isolation and relationships. Born in 1934, Cohen was from Quebec.

Cohen's recording career began in the 60's and 70's. He was not happy with his finances as a writer, so he turned to music. It was during this time he moved to the US. Cohen became a staple in the Andy Warhol crowd. He also became a huge success with fellow singer Judy Collins, who wanted to work with him. She introduced him to television where he did duets. It was then that his album Songs of Leonard Cohen was released and became a hit. In 1970, Cohen toured Europe and made a name for himself.

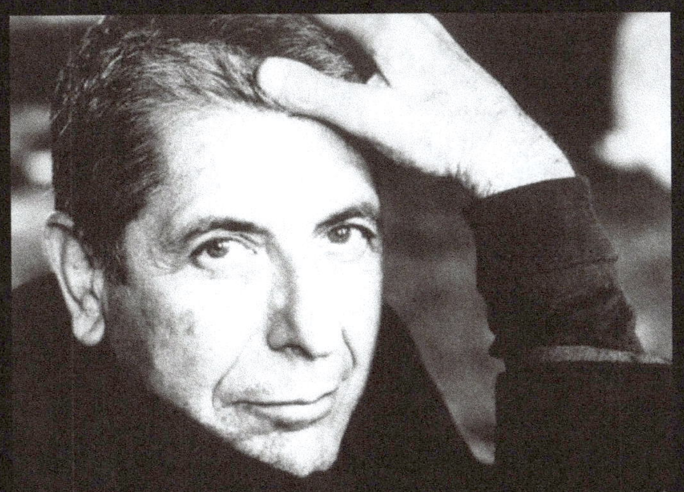

He continued to make a name for himself in the 60's and 70's from albums and touring. Then, in the 80's, he expanded even further with the release of his song Hallelujah. This song was covered by countless artists from numerous countries.

In the 2000's Cohen faced some legal troubles with people selling the rights to his music. Cohen won in the suit and was rewarded nearly 9 mil. In 2006 The Book of Longing was released. It topped best seller lists in Canada. That same year, music was composed for the book, a double CD was released including spoken word poetry with music.

Cohen continued to tour throughout 2010 and 2012. He also released an album in 2012, Old Ideas. This was followed by a world tour in 2012 and 2013.

Cohen passed away November 7th 2016 after a long battle with cancer. He was 82. There is no doubt his impact on the world. His words were true art in poetry and music. He leaves behind two children and two grandchildren. ■

CARPE NOCTURNE
SOUNDS OF THE LIVING DEAD
ALBUM REVIEWS

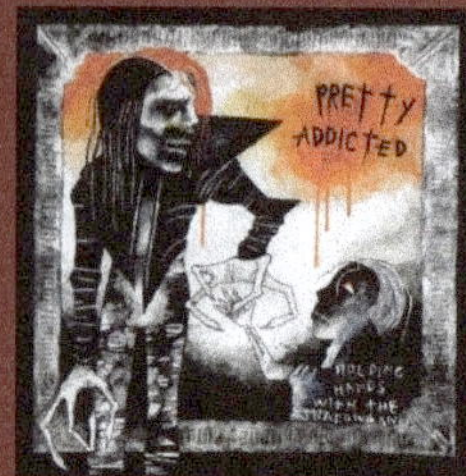

Artist: Pretty Addicted
Album: Holding Hands with the Shadow Man
By Asylum Attendant

Any band that refers to itself as "GDM" or "gothic dance music", features a genderfluid lead singer that resembles a terrifying Mickey Mouse and names their fanbase Crackheads automatically piques my interest. Even still, I did not expect to love Pretty Addicted and their new album Holding Hands with the Shadow Man as much as I do. The album is extremely thought provoking, yet alternative club ready for a night of fucked up merriment. These songs leave an imprint on your mind that you cannot erase and you find yourself bouncing around to some disturbing shit. This is the good kind of scary, folks.

The lead single and album opener "Choose Your Poison" addresses the devastating effects of alcoholism on those that encounter the disease in a loved one. This song is an ultimatum to the alcoholic, with harsh words at the beginning and one final plea to get sober in the middle, necessary (yet futile) and much gentler than the rest of the track. "Piggy" is an inappropriate nursery rhyme about elitists full of greed. The oinking in the instrumental is a cute touch. Maniacal laughter and broken music boxes comprise "Tic Tac Toe", a creepy freak anthem that Marilyn Manson would be proud of.

Singer Vicious Precious revels in calling inauthentic people out on the brutal "Suckerpunch". They are not afraid to display the honesty most of us keep hidden. "Monster (Inside the House)" is a solemn trance track full of self-hatred and vulnerability. This song is unsettling because Vicious is bearing their soul amongst melancholy synths. Their usual venomous vocals are much smoother and melodic here.

Holding Hands with the Shadow Man is like a gothic rave with substance. Pretty Addicted has quickly turned me into a fan with their thrashing beats and unusual lyrics. Just do not listen to this album at 3am like I did unless you look forward to nightmares.

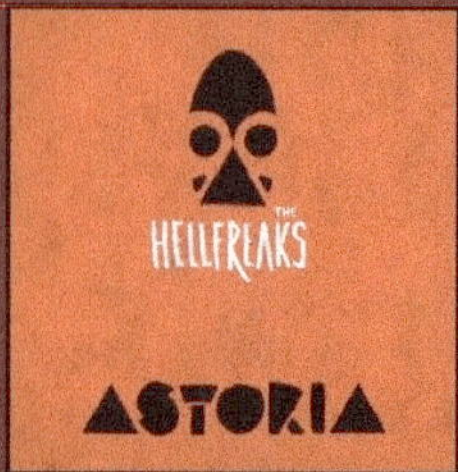

Artist: The Hellfreaks
Album: Astoria
By Samm Sanity

The Hellfreaks; a Hungarian, formally a psychobilly, horrorpop band, has shed their billy roots in their newest album, "Astoria". The album is the first since the band's re-group, and it released in June of 2016.

"Astoria" has a new punk rock sound and it is kick-ass. The album is full of the typical punk beats and sounds, combined with the unique sound and voice of The Hellfreaks. Shakey Sue's vocals are aggressive and totally at home in the punk genre. The boys' riffs

and beats are phenomenal, especially in "Sid and Clyde" and "Little Crime".

Although the band have traded their upright double bass for an electric guitar, there are still subtle hints of their billy past in some of their songs. Such as underlying sounds in "Why Do You Talk" are reminiscent of their past work. While not explicitly psychobilly, the band's billy beginning comes softly through whether intentionally or not. Old fans are sure to love it, as well as gaining new ones. I personally enjoy the new sound; "Back To My Planet" is my favorite from the album. Overall, the album is well put together, full of punk rock kick, and sure to please old and new fans alike.

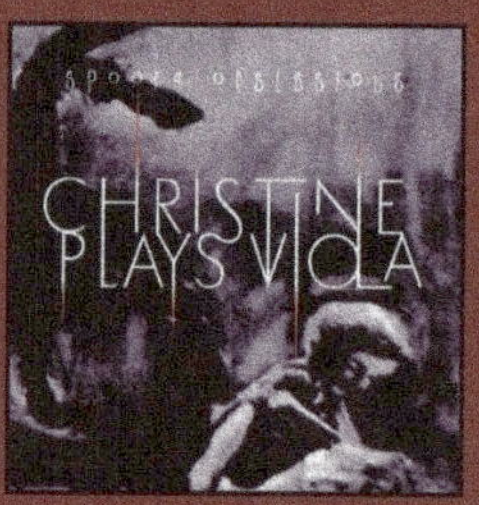

Artist: Christine Plays Viola
Album: Spooky Obsessions
By Sergio Manghina

The great merit of Christine Plays Viola, maybe their best quality, is that they have been able to create something personal, by combining the various souls of post-punk into only one sound. Their own sound. With deep roots firmly planted in 1980s British dark-wave, the band touches chords of the more classic goth-rock and sometimes shows interesting cold-wave influences. In addition they add a peculiar flavour of Italian wave. Christine Plays Viola are not afraid to confront a difficult issue as the so called "near-death experience". Obviously, it is not a comfortable topic, due to its unpleasant implications, but however represents an original central idea inside this concept album.

"Ossessione" opens with an eerie - almost martial – beat that introduces a series of songs that, one by one, go to fill their own blank space in the mosaic. So "Midnight Trauma" has a relentless pace, percussive and mysterious, followed by the solemnity of "Behind A Wicked Mind". "Nefarius" and "Poles Apart" offer two captivating melodies joined with a dream-synth-pop mood. "Murderous Dementia" is one of the highlights of this work, hung to circles of guitar, tense, restless, arcane.

When arrives the moment of "Unneeded Burial" the atmosphere slips into a charming psalm vaguely in death-rock style. Impressive! Bass and drums increase their beats on "N.D.E. (Life Beyond Life)" drowned into liquid synths, merging together melody, rhythm and mystery.

"Slow Sinking In Gloom" is a formidable example of dance-oriented/dark-wave. An absolutely catchy melodic line, even crossed by echoes of the Canterbury sound. At the end, "The Last Sacrifice" is more slow but not less restless and then reappears some death-rock connection, above all in the guitar.

"Spooky Obsessions" has a special listening pleasure, that remembers the solidity of certain discs of the past, those that you listened from the first to the last note, without even a weak moment or a merely filler episode. ■

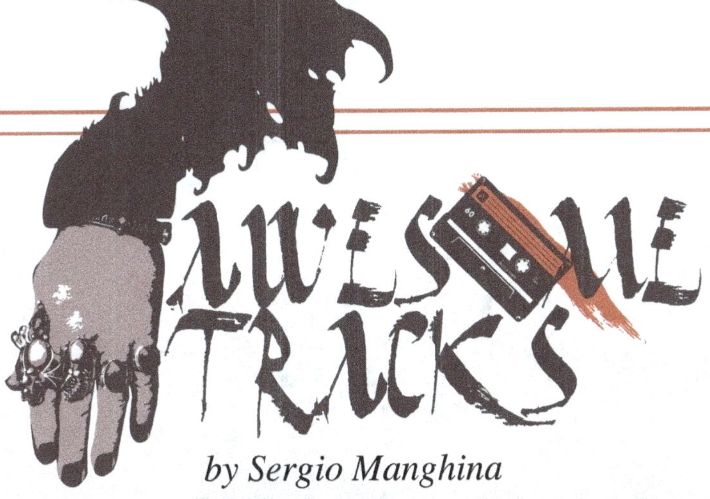

AWESOME TRACKS

by Sergio Manghina

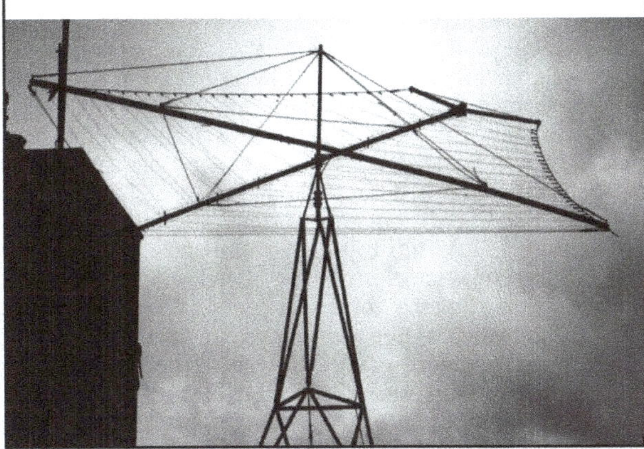

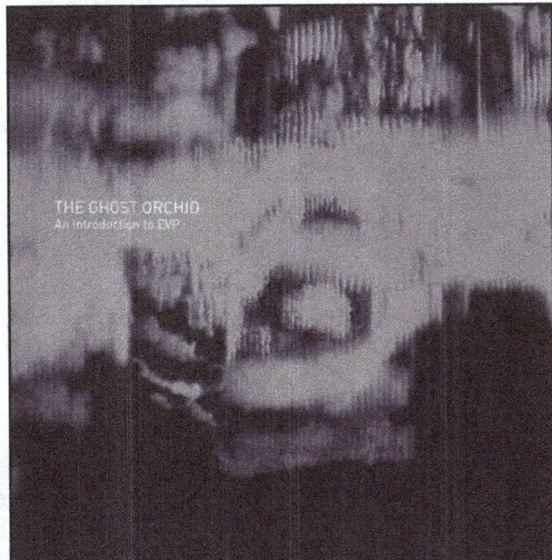

THE GHOST ORCHID: AN INTRODUCTION TO EVP
Label: Ash International 2009
Parapsychic Acoustic Research Cooperative

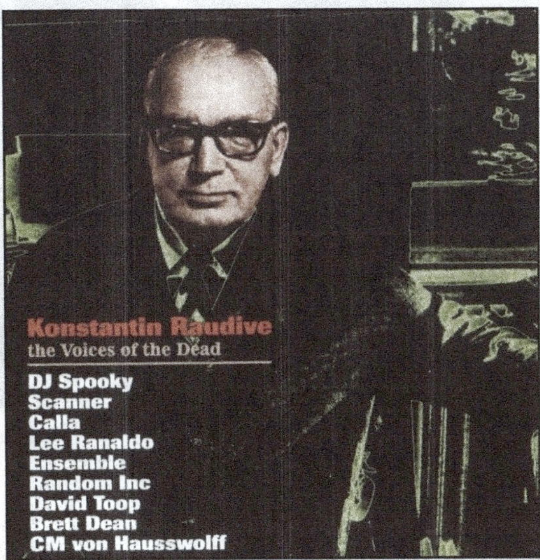

KONSTANTIN RAUDIVE/THE VOICE OF THE DEAD
Label: Sub Rosa 2002

THE CONET PROJECT/RECORDINGS OF SHORTWAVE NUMBERS STATIONS
Label: Irdial 1997
5 CD Box 2013

This is maybe not suitable for people particularly impressionable, but it is very intriguing to everyone else. This is a series of 79 tracks for about 64 minutes of mysterious voices materialized - with no apparent explanation - on the tape recorder. EVP (Electronic Voice Phenomena) are a "real" thing, but still relatively little studied and often denigrated by the usual professional skeptics. Friedrich Jorgenson, Konstantin Raudive and Raymond Cass were the pioneers of this kind of studies. In the fifties, Jorgenson, attributed those phantasmic voices to entities from the afterworld.

The other two explorers of the unknown - Raudive and Cass - also provided further explanations and possible answers. In effect, the new physics supposes the existence of parallel dimensions and some parapsychological scholars hypothesize about beings who sometimes cross the veil between us and them. Another theory explains those voices as triggered by our own subconscious.
"The Ghost Orchid" includes material coming from the Raymond Cass archives and is divided in to various parts, including "Polyglot Voices," "Public Service Broadcasting," "Interruptions." "Singing Voices," "Instant Response Voices" and "Alien Voices." In addition, it gathers some things by Konstantin Raudive, articles and other interesting stuff.

"The Voice of the Dead," by the Belgian label Sub Rosa, is instead dedicated to Konstantin Raudive and contains several remixes of his strange material, realized by artists such as DJ Spooky, Scanner, David Toop, Lee Ranaldo, etc. It could be a good idea to combine "The Ghost Orchid" with "The Voices of the Dead" and "The Conet Project." This last one, captures the essence of another curious phenomenon called "the numbers stations." It is interceptable (with a certain patience) during some sleepless nights on whatever well-built short wave receiver. There are signals from the Twilight Zone out there, so stay tuned... ∎

Anyone who follows America's Got Talent has probably seen her name in lights. Grace VanderWaal won the 2016 AGT at the tender age of 12 and the world is in love with her. Grace captured the hearts and minds of millions with her sweet personality, amazing vocal talent, beautiful lyrics and stunning vocal power. For those of you who have not seen this amazing young lady let me give you a little introduction. Grace, as I have said before, is a 12 year old girl from Suffern, New York. She had been longing to audition for American Idol but to audition she would have to be 16. When she found out that 2016 was going to be the last year of American Idol she decided to go and audition for America's Got Talent. A year before her audition she had picked up a ukulele for the first time and taught herself to play. So she wrote her own song, "I Don't Know My Name", and went to audition. From the very beginning she took the audience's breath away. If you watch the YouTube video of her audition you can see the reactions of individual audience members saying "wow" and standing dumbfounded in the wake of Grace's talent.

Grace's voice is not really something one can compare to anyone else. She has been compared to many different famous singers but her voice really is her very own. At her tender age she has a folksy gravel that can take years of training in Bette Davis or Mae West impersonations. The really amazing thing is that everything she sings comes out so naturally to her and she seems to have fun with it all. Through AGT she wrote her own songs; "I Don't Know My Name", "Beautiful Thing", "Light the Sky" and my absolute favorite "Clay". This unto itself is a feat but the fact that she makes it fun to listen to and that she is so very uplifting in her lyrics make her a bright star in an otherwise very cynical world.

When Grace stepped onto the stage for her first performance you could tell she was nervous. Her ability to break through her nerves and talk to Howie Mandell (who admittedly seemed smitten by her from the beginning), Simon Cowell (who could make the Grim Reaper nervous), Heidi Klum (Project Runway Host) and Mel B (of Spice Girls fame). Her responses were never trite or out of line for a 12 year old but they revealed a young lady who definitely felt she had something to offer the show. "I Don't Know My Name" introduced viewers to

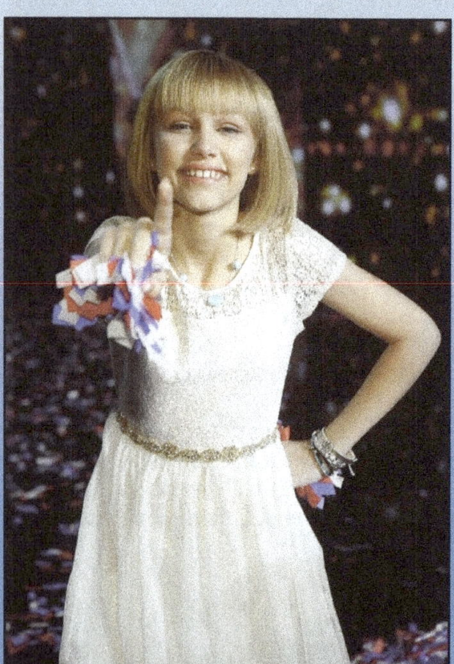
© NBCUniversal

Grace's singing voice, which though not completely does sound a little different from her 12 year old speaking voice. Especially when she drove the final chorus in a powerful drive and completed the song on a strong note. The lyrics were perfect, too. She sings about a young girl who is trying to find herself in a big world that seems to compare her to everyone else and demand to know why she is how she is, but by the end she knows who she is and it is exactly who she needs to be.

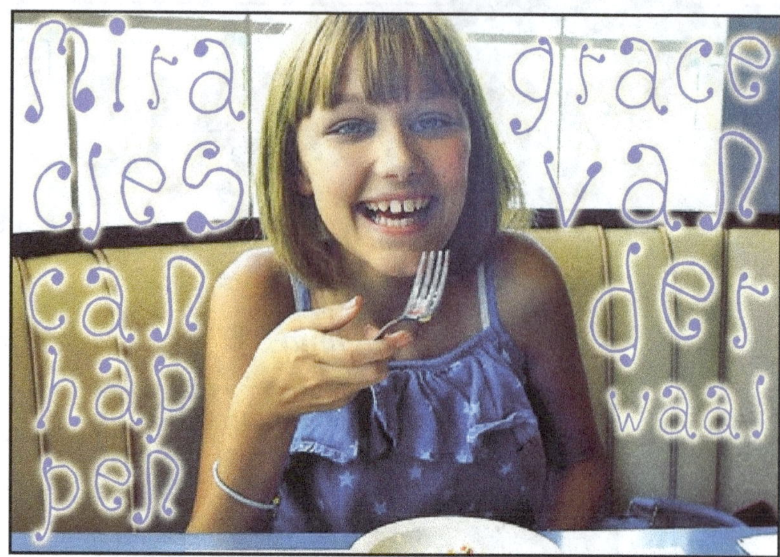

by Kathleen Sharkey

"Beautiful Thing" was a song Grace wrote about her sister who is also her best friend. These touching lyrics about how someone who knows you so well can complete who you are and make everything better really hit me hard because my sister and I have had such a relationship so I can understand where she is coming from. Again Grace's beautiful smoky voice presents the song in a loving and tender dedication, the personal meaning behind it lending love to her vocals. "Light the Sky" was another song that she leant an obvious personal touch to. About how it really doesn't matter what others think about your light because they can just close their eyes if they don't like it. With so many trolls losing their trash on the internet upon this talented young lady this response was very Grace, "I don't care what you think, I am going to let my light shine and you can look elsewhere." The fact that the song draws the listener in as a coconspirator and elevates us to another light in the same sky as Grace. So instead of directly attacking the negative she draws us into her positivity and elevates herself above them all.

"Clay" was Grace's final song. For anyone who has ever been the outsider this song hits home. Grace's voice got even more potent finding a power-chord growl to drive the beat and the heart to the world. It spoke about the idea that we can't change who we are because we are not made of clay and there is no reason we should have to live in a world of horrible words and nasty people. We just have to be the people we are and not allow the negativity to destroy us. I found it to be the most influential of all of her AGT songs.

On September 14 of 2016 Grace won America's Got Talent, $1 Million and her own show at the Las Vegas Planet Hollywood at Caesars. Her shows are to be October 27-30. She is working on an album and as of this writing has decided to give some of her winnings to charity and do the 12 year old thing and use the rest to build an ultimate tree house for her and her sister. This is an amazing young lady and if you haven't gotten a chance to hear her sing definitely check her AGT performances out on YouTube or go to her own YouTube channel (ohneverminditsjustme). She is spectacular and destined for amazing things. But Grace do us one thing, don't grow up too fast, OK? ■

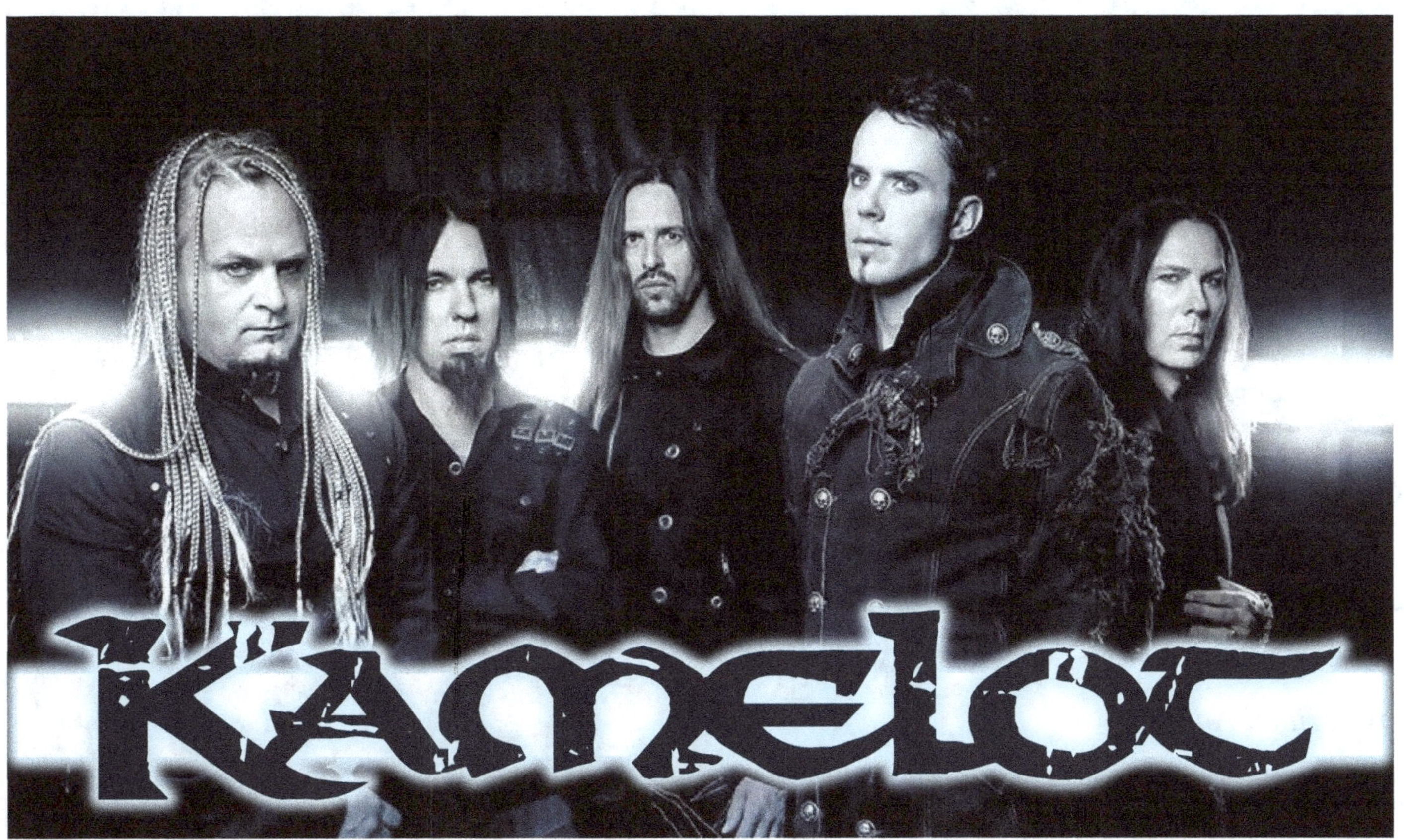

by Chirality

Kamelot is an American Power Metal band from Tampa, FL. The band was founded by Thomas Youngblood and Richard Warner in 1991. Kamelot has released 11 studio albums including two reissues. They formed unofficially under Camelot around 1988 and then soon became the Kamelot we know today.

Three years after forming they were signed to Noise Records and released their album Eternity in 1995. Dominion was then released in 1997. Siege Perilous was then released in 1998. This year also led to a change in vocalists from Warner to Roy Khan and drummer Casey Grillo. The band started a tour that year under the new lineup. They mostly played shows across Europe and then returned to work on the next album, The Fourth Legacy.

The Mid 2000's showed a lot of change for the band and they did a massive tour covering most of Europe. It was here that their live album Expedition was made. Karma, the bands 5th album, was released soon after. Epica was then released in 2003 and followed another tour across Europe and Japan. The Black Halo followed in 2005. 2005 also saw the band's first music video "The Haunting (Somewhere in Time)" and "March of the Mephisto" from The Black Halo album.

In late 2006 the band went to Germany to record Ghost Opera. Ghost Opera summoned a massive world tour covering all of Europe and the U.S. In 2008-2009 they played numerous festivals such as Wacken and Tuska Open Air Festival. In 2010 Khan fell seriously ill. He was soon replaced by Tommy Karevik. Silverthorn was released in 2012 and was the first album with Karevik. This also summoned another tour across the U.S. and Europe and the album made the Billboard charts at 79. In 2015 they were at it again with Haven. This album debuted at 75 on the Billboard charts and received critical acclaim. It was also confirmed that in 2017 they will be attending the Metal Cruise called 70000 Tons of Metal.

Kamelot can sort of fit into the likes of Within Temptation, Nightwish and so many others but they have been able to branch off and become their own and with the release of Haven show they have indeed grown into their own after so many years. Taken with bits of darkness, goth, fantasy and old lore seems to be the make up for this band. I urge everyone to check them out on Facebook or their website.

http://www.kamelot.com ■

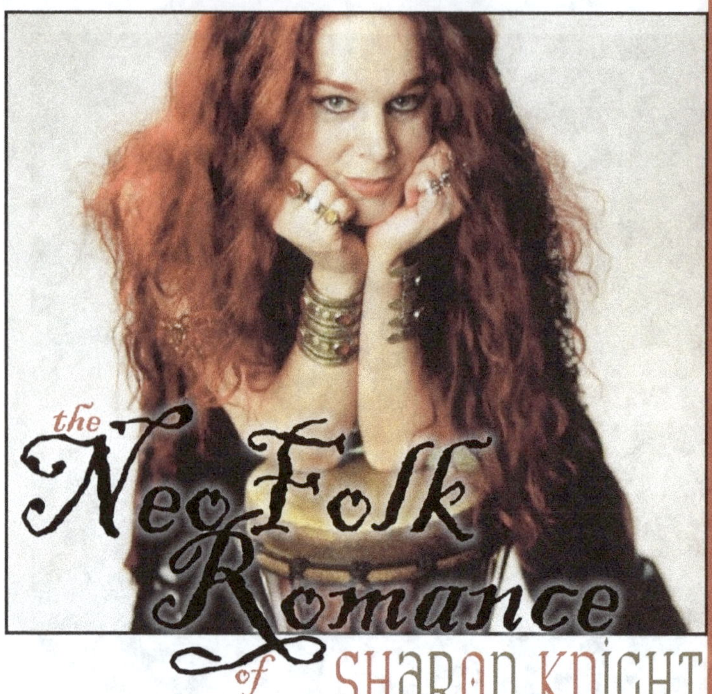

by Jezibell Anat

San Francisco native Sharon Knight is a singer, songwriter and multi-instrumentalist who is often compared to Stevie Nicks and Loreena McKennitt. She and her partner Winter perform at festivals, masquerades, conventions, cafes, shops, and house concerts. They have performed main stages at Faerieworlds in Oregon Sherwood Faire Celtic Music Festival in Texas, and the New York Faerie Festival as well as at many Celtic/mythic/fantasy festivals across North America. They describe their music as Neofolk Romantique, which came out of a fusion of their musical backgrounds.

It was love at first sight, when Sharon and Winter met at a Pagan festival called Ancient Ways in Northern California. However, it took them three years to get together because they were both with other people.

Sharon elaborates, "We were intrigued indeed that the other was both musician and magician. We finally acknowledged the obvious one night at a mutual friend's dinner, when, thanks be to alcohol, I opened up my mouth to say that I had always wanted to be with him. I remember my brain thinking "woah, look what my mouth just did!" And I am glad it did, for he was planning to move away with his girlfriend within the month. We both broke up with our respective partners the next day and never looked back. The music part kicked in a short while later."

Sharon had begun her career playing Celtic folk music. When she started to write her own songs, she wanted to explore more mythic themes than were in traditional music. Winter, a native of Kassel, Germany was a rock and blues musician who brought a grittier, more energetic edge. As they began their collaboration, they were increasingly told "That's not Celtic!"

Since they did not want to be constrained by that genre, they created a new title for their style, Neofolk Romantique, so that no one else could define them. Now they describe their music as Celtic-inspired songs for poets, adventurers, and lovers of mystery.

They still include traditional songs in their repertoire, but feel that claiming their own genre has helped them make room for the full scope of their artistic vision. Their music sounds more like "Folktales that ran away with the Faeries at the turn of the century and took cover in an old trunk bound for the circus, which was then commandeered by pirates."

They spent 2016 promoting their recent release Portals, envisioned as an otherworldly traveling carnival, where each performer wields a magic capable of opening windows to the realms of myth and dream. Portals features guest performances and showcases Winter's bluesy guitar chops.

This album is filled with rich, sensual songs, including "Scent of Your Skin" about love, longing, and the evocative power of fragrance. This Middle Eastern piece features the oud and is great for belly dancing. "Slippers of Rose" is a lovely heartfelt waltz about Sharon and her father where she sings, "I was your princess in shimmering silk and you were my Gentleman King."

Sharon admits that her songwriting process is completely random. "Sometimes a lyrical snippet will come, other times a melody. And sometimes it is just an Idea that must be wrangled into song form. It isn't always about inspiration, sometimes it is just writing something, anything, for the sake of writing, and being okay with the ones that aren't good."

My favorite song on Portals is "Melusina" because it's based on one of my favorite tales, the medieval French legend of a siren who is half-woman, half-serpent. "Melusina" is a folk/Pagan/rock song about living between two worlds and includes the lines "Through beauty and through sorrow/We crack the masks of certainty. " I identify with this all too well. (Interestingly Melusina is also the image on the Starbucks cup.)

"Porcelain Princess" tells the story of a marionette who is in love with her puppet master and knows she would come to life if he returned her affection. Sharon says, "This particular song came together pretty quickly. It is about feeling invisible, yet yearning to feel fully alive, to be seen by those who matter to us. I remember very clearly when I wrote the beginning skeleton of the song...at the very beginning of my touring music career, and I felt very much like an outsider, like "the new kid". Everyone else there knew each other, had history, and were enmeshed in friendships that I longed to be a part of."

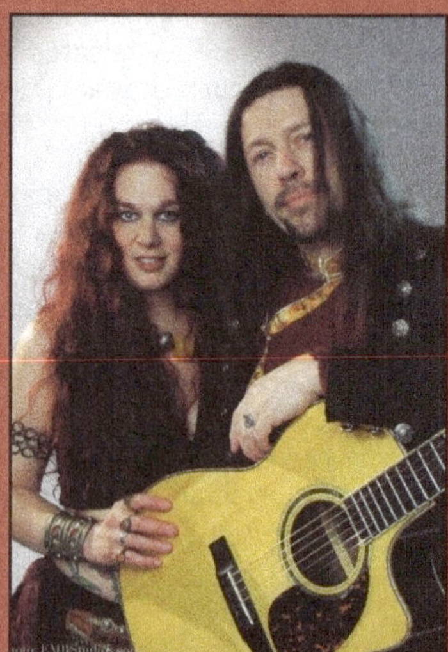

Sharon and Winter also created a lavish music video for this song, directed by Paul Nordin of EMB Studios. Sharon adds, " I am pleased to say that I now do have friendships with many of these folks whose connections I envied at the time. The exclusion never came from them, only within myself as I sought to find a place in a new life. "

Sharon and Winter have formed a band, Pandemonaeon, which blends Middle-Eastern themes with dark trancy rock and metal accents. Pandemonaeon will be appearing at Caldera Music Festival in 2017.

Here is the link to the video of Porcelain Princess https://www.youtube.com/watch?v=KptG3ONbYe8. For more about Sharon and her music, visit her website http://www.sharonknight.net/about-2/

All photos by EMB Studios ◼

For the Love of Music

A Look at the Career of THE PRETTY RECKLESS Frontwoman Taylor Momsen

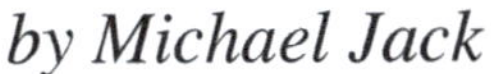

by Michael Jack

I remember when I first stumbled across The Pretty Reckless. I was YouTube surfing, and clicked on the video for "Make Me Wanna Die." What I discovered was a female fronted rock/metal band that was edgy, had great aesthetics, and tilted ever so slightly to the side of Goth. The song was amazing, more traditional metal, with a good heaping of teen angst thrown in. The frontwoman, as I would soon discover, was none other than Taylor Momsen, an established actress. She is most known for her role of Jenny Humphrey on "Gossip Girl," but I knew her best as Cindy Lou Who, the young girl who melted my heart singing, "Christmas, Why Can't I Find You?," in Ron Howard's "How the Grinch Stole Christmas." Now, here she was, still only sixteen years old, stripping her clothes off, screaming, "you make me wanna die," as she walked fearlessly towards a burning mansion. My curiosity hit hyperdrive, and I began searching everything Taylor Momsen and The Pretty Reckless.

Fearless may be a very good word to describe Taylor Momsen, but not exactly as you might think. Yes, she performed in "Heaven Knows" wearing nothing but a painted black cross across her body with an arrow pointing down. Yes, she sang as a strung out morally questionable party goer in "My Medicine." Those were more bold than fearless. Taylor Momsen had a rising acting career. She starred in movies like "Spy Kids 2," and "Underdog." They weren't exactly blockbusters, but they did earn Taylor some young acting award nominations. There was also "Gossip Girl." She also had a distinguished modeling career, including being the face of Madonna's Material Girl fashion line. To say she had "opportunities for eternity," seemed exactly right. At the age of sixteen, Taylor Momsen gave it all up to pursue a music career, which was her true passion.

Taylor's newly formed band, The Pretty Reckless, saw some early lineup changes, but soon found themselves opening up for the Veronicas on their 2009 North

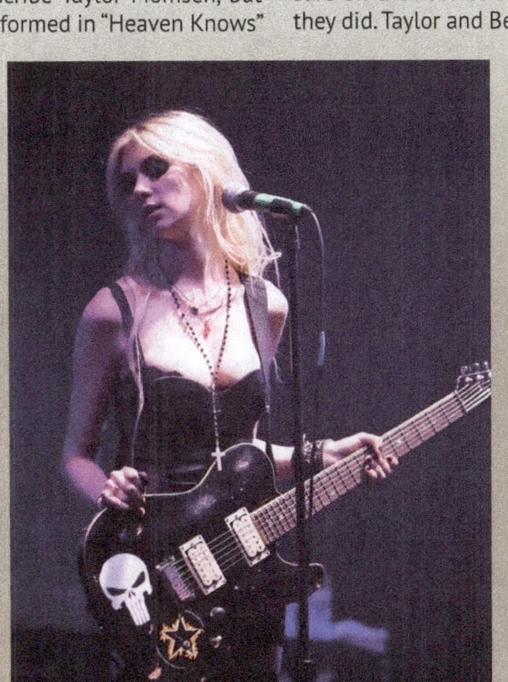

American tour. This was even before the band had released their first album. The Pretty Reckless also performed on the entire 2010 Warped Tour, but their first full-length release wouldn't come until August of that year. Taylor Momsen never looked back. The band just released its third full length album, "Who You Selling For." The first single, "Take Me Down," reached number one on Billboard's Mainstream Rock Chart. This makes four consecutive number ones for The Pretty Reckless. The current record is five, held by Three Days Grace. It is also the most number one singles ever from any female fronted band. Taylor Momsen is still only 23 years old. Think about that for a moment.

The new album, "Who You Selling For," is a little more laid back than previous works, a little more bluesy, and a little more country. It is still undeniably metal, and will still get your fists pumping, but the entire body of work may surprise listeners. Taylor, and fellow co-writer and guitarist Ben Phillips, strayed a little further from that pure rock path this time. When asked how they approached this album, the answer is always the same…they "try not to try." The two of them put no pressure on themselves to create something greater than the last thing they did. Taylor and Ben just simply let the music flow, and see where it takes them. What resulted this time was "Who You Selling For," and it is another impressive album from a band who is quickly rising to the top of the Rock industry.

If you think all of this success has gone to Taylor Momsen's head, you are completely wrong. I think that is what surprises me most about her. Taylor is very introspective. Despite the brazen personas you see in the music videos, the real woman is a quiet homebody Netflix junky. She writes her songs for her, not because she wants to sell records. If asked to explain the meaning of her lyrics, Taylor will tell you to interpret them yourself. A song means different things to different people, and she wants to leave it that way. Her music is a love, and she does it for herself. She is just fortunate enough to be able to make a living from doing so. Success hasn't changed her, and that is the best part. She still does this simply for the love of music. ∎

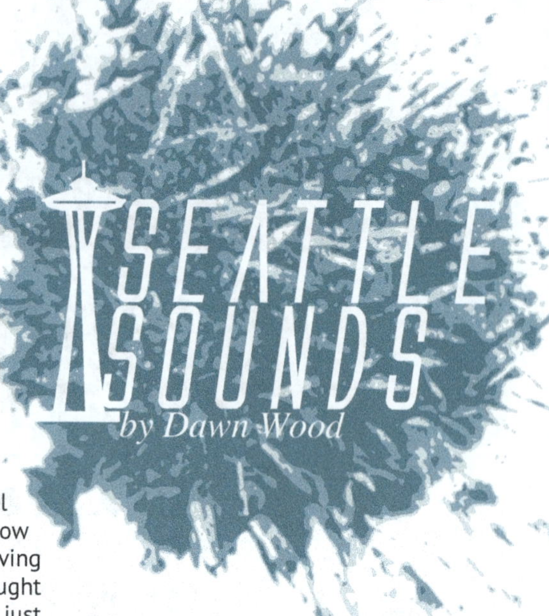

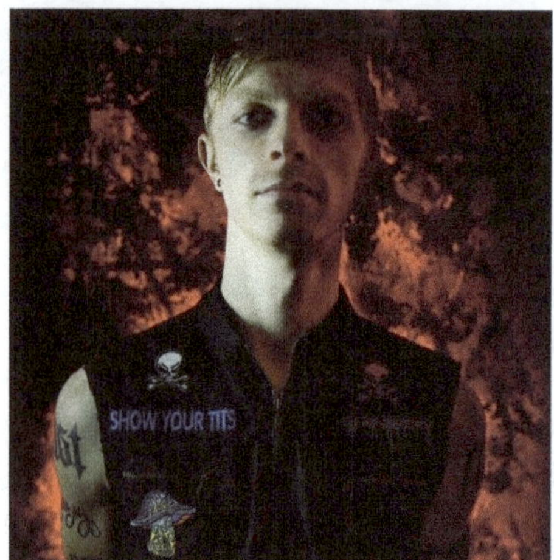

Drummer Galen Waling is a rising force in the Industrial realm of music today. You may not recognize his name right off the bat NOW, but if you are familiar with the Industrial Scene, you have probably heard Galen in action. Galen has brilliantly marketed himself as a session and "drummer for hire" in a scene where "Industrial/Rock" drummers are either non-existent, misplaced by the lack of talent necessary to make the music truly shine, or are in numerous bands. Galen is known as a theatrical, hard-hitting drummer with sharp skills and precise timing. He has risen to a position to play amongst the greats in the Industrial Industry. He has toured with Left Spine Down, Sounds of Mass Production (SMP), Stiff Valentine, Unit:187, Julien-K, PIG and has been a live drummer for: Desillusion, Mixed Messages, Pill Brigade, Murder Weapons and Syztem 7 in the Seattle Industrial scene.

One of the nicest and most accurate quotes that I find which perfectly describes Galen was quoted by Justin Bennett from Skinny Puppy and My Life with the Thrill Kill Kult: "Not only is Galen an amazing drummer with powerful chops and showmanship, he's a cool cat to have around on tour. He's a true talent and team player, the two fundamental necessities that make one a valuable addition to any touring band." - Justin Bennett

I had a chance to ask Galen some questions about his career and upcoming exciting news in his world.

[Carpe Nocturne] Galen, what was your first introduction to the music scene?

[Galen Waling] In general, I got in to the music scene at a very young age. Music was always played in my household and one of our family friends had a drumset he let me play on, so I got an introduction there.

If we are talking industrial, that would probably be when I joined up with Desillusion.

[Carpe Nocturne] Have you always strove for multiple drumming gigs? Do you ever wish you were just in one project or band?

[Galen Waling] When I first started gigging, I didn't even think about being in multiple bands. It wasn't until I saw drummers like Angel (Dope, Genitorturers) and noticed how much fun it seemed they were having playing for all these cool bands. I sought out a few extra gigs at first, and then it just took off from there once people knew I was available. I really enjoy the experience I get from playing for so many different, eclectic, talented musicians.

[Carpe Nocturne] What keeps you grounded and motivated?

[Galen Waling] Playing and practicing drums. Practicing is really important to me. It allows me to see through my hard work the progress I make, whether it's a little or a lot at a time. That to me is motivating. Being the best musician you can be. And have fun!!!

[Carpe Nocturne] Tell us about your upcoming projects?

[Galen Waling] There is a lot of fun stuff coming up. I can't go into too much detail, but some cool gigs coming up with 16Volt, Julien-K, & Ludovico Technique. Hopefully some of the other bands I've had an opportunity to play for like PIG, En Esch and Left Spine Down will tour as well. I like to stay busy!

[Carpe Nocturne] How did you get involved in drum school instruction? How has teaching others this skill influenced you?

[Galen Waling] I got involved with teaching kind of unintentionally. I've taken private lessons since grade school with the same teacher, Chase Cull, and still do when I have the time to this day. Anyway, Chase had some touring and vacation time coming up and asked me to fill in while he was away. I thought it would be a great opportunity to pass what knowledge I've learned on to others. Not only that, every musician learns and interprets differently whether they are a beginning or advanced student. There is something to learn from everyone.

[Carpe Nocturne] Where do you see yourself in 5 years?

[Galen Waling] My goal is to have played at least one stadium gig.

[Carpe Nocturne] Anything else you would like to promote?

[Galen Waling] Gotta do it. Self promotion! Please contact me if you are interested in having me play for your band or project! Also, please check out my website at www.galenwaling.com

Check Galen out on his website and with PIG:
@pigindustries
Left Spine Down: @leftspinedown
16 Volt: @16volt
Julien-K: @julien-k ■

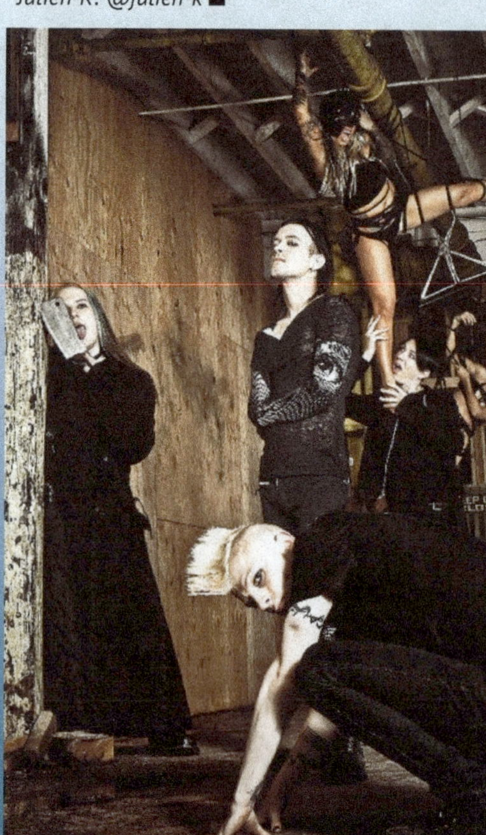

Bring On the Belgians!

In the beer world, it is commonly agreed upon that the best beers come out of Belgium. For a smaller country, Belgium boasts 180 breweries, and a craftsmanship that is unequaled. The most famous of these breweries are the ones run and operated by Trappist Monks, who have perfected their craft over many centuries. Currently, there are only eleven Trappist breweries in the world, six of which reside in Belgium. This wonderful beer producing country also has many Abbey breweries, which work in conjunction with or are affiliated to various monasteries. The Abbey breweries, in my opinion, are every bit as good as the actual Trappist ones, and are most popular for their Dubbel, Tripel, and White styles of beer (although they brew many others).

For this edition of the Gothic Brewer's Guide, I decided to step away from my normal format, and pay homage to the greatest beer producing country in the world. Belgian styles are often imitated, but never quite duplicated. Belgian beers often pack a punch with a high ABV, and are not meant to be used as a session. They are also the most expensive beers on the market, and often retail for over $100 a case, if you are ambitious enough to buy one. For this article, I decided to stick with beers that have a large international distribution, and are easy to find. I'm not trying to have someone book a flight to Belgium just to try a beer on my recommendation (although you won't be disappointed with that trip at all).

Seasonal: Chimay Blue

If you are a beer connoisseur, or are simply familiar with Chimay Blue, you are already screaming foul. Chimay Blue is sold year round. However, did you know this Belgian Strong Dark Ale originated as a Christmas beer? It was so well received, the Trappist Monks began offering it year round.

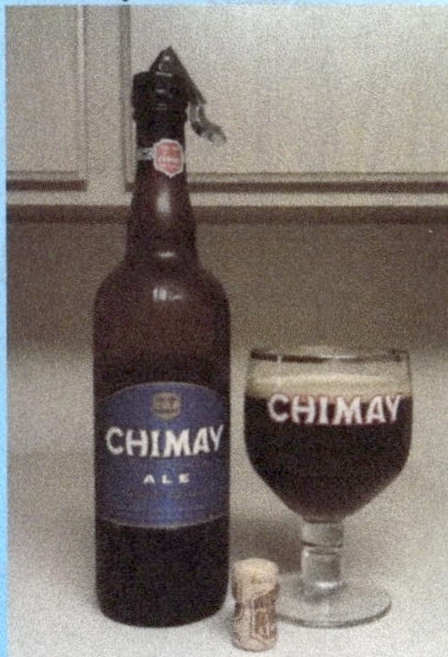
Chimay Blue

Chimay is the oldest Trappist Brewery in the world, and to me, this is their best product. It was also my introduction to authentic Belgian beers, and I have never looked back.

Chimay Blue is a darker ale, as the style suggests. The flavors are very complex, and it is difficult to pick them all out. This is because they all blend perfectly together. What you can expect is hints of caramel, fruits like raisins and plums, and definitely malt. This beer has a heavier body, but is not filling. There is carbonation, but not too much. It has a 9% ABV, but it does not taste boozy. The Chimay Blue is the epitome of balance and smoothness for a beer, and that is impressive considering the style. Chimay Blue is a must try for beer lovers.

Year Round: St. Bernardus Abt 12

St. Bernardus is considered an Abbey brewery, but it has the closest ties to actual Trappist styles. In fact, their recipes come from the St. Sixtus Trappist Monastery in Flanders, Belgium. When St. Sixtus decided they would stop brewing beer for public consumption in 1945, they gave their

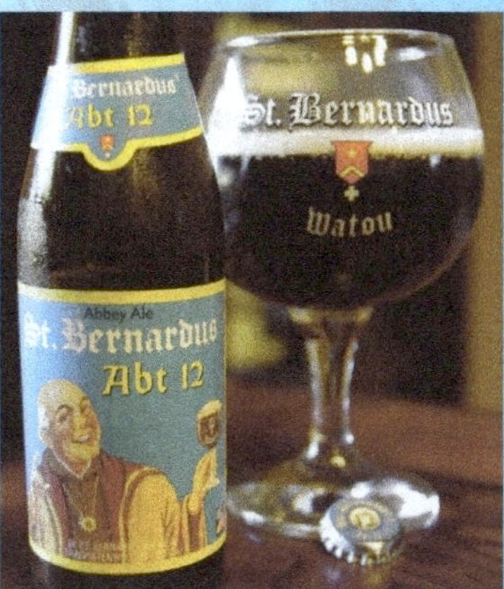
St. Bernardus Abt 12

license and recipes to a local cheese factory. St. Bernardus Brewery was born. Since that time, St. Bernardus has grown to become one of the most respected and renown breweries in the world. Their famous Quadrupel, the Abt 12, regularly sits near the top of the list of greatest beers in the world by every authority.

As I mentioned in my opening, the Abbey Breweries are famous for their Dubbels and Tripels. The Abt 12 is a Quadrupel, which means it is has bolder flavors, and a higher alcohol content. Like most Belgian beers, this is an ale. It is also very dark in color, but not opaque. To look at it, you might almost think someone poured you a cola. The aroma is sweet, there are tastes of fruit like plums and figs throughout, yet this beer is not overly sweet. In fact, the taste is very difficult describe. I have seen it described as witchcraft, and that might be the closest thing to accurate. From personal experience, I can tell you I never understood what a beer could taste like until I tried the Abt 12. It's life changing. This mouth warming Quadrupel is 10% ABV, but you would never know. It is smooth, mysterious, and just something you need to experience.

Theme: Delirium Tremens

From Huyghe Brewery in Melle, Belgium, the Delirium Tremens is widely considered one of the best beers in the world. In fact, in 2008, it won the World Beer Championships in Chicago and is listed as number one in the "50 Greatest Beers in the World" book by Stuart Kellen. Huyghe Brewery is not associated with any monastery. They have just spent over a hundred years perfecting

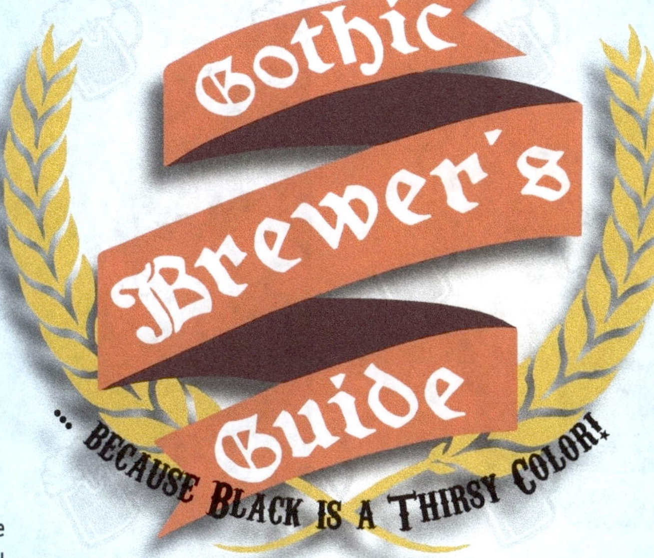
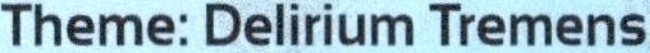
by Michael Jack

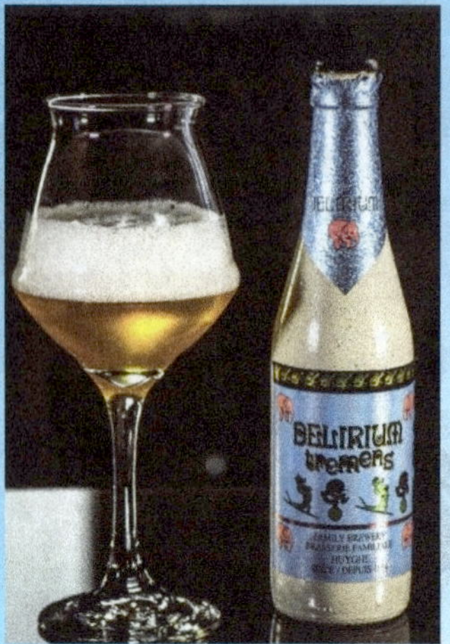

Delirium Tremens

their Belgian styled craft.

The Delirium Tremens is a stronger Belgian Blonde that is extremely easy to drink. It pours to a murky golden color with a fluffy head. Precipitation can be seen like you would expect from a wheat beer. The Delirium Tremens is creamy but does not feel dense to the palate. Notes of pepper and lemon are subtle, but it is the yeast that dominates the taste. It has a slightly floral aroma that is very inviting. The Delirium Tremens is a beer you will want to drink all night long, but use caution. This Belgian Blonde is 8.5% ABV, so I don't recommend more than two. There is always tomorrow night to drink more.

Personal Recommendation: Allagash White

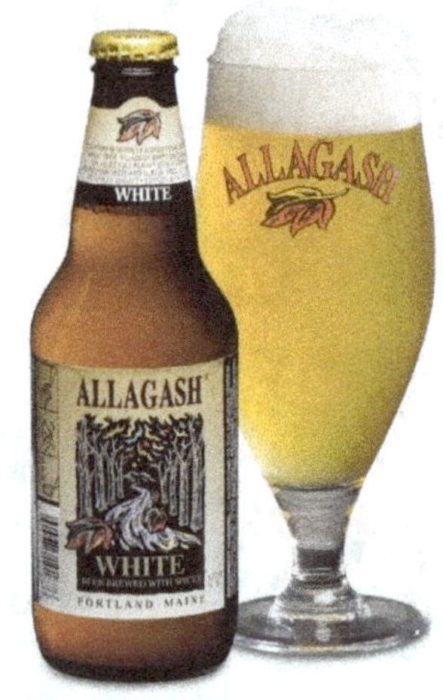

Allagash White

As Belgium has set the standard for beer craftsmanship, the rest of the world is trying to catch up. More breweries are adapting the styles of the Belgians, and are diligently trying to duplicate their styles. In the U.S., almost every brewery now offers at least one Belgian styled beer. I have had many good ones, and many bad ones. There is one, however, that stands above the rest. It is considered the gold standard of American Belgian styled beers. From Portland, Maine, Allagash Brewery has not only managed to replicate a Belgian White, but they have perfected it.

The Allagash White is brewed in a classical Belgian Wheat style. With spices of coriander and Curacao orange peel, this beer tastes exactly like it was imported from Belgium. It is crisp, refreshing, and everything you would expect from a lighter beer. The color is a cloudy golden straw with a bright white head. The aroma is subtle, slightly sweet, with slight hints of clove. Overall, the flavor is very balanced, and it goes down very easily. You may finish the beer before you release you have even begun. It's that smooth. The Allagash White is 5.1% ABV, and by all means can be used as session if your wallet allows. Like the authentic Belgians, this beer comes with a higher price tag. Just like the authentic Belgians, it's worth it. ∎

**Become a writer for
Carpe Nocturne
info@carpenocturne.net**

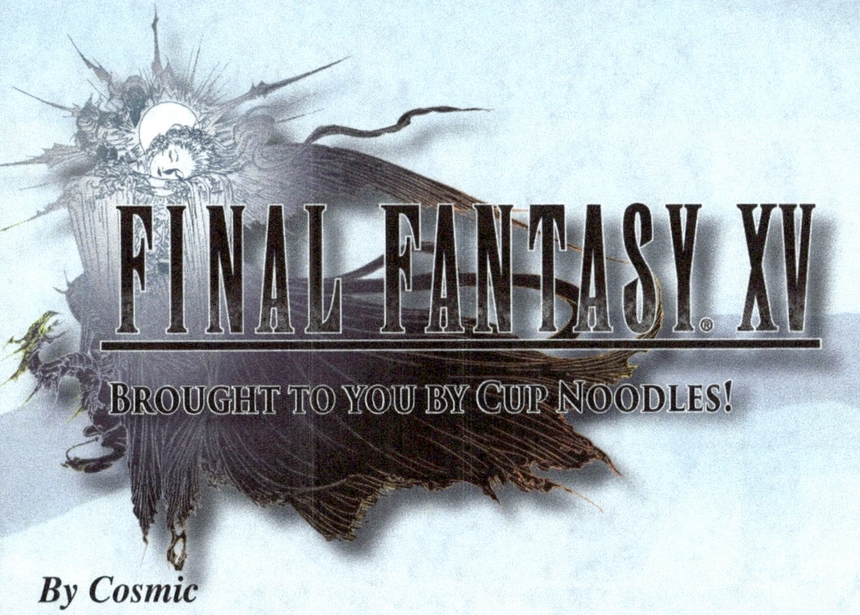

FINAL FANTASY XV

BROUGHT TO YOU BY CUP NOODLES!

By Cosmic

After 30 some-odd hours of playing the latest installment of the contradictorily-named series, I've finally decided whether or not Final Fantasy XV is a good video game. This was a game that was literally ten years in the making, having originally been titled Final Fantasy Versus XIII way back when the Playstation 3 was still new and the verdict was still out on this new-fangled DLC thing and whether or not it would be sticking around. That being said, I didn't want to give the game an unfair chance before coming to a resounding opinion. As of this writing, I've yet to finish the game... but I'm also not exactly certain if it's worth finishing.

That sounds bad, doesn't it?

The truth is, though, I actually enjoyed the hell out of Final Fantasy XV. The story concerns itself mostly with the lengthy road trip taken by a young prince and his three bodyguards. The player controls Prince Noctis, and the other three characters serve mostly as autonomous support in your party, a feature which is the first of many deviations in standard Final Fantasy fare. Bad things happen, and your goal changes from simply driving your awesome customized coupe to your wedding to instead being tasked

Pictured: The most important feature of the game.

with... stopping the evil Empire? Collecting magic swords? Fighting deities? Therein lies the first major problem with the game: it's nearly invisible and very vague plot. You are given a gorgeous and impeccably-rendered world to explore at your leisure, but no real reason to be invested in it. Sidequests flood your to-do list early on and there is a lot to keep you occupied without ever stepping foot onto the main storyline. Ironically, it is here where the game shines. The sandbox is easy to get lost in as you ride Chocobos, fish, and cook deliciously rendered food. Along the way, your J-Pop Band-looking party starts to endear themselves with humanizing and genuinely funny dialogue. You camp with them, you fight baddies with them and you grow with them. By the time you're 30 hours in it feels like the boys have gone through a lot together, and it was at this point that I felt ready to tackle the main storyline.

And it was here that Square-Enix absolutely crushed me. I'd already willingly overlooked a lot of silly moments, such as bizarre product placement that ripped me straight from the immersion of the fantasy. First, the American Express stickers on the door to every shop. How can there be American Express in a fantasy world with no America? Then, there was an entire quest related to the acquisition of ingredients for Cup Noodles. Apparently, the headquarters for Square-Enix in Japan is located right across the street from Nissin, and a lot of cross-promotional marketing took place for both products. A quick Google search will take you to surreal CG advertisements for Cup Noodles as presented by the characters of Final Fantasy XV. Such was the involvement of Nissin in the production of this game that I found myself climbing a gorgeously-rendered volcano for the aforementioned Cup Noodles ingredients. A volcano. For Cup Noodles. And the craziest part is that I actually had fun doing it. The volcano was breathtaking, and climbing it in game was actually a rewarding challenge. Standing before the mouth of a gaping cave in the mountain, I wondered just how timeless this game would be if I were there to fight a dragon or an evil deity instead.

Which brings me to the disappointing paradox that is Final Fantasy XV. By the time I continued with the main quest I found myself wishing for another Cup Noodles quest. The story took me to a fabulous Venetian city where I was tasked with reuniting with Noctis' fiancé. At this point you're treated to some interesting political intrigue surrounding the warring nations of the game, but the rest is unintelligible. Lunafreya, Noctis' bride-to-be, explains the game's lore with dialogue such as, "I know what you must know – that the King of Kings must drive the darkness from our star!" This kind of writing for such a vital character makes the plot vague and uninteresting, and it seemed this was the case for most of the characters responsible for story exposition. Your four party members throw casual American slang at each other in the comfort of one another's company (to enjoyable effect) and yet Final Fantasy XV fills its main storyline with Exposition Fairies who can't be bothered to speak more sensibly than the most cryptic wizards in Lord of the Rings.

Perhaps I'm being a bit unfair in not finishing the game, but the immersion factor was completely lost for me by the half-way point in the story. Any emotional investment I had in the characters was sapped completely by hackneyed writing and dialogue that would probably make George Lucas cringe. Tragically-themed cutscenes that were pitifully derivative of previous Final Fantasy games (yes, *that* Final Fantasy game) attempted to create emotionally memorable events but instead came across as cheap and insulting considering where Square drew their visual inspirations from. By the time the so-called climax was over I had lost all interest in Final Fantasy XV.

If I ever pick the game back up again it might be because I feel the burning desire to make some Cup Noodles. ∎

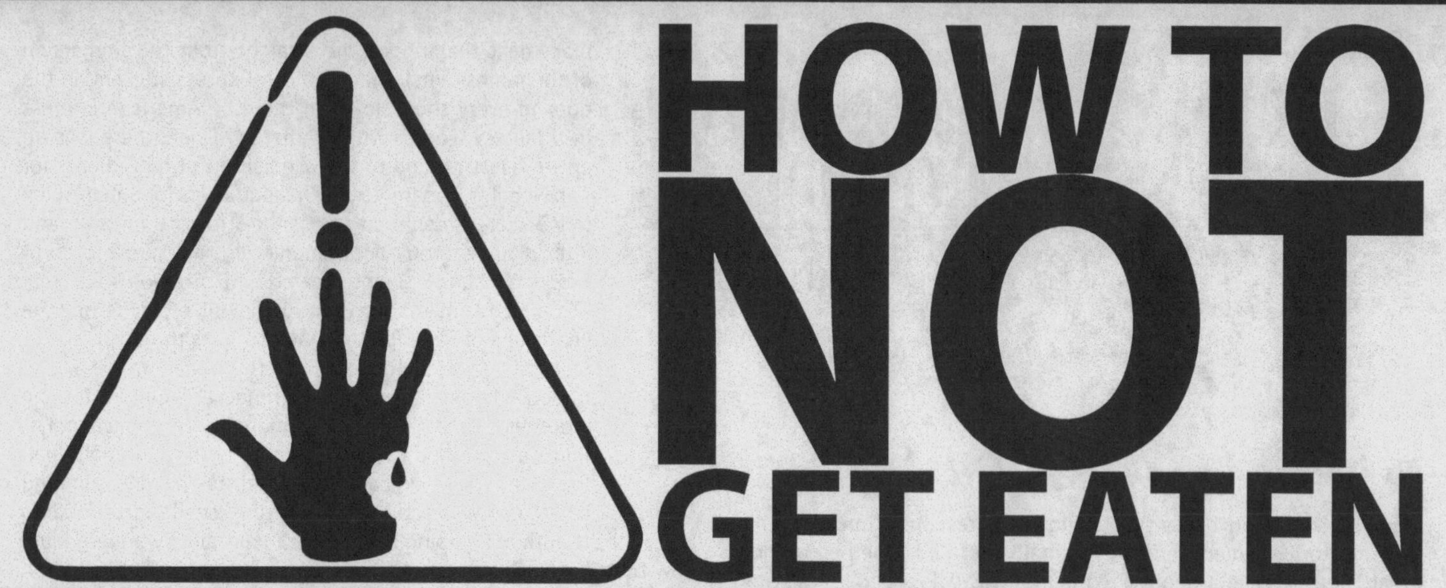

HOW TO NOT GET EATEN

by *Xxx Zombieboy xxX*

For this entry in surviving the zombie apocalypse, I want to focus on a trend that is growing on the internet, which largely preys upon a lack of information and fear of needing but not having. That is how to put together a "bug out bag." Having gone over dozens of websites and reading a number of survival books, there are some things I agree with and many I don't. I try to design my own with a few things in mind.

First, is mobility. You cannot weigh yourself down. You are going to have to be able to run, swim, jump over obstacles and scale obstacles with your bag. Therefore, it must be light.

Two, this cannot be the only thing you rely on. A bug out bag is only to get you started. It will not last forever, nor will the items you bring. So, keep that in mind. If the survival situation is prolonged, then a good bag will give you a head start. It will not, however, keep you going forever.

With these things in mind, the following is what I have surmised to be the best way to get going. One final note, I did not include weapons. Weapons are a separate issue, though some items listed may be used as such, but that is not their principal purpose.

1) A Fire Source – Your best option here is to learn how to use a fire starter such as flint and iron. A fire striker is small and light weight. Always have one. It would not hurt to also have a back up disposable lighter. Again, lightweight and most last a decent amount of time, at least until you find more. Also, I always say having a box of plain old stick matches is a good idea. Bottom line; always have at least one fire source.

2) A Light Source – Get yourself a small LED flashlight. There are literally thousands of tactical flashlights on the market, all saying that they are the best. Myself, I still love the Maglite. Some are more weatherproof than others, so that is a consideration. However, do not weigh yourself down with a huge and powerful light. A simple flashlight will do, and one change of batteries. But only one. These get heavy if you burden yourself.

3) A Knife – The good old Swiss army knife is always a good suggestion. Time honored for a reason, these always have a use. I do not recommend some crazy huge version with tools you will likely not need or use. One with a saw blade is not a bad idea. However, the most important thing is a good and decent utilitarian blade. Not a weapon. A tool. You will use the hell out of it so make it a good one!

4) First Aid – I could and likely will write an article about this alone. Therefore, I am only going to cover the basics. Painkillers are a must. You are likely to get headaches and injuries for many different reasons. Do not weigh yourself down with some crazy huge kit however. Remember that this is to get you started, not to turn you into a moving hospital. So make sure you have painkillers. Basic wound dressings are a good idea. I also highly recommend allergy tablets, blood clotting powder, and any antibiotics you may have. Remember that these later do expire. Finally, and perhaps most important, would be some form of anti-bacterial cleanser.

5) Toiletries – Get a small travel kit. Keeping clean is extremely important. Just the basics. No makeup. No hair gel. Get soap, a toothbrush, and toothpaste. Nail clippers and a small pair of scissors may be worth the extra weight. Soap above all else however.

6) Cooking – A small pot and a metal spork are all I suggest. The pot should be very sturdy and able to be put right in a fire. Don't bother with plates and bowls and a plethora of silverware. These things will weigh you down significantly. Just one small pot and one small utensil. That is all you need for starters and you can prepare almost anything in this.

7) Blanket – OK this is a large item but I am a huge fan of Navajo blankets in survival situations. They are strong, warm, and a decent cushion on bare ground. You may also consider one of those space survival blankets. They are very lightweight and can also be used to signal.

8) A small mirror – For signaling and self-use.

9) Life Straw – I did an article already on water purification and these little guys are invaluable. You can use them almost anywhere and they take very little time and space. Get two.

10) Can Opener – You do not need a huge and heavy one. You can get the small ones that have been military issued for decades and they work fine. They are called the P-38 and cost about a dollar at any surplus military store.

11) Bandana/shemagh – I recommend both. Each has dozens of uses and takes very little room.

12) Reusable rain poncho – Getting soaked can be very problematic. You can even build a temporary shelter with a good one. Don't bother with the cheap one-use ones. Get a decent one. You will need it.

13) Fishing kit – You can get a small one and use it over and over. The old adage about teaching someone to fish and feeding them for life is absolute truth. They take very little space, and can be invaluable.

14) Flash Drive – Spend the money and get a really strong and weather resistant hard drive. Put photos, documents, identification and music on it. Keep it safe, and keep some space on it. You never know when you might need such a small piece of useful technology.

15) Paper clips – These little babies have dozens of survival uses. Dozens. Keep a handful in your kit.

16) Plastic zip lock baggies – Use them to store all of these things. They can be reused in the field for carrying any number of items including food you may catch or gather.

17) A small pencil and small notebook. You may need to take quick notes from other survivors or keep track of things. Just a small pad and a stub of pencil. That is it. Do not burden yourself with a big journal.

18) Money – Stash a few hundreds. You never know.

19) Food – This is a difficult one to discuss. I do not think you should carry a huge amount. Enough to get you started. Something that lasts a long time and will provide you with energy. A few energy bars perhaps and some nuts but do not take a huge box of MRI's or a bunch of canned goods. These may be OK if you are going off in a vehicle. That changes the game. However, do not weight down your bug out bag with a ton of food. And salt. Always bring salt.

20) Canteen – Not necessarily in the bag itself, but a good old-fashioned military canteen on your belt is a good idea.

21) Clothing – This changes from environment to environment. Pack accordingly. Over all I suggest one change of pants, one change of shirt, two pairs of underwear and two pairs of socks, and that is getting generous.

22) Duct tape – wrap maybe three feet around the pencil. Don't bring a whole roll.

23) Vitamins – You can get a long way with a single bottle of GOOD vitamins. Do the research and distinguish which multivitamin is good and which is a bunch of crunchy herbal crap that you will just piss out. You may consider just putting them in a zip lock bag to save space. They can also be noisy if they rattle in a bottle.

24) Magnifying glass – You can get a small and hearty one that you can use for making fires amongst other things.

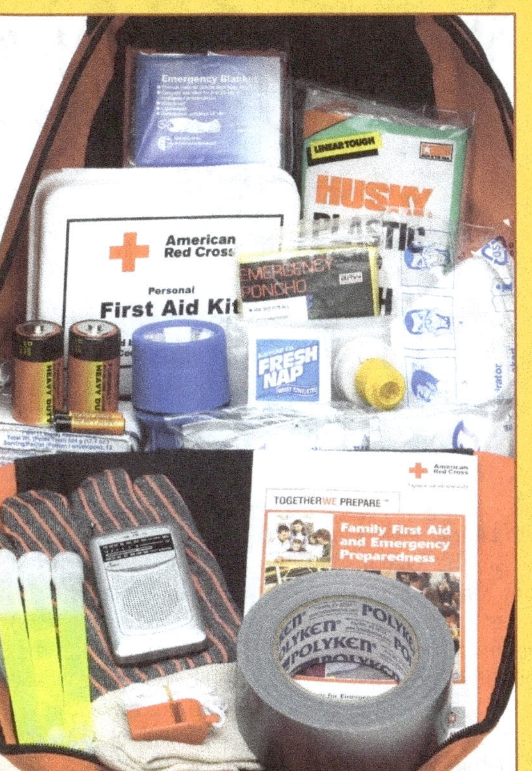

25) Aluminum foil – a few sheets wrapped down into a small square. Good for wrapping, reflecting, cooking, etc.

26) Glasses – If you have any vision issues, have at least one back up pair of glasses. The same goes for any medications you may require to stay alive. Have extra ready of any of these things.

There are some other items that you may consider. These are not as essential as the ones above so use your best judgment.

1) Universal USB solar charger – Technology and survival are changing all the time. It may be that technology is the savior. Or it may be more weight and useless. Consider the state of the world and the state of the emergency.

2) Sleeping Bag – This one I am usually not into including. They are bulky and largely more trouble than they are worth. However, if you are surviving in extreme cold climates, you may have to include one.

3) Tarp – These are very useful for building shelters and can be used to collect water.

4) Cooking stove – I say learn how to cook with the fire that you have learned how to make. However, there are some very small and lightweight ones out there. Use your best judgment.

5) Spices – Not a true necessity perhaps, but a little comfort can go a long way, and these can take up very little room in small zip lock bags.

6) Compass – You may wonder why this is not in the essential list. With some training, it IS non-essential. There are other ways to navigate. However, I was on the fence with this. A small one perhaps may be added to the essential list, and a larger one to this list. However, make sure you know how to use one, or it is absolutely a waist of space to you.

7) Feminine Hygiene products – Don't jump down my throat, but I was on the fence with this one as well. Again, use good judgment. Do not pack tons of these.

8) Toilet paper – A small amount may be very useful, but let's face it, you will blow through this quickly. You simply cannot bring enough to sustain. Try to find more or learn to use non-poisonous leaves.

9) Paracord – Many survivalists swear by it, and they are not wrong. Just do not bring enough to weight you down!

10) Comfort Items – Now this may seem ridiculous, but I will always bring a small bottle (SMALL!!) of whiskey, and a pack of smokes. Perhaps some caffeine pills as well. Sanity is a thing, and if I get surrounded with no way out, I am taking that shot and lighting up.

That's it kids. My suggestion on the absolute essentials and some secondary considerations. Where you are, the type of zombies, your personal training and about a thousand other variables may alter this list. Again, as I have said over and over, use your best judgment! ∎

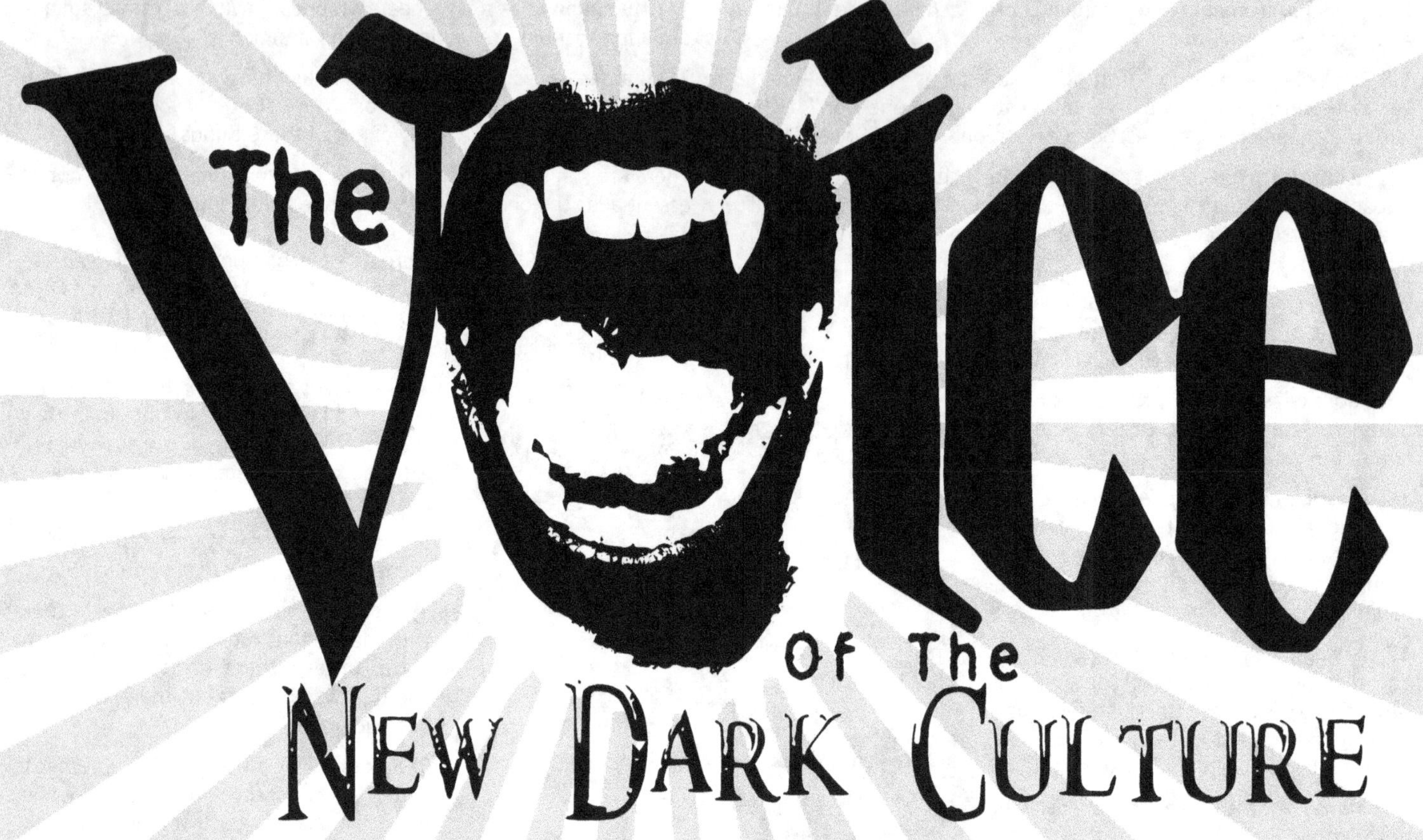

by Chirality

Dating in the new millennium has proven to be interesting. With sites like Tinder, Ok Cupid, and Plenty of Fish, the search for a perfect match has changed, and maybe not for the better. The worst part too is being someone who is alternative looking for someone. I will use my own experiences here to let you know how hard it is to find that special someone in your life.

I am divorced, and my divorce has been final since 2012. I had a few boyfriends, some scene and some not. The ones in the scene seem to be really disastrous, so I figured I would go out on a limb and make an Ok Cupid profile. I noted myself as not only "plus sized" but alternative. Yup, fat and alt. OMG! I was getting a lot of responses from guys who were "impressed" at my honesty, and loved Gothic girls. They all "loved" Gothic girls.

I went on a few dates, and some I even gave a few weeks. The first one we will call Dave. Dave was an accounting student. He wore his hair nice, had nice little glasses and seemed sweet. He seemed to like my alt lifestyle, but it also seemed to unnerve him. Dave seemed surprised that I wanted a family and to settle down (remember kids, Gothic woman are loose, slutty and wild in the bedroom). So when I smashed his dream, he seemed disappointed. I remember one day being in Walmart of all places and falling in love with a pair of sneakers that were black and pink with tiger stripes. Dave said, "Wow you are different, aren't you?" What was your first guess sporto? I never made myself out to be anything I am not.

The second, we will call him Scott. Scott worked for a very well to do television station in a very big city. He has nice blonde hair and blue eyes (this is not saying blonde dudes can't be Goth, but just follow me here). We went out. Scott assumed since I was Goth I was more into the S&M aspect, which I am, but it is neither here, nor there. He was very well to do and his life showed it. Now here comes me with my black hair, tattoos and piercings. Scott told me he was ok with my lifestyle and alt choice, but soon he started to talk about putting me into pink dresses and making my hair it's natural blonde color. I had started to feel a little creeped out. Then the comments on the tattoos came and that was it for me. I am who I am. The funny thing is two years later he still texts me.

And then there was guy number 3 who was very "normal" but not. Let me tell you too, all these guys were NOT normal either. They had some odd sexual fetish (I don't judge) or like one, smelled his hands. I am all for odd and not normal, but when you question my oddness then we have an issue.

Finally, I hope I have found the person who is in the scene and accepts my dorkiness and individuality. I am not just "Goth." I am made up of so many things. Gothic women are not just one thing. They are enchanting and beautiful but we are NOT a fetish. I do not walk into CVS with a corset and fishnets. I have encountered two things. Guys realize that this Goth girl is in fact kinda "normal," or they find out I am exactly who I say I am, and that freaks them out. The novelty wears off as does the fetish. Who doesn't love Gothic women? But we are so much more than our outfits. ∎

Get your album
professionally reviewed
music@carpenocturne.net

www.ingramcontent.com/pod-product-compliance
Lightning Source LLC
Chambersburg PA
CBHW082248060726
47592CB00021B/3304

9 781941 901304